Fantasies

of the

Master Race

Literature, Cinema and
the Colonization of American Indians

Ward Churchill
Edited by M. Annette Jaimes

Common Courage Press   Monroe, Maine

ISBN: 0-9628838-6-7 paper

ISBN: 0-9628838-7-5 cloth

Common Courage Press
P.O. Box 702
Monroe, ME 04951
207-525-0900

"Literature as a Weapon In the Colonization of the American Indian" was originally published as "Literature and the Colonization of the American Indian" in *Journal of Ethnic Studies,* Vol. 10, No. 3, Fall 1982.

"Carlos Castaneda: The Greatest Hoax Since Piltdown Man" was originally published as "Debacle in Academe: Carlos Castaneda as Literary Hoax" as a monograph by the American Academy of Higher Education, 1985.

"Ayn Rand and the Sioux: Tonto Revisited" was originally published in *Lakota Eyapaha,* Vol. 4, No. 2, June 1980.

"*Creek Mary's Blood:* A Comparison to *Hanta Yo*" was published with variations in *Journal of Ethnic Studies,* Vol. 12, No. 3, and as "The Fictionalization of History in *Creek Mary's Blood*" in *Organization of American Historians Newsletter,* Vol. 13, No. 5, February 1985.

"It Did Happen Here: Sand Creek, Scholarship and the American Character" is forthcoming in *American Indian Culture and Research Journal.*

"*That Day in Gordon:* Deformation of History and the American Novel" was originally published in *Western American Literature*, Vol. 22, No. 1, Spring 1987.

"'Friends of the Indian:' A Critical Appraisal of *Irredeemable America: The Indian's Estate and Land Claims*" was originally published in *New Studies on the Left*, Vol. 13, Nos. 3-4, Summer-Fall 1988.

"*Interpreting the American Indian:*A Critique of Michael Castro's Apologia for Poetic Racism" was originally published in *Wicazo Sa Review*, Vol. 1, No. 2, Fall 1985 and *Journal of Ethnic Studies*, Vol. 13, No. 4, Winter 1985.

"*Beyond Ethnicity:* Werner Sollors' Deepest Avatar of Racism" was originally published in *New Scholar*, Vol. 10, Nos. 1-2, Fall 1986.

"The New Racism: A Critique of James A. Clifton's *The Invented Indian*" was originally published in *Wicazo Sa Review*, Vol. 6, No. 2, Spring 1991.

"A Little Matter of Genocide: Sam Gill's *Mother Earth*, Colonialism and the Expropriation of Indigenous Spiritual Tradition in Academia" was published in part as "A Little Matter of Genocide: Native American Spirituality and New Age Hucksterism," in *Bloomsbury Review*, Vol. 8, No. 5, October/November 1988 and in *American Indian Culture and Research Journal*, Vol. 12, No. 3, Summer 1988.

"Spiritual Hucksterism: The Rise of the Plastic Medicine Men" was originally published in *Z Magazine*, December 1990.

"Fantasies of the Master Race: Categories of Stereotyping of American Indians in Film" was originally published in *Book Forum*, Vol. 3, No. 3, 1981.

"'Lawrence of South Dakota': Perspectives on *Dances With Wolves*" was originally published in *Z Magazine*, May 1991.

"Hi-Ho Hillerman...(Away)" is forthcoming in *Z Magazine*.

Third Printing

Previous Books by Ward Churchill

Marxism and Native Americans (1983)

Culture versus Economism: Essays on Marxism in the Multicultural Arena (with Elisabeth R. Lloyd, 1984)

Agents of Repression: The FBI's Secret Wars Against the Black Panther Party and the American Indian Movement (with Jim Vander Wall, 1988)

Critical Issues in Native North America (1989)

The COINTELPRO Papers: Documents from the FBI's Secret Wars Against Dissent in the United States (with Jim Vander Wall, 1990)

Critical Issues in Native America, Vol. II (1991)

for our maternal grandfathers

Philip H. Allen, Sr.

Pedro W. Guerrero

Contents

Introduction

Weapons of Genocide

Literature crafted by a dominating culture can be an insidious political force, disinforming people who might otherwise develop a clearer understanding of the struggles for survival faced by an indigenous population. This volume of essays written over the last ten years is offered to counter that disinformation, and move people to take action on issues confronting American Indians today.

But what is the great harm done in altering a few facts to make a good historical novel? In *Fantasies of the Master Race*, Ward Churchill lays waste to the innocence of this question, stating: "The stereotypes [in both historical novels and documentary accounts of events] assume a documented 'authenticity' in the public consciousness...For stereotyped and stereotyper alike, it becomes dehumanizing and a tool to justify murder under the guise of aesthetic freedom...The [stereotypes] of American Indians in American literature may be seen as an historical requirement of an imperial process." As Russell Means has put it:

> If our culture is dissolved, Indian people *as such* will cease to exist. By definition, the causing of any culture to cease to exist is an act of genocide. That's a matter of international law; look it up in the 1948 Genocide Convention.

What are the more insidious stages of genocide? As Churchill points out, genocide can have several distinct stages. During each phase of the genocide of American Indians, literature, film, and the assimilation of culture have played critical roles. Literature from the very first

1

arrival of white people on the continent has been written in the service of dominating American Indians "to provoke and sanctify systematic warfare..." Later, literature enhanced the public zeal in "civilizing" the savage. In the final stage, literature and the stereotyping of culture establishes complete control "over truth and knowledge. It finally replaces troops and guns as the relevant tool of colonization."

Each part of the book focuses on a particular device—from the outright invention of spiritual rituals to the rewriting of history—designed to obliterate Native American culture and people, or to absorb them into a system of Euroamerican values. The essay on Carlos Castenada serves as an example that these fabrications are used in the highest echelons of academia to obtain doctorates, fame, and wealth.

A warped brand of rugged individualism, so dearly espoused by the followers of Ayn Rand, has been projected onto the American Indian in *Hanta Yo*. In "Ayn Rand and the Sioux," Churchill meticulously shows how these destructive values are antithetical to American Indian cultures.

But it's not just the political right which has altered American Indian values for its own purposes. White values of every stripe have steamrolled over the indigenous population. In the last essay in Part Two, Churchill reviews how the values and rights to self-determination are subordinated to the need to believe in a socialist revolution. Implicit in these pieces is a warning: truth must come before ideology, and those who seek to understand the world and fight for justice must not allow themselves to reverse that priority.

"History is the propaganda of the victors," it was once said, and there is much scholarship on American Indians to prove it. Treatment of the Sand Creek Massacre in "It Did Happen Here" provides fascinating insight not only into how the event was handled at the time—both by those who condoned it and those who condemned it—but also reveals that rewriting and justification is still needed by the victors one hundred years after the event. The method used to describe the massacre will be familiar to any student of propaganda. Churchill shows that rather than denying the event or defending the slaughter outright, the scholar treats the tragedy as an "excess." This allows the event to be seen as an aberration and even preserves the intent of the killers as "noble." This characterization precludes any need to examine the event as part of a systematic policy of genocide.

"That Day in Gordon: Deformation of History and the American Novel" will serve as a rude awakening for anyone who believes that rewriting history does not occur with contemporary events.

A great deal of damage can be carried out under the cloak of benevolence. "Friends of the Indian" have furthered the control of American Indians by whites. As an example, Churchill cites the authors of *Irredeemable America: The Indian's Estate and Land Claims,* who harm indigenous struggle by making the land claims struggle out to be a hopeless cause not worth fighting for.

Racism also hides behind benevolence. *"Interpreting the American Indian:* A Critique of Michael Castro's Apologia for Poetic Racism" shows how the conflict between the colonizer and the colonized has evolved. As Churchill puts it, "members of the dominant culture are unable to retain their sense of distance and domination from that which they dominate." The conflict becomes not only an attempt at extermination, but takes on a new task of absorbing the indigenous culture into the culture of the dominant group. In *"Beyond Ethnicity:* Werner Sollors' Deepest Avatar of Racism," and "The New Racism: A Critique of James A. Clifton's *The Invented Indian"* resurgent academic racism completely muddles the issues in an attempt to define from a Eurocentric perspective nonwhite cultures.

But what's wrong with white people incorporating Native American spirituality into their own beliefs? Churchill shows that this interest can wrest control of the culture from those who created it. By examining the hunger for the antics of Sun Bear and some non-Indian cohorts in "Spiritual Hucksterism," the stark, pathetic emptiness of much of Euroamerican spiritual life is revealed. This process of white dabbling in American Indian spiritual rituals represents the ultimate absorption. Native American spirituality becomes a commodity in the Euroamerican market place, to be bought and sold alongside other "New Age" items.

Others seek to rob American Indian culture outright. In "A Little Matter of Genocide:" Churchill looks at the work of Sam Gill, a blatant attempt to deny American Indians one of their most central beliefs—that the Earth is the mother of all life.

White domination is so complete that even Indian children want to be cowboys. It's as if Jewish children wanted to play nazis, Churchill states. In the book's final section, a look at more popular portrayals of American Indians show how this pernicious feat has been accomplished.

But what could possibly be wrong with *Dances with Wolves*, Kevin Costner's "western with soul," as one reviewer called it? Or with Tony Hillerman's mystery novels which represent "a forceful advocacy of the Native American cause," to quote another reviewer? How could they possibly be examined in a volume that looks at literature as a weapon of genocide? For answers to these questions, you'll just have to read the book.

—M. Annette Jaimes
Boulder, CO
November, 1991

Preface

The Open Veins
of Native North America

It is perhaps helpful to provide a backdrop to the analysis of literature examined in this volume by reviewing some factual information on the contemporary colonial context in North America. These facts should make clear that the very core of the U.S. imperial structure lies not abroad in the third world, but right here "at home." Although mainstream ideologues ranging in outlook from reactionary republicanism to revolutionary marxism are wont to decry as "misleading and rhetorical" any application of terms like "colonization" to the North American context itself, the reality of circumstances on this continent demands such usage. As this is written, more than 400 indigenous peoples continue to exist within the borders of the 48 contiguous states.[1] About half of these peoples retain nominal possession of some reserved portion of their original territory, a pastiche of areas altogether comprising approximately 3 percent of the acreage in the "lower 48." Moreover, these indigenous peoples— having never ceded it in any of the 371 ratified treaties by which the United States acquired deeds to the remainder—still retain unassailable legal title to about ten times the area now left them.[2] Put another way, the United States lacks even a pretense of legitimate ownership over approximately one-third of its main continental land mass. In all of this vast and unceded area, the U.S. is an occupying power, pure and simple. Official conceptions of territorial integrity demand that it remain that way.

While pushing Indians off 90 percent of the land they'd retained by treaty—instruments by which the

United States formally and repeatedly recognized indigenous peoples as being fully sovereign nations in their own right—federal officials carefully saw to it that indigenous populations were restricted to what was then thought to be the least useful and productive portions of North America, mostly arid and semi-arid parcels deemed unfit for ranching and agriculture, and typically lacking in timber and other renewable resources.[3] It is one of history's supreme ironies that this same "worthless" acreage turned out to be extraordinarily rich in minerals, overlying about two-thirds of all known uranium reserves within the boundaries of the continental United States, as much as a quarter of the readily accessible low sulphur coal, 15 to 20 percent of the oil and natural gas, and appreciable deposits of copper, bauxite, zeolite and other strategic and commercially crucial ores.[4] These minerals, plainly belonging to other nations, constitute the bulk of what federal economic planners now like to refer to as "U.S. domestic reserves." Without these resources, U.S. business-as-usual could never have been created, and would come to a halt in a hot minute.

Using the term "colonization" to describe such facts risks instilling a certain unsettling (and "destabilizing") cognitive dissonance among the Euroamerican citizenry. After all, they themselves had engaged in an anti-colonial struggle, a theme in history which has (incorrectly) legitimated their claim to "the land of the free and the home of the brave." Rather than risk this dissonance, U.S. propagandists have contrived a whole new set of terms to mask the nature of U.S.-Indian relations. These have centered on semantical contentions that the United States, rather than occupying and colonizing Native America, has assumed a permanent "trust" responsibility over Indian land and lives, a responsibility imparting "plenary (full) power" over native property.[5] The employment of such euphemisms has allowed projection of an illusion that federal interaction with Indians, while em-

bodying a number of errors and excesses during the 18th
and 19th century settlers' wars, has long been and remains benevolent, well-intended and ultimately "for the
Indians' own good."

The true cost to native people bound up in the complex of relations anchoring the U.S. status quo is revealed
in the federal government's own statistics. By any reasonable computation, a simple division of the known remaining resources of Native America by the approximately 1.6
million Indians (.6 percent of the total population) reflected in the last U.S. census should make Indians the
largest per capita land holders in all of North America;[6]
they should in other ways as well comprise the continent's
richest "ethnically-defined population group," both in aggregate terms and on a per capita basis. Instead, they are
by far the poorest overall, experiencing the lowest annual
and lifetime incomes, poorest housing and sanitation conditions, lowest level of educational attainment and highest rate of unemployment.[7] The single poorest county in
the United States over the past fifty years has been
Shannon, on the Pine Ridge Sioux Reservation in South
Dakota. Counties on half a dozen other Indian reservations distributed across a wide geographic area make
regular appearances among the ten poorest recorded by
the U.S. Departments of Labor and Commerce.[8]

Correspondingly, Native Americans currently experience the most pronounced symptoms of poverty evidenced by any overall population group on the continent:
twelve times the U.S. national rate for incidence of mal-
nutrition, nine times the rate of alcoholism, seven times
the rate of infant mortality, five times the rate of deaths
by exposure, several times the rate for incidence of bu-
bonic plague, tuberculosis, typhoid, diphtheria and other
readily preventable diseases. Children still die regularly
from whooping cough, strep throat and measles. The
present life-expectancy of a reservation-based male is 44.6
years; reservation-based women can expect to live less

than three years longer. Indication of the level of despair inculcated among native people by such conditions may be found in the extreme rates of alcoholism, drug addiction, familial violence and teen suicide in every North American Indian community.[9] The government response has been to imprison one in four native men and to impose involuntary sterilization upon perhaps 40 percent of all Indian women of childbearing age.[10] The setting resembles, properly enough under the circumstances, colonization which pertains to certain locales within the third world rather than those one might expect to encounter in the midst of a country enjoying one of the world's most developed standards of living.

The vast gulf separating the potential wealth possessed by Native America on the one hand, and its practical impoverishment on the other, resides squarely within what writer Eduardo Galeano has in another context aptly termed the "open veins" of the colonized.[11] In other words, the federal government has consistently used its unilaterally asserted position of "benevolent" control over indigenous affairs and property to pour the assets of native nations directly into the U.S. economy rather than those of native peoples. A single illustration will suffice to tell the tale. Very near the starving residents of Shannon County, on land permanently guaranteed by the United States to the Lakota Nation through the 1868 Fort Laramie Treaty, the Homestake Mining Corporation alone has extracted more than $14 billion in gold over the past half-century.[12]

Multiplying the Homestake Mining example by scores of U.S. corporations doing business on Indian land barely begins to convey the dimension of the process. Stripped to its essentials, the entire fabric of the "American way of life" is woven from the strands of these relations. They constitute an order which must be maintained, first, foremost, and at all costs, because they more than any other definable factor constitute the absolute bedrock upon which the U.S. status quo has erected and maintains itself.

Things are never, of course, described so straightforwardly in official circles. They are packaged to appear to be quite the reverse. A salient example, beginning with the passage of the 1934 Indian Reorganization Act (IRA), has been the unilateral displacement of traditional indigenous forms of governance by a "tribal council" model. Devised in Washington, DC, it was imposed over the vociferous objections of the bulk of those to be ruled by it.[13] The IRA councils owe their allegiance not to their ostensible constituents, but to the federal apparatus which created their positions and installed them, and which continues to fund and "advise" them. From the outset, these councils accepted a tacit *quid pro quo* attending their positions of petty power and imagined prestige. Theirs have been the signatures affixed to resolutions extending "Indian" approval to leases paying their people pennies on the dollar for mineral wealth lying within their lands, waiving environmental protection clauses in mining contracts and all the rest. Theirs have been the "Indian" voices adding illusions of "consensus" to the federal and corporate chorus proclaiming every agonized step in the ongoing subjugation and expropriation of Native America as "giant steps forward," denouncing those who insist upon indigenous alternatives as "barriers to progress."[14]

Altogether, this structure of puppet governance had become so entrenched and effective by the mid-1970s that it was cast under the rubric of "Indian self-determination." This inherently anti-colonialist term defined by contemporary international law was stood neatly on its head. Advanced in its stead was a statutory formulation wherein all policy decisions affecting Indian country would forever fall within the sphere of federal authority. Implementation of these policies would, to the maximum extent possible, be carried out by native people hired specifically for this purpose. (This was dubbed "Indian preference.")[15] As indigenous people became increasingly self-colonizing during the 1970s and '80s, it became ever more possible to neutralize indigenous opposition to internal colonization by juxtaposing it to the posturing of members of the growing gaggle of IRA "leaders" or preferred employees of the federal bureaucracy. All of them were prepared at the drop of a hat to confuse critics through avid endorsement of the system. In addition, these "leaders" publicly dismissed Indian activists—usually in the face of overwhelming evidence to the contrary—as "self-styled and irresponsible renegades, revolutionaries and terrorists" who lacked standing or credibility within their own communities.[16]

Within this deliberately contrived framework of duplicity and false appearances, any real potential for coherent non-Indian understanding of the situation becomes difficult. Taking the further step of engaging in effective opposition to federal Indian policy has become thoroughly diffused and dissipated, even among those most seriously committed to combatting U.S. colonial activities in Central America, Southern Africa, the Middle East and elsewhere. In effect, the officially-sponsored scenario fosters mainstream perceptions that if Indians themselves cannot agree on the nature of their oppression, or for that matter whether they are in fact oppressed, then non-Indian intervention on their behalf is pointless at best. Worse, based on the notions extended by the government and its "cooperating" cast of Indians that Native America is already largely self-governing and self-determining, non-Indian efforts to foster changes in U.S.-Indian relations can be cast as presumptuous and counterproductive.

The primary means by which the structure of U.S. internal colonialism is defended has come to be sophistry. The aversion of even the possibility of developing non-Indian opposition to what the federal government is doing is accomplished by projecting a carefully-perfected image that the system of colonial oppression no longer "really" exists. Culmination of the process will rest on inculcating the population at large with a subliminal "understanding" that the only "genuine," "authentic," "representative" and therefore "real" Indians are those who "fit in" most comfortably. "Real" Indians, in other words, conform most closely to the needs and expectations of the "larger society." "Real" Indians provide "voluntary" and undeviating service to those "greater interests" associated with the non-Indian status quo. An integral part of this capstone project requires an extensive literature and film industry to win the hearts and minds of non-Indians. It is the history and current efforts of this project which define the central theme of this book.

—Ward Churchill
Boulder, CO
November, 1991

Notes

1. See Stiffarm, Lenore and Phil Lane, Jr., "The Demography of Native North America: A Question of American Indian Survival," in M. Annette Jaimes (ed.), *The State of Native America: Genocide, Colonization, and Resistance*, South End Press, Boston, 1992.

2. Details, plus maps illustrating the disposition of these territories, may be found in Churchill, Ward, "The Earth is Our Mother: Struggles for American Indian Land and Liberation," in *The State of Native America, op. cit.*

3. The texts of all 371 ratified treaties may be found in Kappler, Charles J. (ed.), *Indian Treaties, 1778-1883,* Interland Publishing Co., New York, (Second Printing) 1973. Constitutional requirements for U.S. treaty-making, and the corresponding implied status of entities with which the federal government relates, are covered in Cohen, Felix S., *Handbook of Federal Indian Law,* University of New Mexico Press, Albuquerque, 1979, pp. 33-67. On the expropriation of treaty-secured land, see McDonnell, Janet A., *The Dispossession of the American Indian,*

1887-1934, Indiana University Press, Bloomington/Indianapolis, 1991.

4. On resource distribution, see generally, Garrity, Michael, "The U.S. Colonial Empire is as Close as the Nearest Reservation," in Holly Sklar (ed.), *Trilateralism: The Trilateral Commission and Elite Planning for World Government,* South End Press, Boston, 1980, pp. 238-68. Also see Jorgenson, Joseph (ed.), *Native Americans and Energy Development II,* Anthropology Resource Center/Seventh Generation Fund, Cambridge, MA, 1984.

5. Elaborations of the "plenary power" and "trust" doctrines as they pertain to Native Americans will be found in Deloria, Vine Jr., and Clifford M. Lytle, *American Indians, American Justice,* University of Texas Press, Austin, 1983.

6. U.S. Bureau of the Census, *1980 Census of the Population, Supplementary Report: American Indian Areas and Alaska Native Villages,* U.S. Government Printing Office, Washington, DC, 1984.

7. See, for example, U.S. Department of Health, Education, and Welfare, *A Study of Selected Socio-Economic Characteristics of Ethnic Minorities Based on the 1970 Census, Vol. 3: American Indians,* U.S. Government Printing Office, Washington, DC, 1974.

8. See U.S. Department of Education, Office of Research and Improvement, National Institute of Education, *Conference on Educational and Occupational Needs of American Indian Women, October 1976,* U.S. Government Printing Office, Washington, DC, 1980. Also see U.S. Senate, Committee on Labor and Human Resources, Subcommittee on employment and Productivity, *Guaranteed Job Oppoortunity Act: Hearing on S. 777,* 100th Congress, 1st Session, U.S. Government Printing Office, Washington, DC, 1980.

9. See generally, U.S. Department of Health and Human Services, *Chart Series Book,* Public Health Services, Washington, DC, 1988 (HE20.9409.988). Also see U.S. Congress, Office of Technology Assessment, *Indian Health Care,* U.S. Government Printing Office, Washington, DC, 1986 (OTA-H-290).

10. The government has admitted a significant portion of this

program; see Larson, Janet, "And Then There Were None" in *Christian Century*, January 26, 1977. Also see Dillingham, Brint, "Indian Women and IHS Sterilization Practices," *American Indian Journal*, Vol. 3, No. 1, January 1977. The best summary may be found in Women of All Red Nations, *Native American Women*, International Indian Treaty Council, New York, 1978. A more detailed overview appears in Jarrell, Robin, "Women and Children First: The Forced Sterilization of Native American Women," undergraduate thesis, Wellesley College, 1988.

11. Galeano, Eduardo, *The Open Veins of Latin America*, Monthly Review Press, New York, 1975.

12. On Homestake, see Weyler, Rex, *Blood of the Land: The U.S. Government and Corporate War Against the American Indian Movement*, Everest House Publishers, New York, 1983, pp. 262-3.

13. For a detailed account of the passage of the IRA and various federal conceptions underlying it, see Deloria, Vine Jr., and Clifford M. Lytle, *The Nations Within: The Past and Future of American Indian Sovereignty*, Pantheon Books, New York, 1984.

14. An excellent assessment of the functioning of IRA governments may be found in Robbins, Rebecca L., "Self-Determination and Subordination: The Past, Present and Future of American Indian Governance," *The State of Native America, op. cit.*

15. Analysis of the international legal conception of "self-determination," and the deficiencies of federal legislation in meeting these definitional standards, may be found in Morris, Glenn T., "International Law and Politics: Towards the Right of Self-Determination for Indigenous Peoples," in *The State of Native America, op. cit.*, For an elaboration of Native American conceptions of the term's meaning, see Robbins, Rebecca L., "American Indian Self-Determination: Comparative Analysis and Rhetorical Criticism," *Issues in Radical Therapy/New Studies on the Left*, Vol. XIII, Nos. 3&4, Summer-Fall 1988, pp. 48-59.

16. See Churchill, Ward, "Renegades, Terrorists and Revolutionaries: The Government's Propaganda War Against the American Indian Movement," *Propaganda Review*, No. 4, April 1989.

Part I

Literature Then and Now

Literature as a Weapon in the Colonization of the American Indian

To retrench the traditional concept of Western history at this point would mean to invalidate the justifications for conquering the Western Hemisphere.

—Vine Deloria, Jr.
God is Red

During the late 1960s, American writers made inroads into advanced literary theory by announcing their intent to offer the journal as novel/novel as journal. Norman Mailer embarked overtly upon such a course of action with his *Armies of the Night* in 1967; Tom Wolfe published his *The Electric Kool-Aid Acid Test* the same year. Such early efforts were soon followed by a proliferation of journalist/novelist works including Kurt Vonnegut's *Slaughterhouse Five* and the great synthetic gonzo excursions of Hunter S. Thompson. According to popular wisdom of the day, a new literary genre had been born, a writing process defining the emergent contours of American letters.

One might be inclined to agree with the assessment that this intentionally eclectic stew of fact and fiction constitutes a representative image of what is characteristically American in American literature. One might, with equal certainty, dispute the notion that such a posture is new to the scene, particularly since the deliberate presentation of fictionalized material as fact has marked the nature of American writing almost since the first English-speaking colonist touched pen to paper. A symbiotic relationship has been established in America between truly fictional writing on the one hand and ostensibly factual

17

material on the other. Perhaps it is true that this principle prevails in any literate culture. America, however, seems demonstrably to have gone beyond any discernible critical differentiation between fiction and nonfiction, a condition which has led to an acute blurring of the line between truth and art. How can this blurring, which might initially appear to be an aberration, be accounted for?

In locating the roots of such a situation, it becomes necessary to examine the content of early archetypal works originating in the Atlantic coastal colonies. By doing so, it is possible to distinguish a common denominator in terms of subject matter between the various modes of writing (formal journals, reports, histories and narrative accounts for the most part) then extant. This subject matter is the indigenous population of the region.

Was this early colonial preoccupation with fixing as "fact" the realities of things Indian through fictive modes a temporary phenomenon, or has it exhibited a longevity beyond the colonial period? An examination of 19th-century American writing, including the emergence of the novel and epic poetry in North America, provides an answer, albeit in cursory fashion. Interestingly, as fictional literature evolves in America, it is relatively easy to point both to its concern with the pronouncements of earlier nonfictive material as well as to the beginning of an active withdrawal of information from the factual treatments of the day. As American fiction developed during the 19th century, it provided a return of information (if only themes) to be pursued in nonfiction fora. The American Indian emerges as the common denominator blending these two types of writing.

Are such literary trends merely aspects of historical Americana or do they retain a contemporary force and vitality? An examination of several recent works in American letters tends to reveal that not only is the Indian-in-American-literature genre alive and well, but also that it has undergone something of an arithmetic progression, assuming a position occupying simultaneously both fictional and nonfictional frames of reference. Works secretly composed of pure imagination and conjecture are presented as serious factual writing; works of acknowledged fictive content are presented as authentic accounting of the true story. The journalist is and has always been novelist, the novelist has always pretended to journalistic truth in relation to the Native American, a condition which, in this sense at least, has served to define American literature itself.

We are not thus confronted with customary understandings of the status and function of literature. When fact and fiction fuse into an intentionally homogeneous whole, mythology becomes the norm. However, those who read, write and publish American literature are unfamiliar with and quite unwilling to acknowledge their truth as myth; it is insisted upon in most quarters that the myth *is* fact. This begs a final question: why is this insistence that a myth is fact so tenaciously maintained?

Viewed from the perspective of colonial analysis, the handling of the American Indian in literature ceases to be an enigma. With literature perceived as a component part of a colonial system, within which Native America still constitutes expropriated and subjugated peoples, the reworking of fact into convenient or expedient fantasies by the colonizer is a logical process rather than an inexplicable aberration. The merger of fact and fiction which was treated as such a rarified accomplishment by Mailer, Wolfe, Thompson, *et al.*, was already a time-honored practice in a colonial nation that has always insisted upon viewing itself as free of the colonial aspirations marking its European antecedents. As noted previously, to uncover the roots of these issues in American writing, we must examine the early historical record.

The Colonial Period:
"Nonfictional" Accounts

In May of 1607, three small ships sailed up the James
River from Chesapeake Bay in search of a site for the first
permanent English colony in North America. The pro-
spective settlers chose a peninsula that had the clear
disadvantage of being low and swampy. But it did provide
a good anchorage, and the fact that it was a virtual island
made it defensible against possible attacks by hostile
Indians. By giving a high priority to physical security, the
colonizers showed an awareness that this was not an
empty land but one that was already occupied by another
people who might well resist their incursion. Unlike
earlier attempted settlements, Jamestown was not so
much an outpost as a beachhead for the English invasion
and conquest of what was to become the United States of
America.

George M. Frederickson
White Supremacy

The need for physical security while carrying out an
invasion not only determined where and how early settlers lived but also what they wrote—the beginning of
American literature. This has held true virtually since the
first English set foot upon the soil of the North American
continent. As early as 1612, Captain John Smith was
offering observations on native peoples to an eager audience in the mother country:

They (the Indians) are inconstant in everything, but what
fear constraineth them to keep. Crafty, timorous, quick
of apprehension and very ingenious, some are of disposition fearful, some bold, most cautious, all savage...they
soon move to anger, and are so malicious that they seldom
forget an injury: they seldom steal from one another, lest
their conjurers reveal it, and so they be pursued and
punished.[1]

Smith's commentary was followed in short order by that of Alexander Whitaker:

> Let the miserable condition of these naked slaves of the devil move you to compassion toward them. They acknowledge that there is a great God, but they know him not, wherefore they serve the devil for fear, after a most base manner...They live naked of body, as if the shame of their sin deserved no covering...They esteem it a virtue to lie, deceive, steal...if this be their life, what think you shall become of them after death, but to be partakers with the devil and his angels in hell for evermore?[2]

In 1632, Thomas Morton added to the growing list of English language publications originating in the Atlantic Seaboard colonies concerned with the indigenous population:

> Now since it is but foode and rayment that men that live needeth (though not all alike), why should not the Natives of New England be sayd to live richly, having no want of either: Cloakes are the badge of sinne, and the more variety of fashions is but the greater abuse of the Creature, the beasts of the forest there deserve to furnish them at any time when they please: fish and flesh they have in great abundance which they roast and boyle...The rarity of the air begot by the medicinal quality of the sweet herbes of the Country, always procures good stomaches to the inhabitants...According to humane reason guided onely by the light of nature, these people leade the more happy and freer life, being void of care, which torments the minds of so many Christians: they are not delighted in baubles, but in useful things.[3]

And, in 1654, Edward Johnson penned the following concerning the English colonists' 1637 extermination of the Pequot:

> The Lord in his mercy toward his poor churches having thus destroyed these bloody barbarous Indians, he returns his people safely to their vessels, where they take

account of their prisoners. The squaws and some young youths they brought home with them, and finding the men guilty of the crimes they undertook the war for, they brought away only their heads.[4]

Each of the remarks cited here serve at least a twofold purpose: first, each contributed decisively to establishing Native Americans as a topic for English-language writing originating in the Americas (in fact, it becomes difficult to conceive of a colonial writing not preoccupied with things Indian). Second, each established the groundwork for a stereotype which assumed increasing prominence in American literature.

Smith's writing played upon the persistent image of the Indian as a sort of subhuman, animal-like creature who was a danger to hardy Anglo frontiersmen. Whitaker reinforced an already pervasive European notion of the Indian as godless heathen subject to redemption through the "civilizing" ministrations of Christian missionaries. Morton's often confused prattle went far in developing the "noble savage" mythology in the Americas. Johnson mined the vein of a militaristic insistence that the native was an incorrigible (even criminal) hindrance to European "progress" in North America, a miscreant barrier to be overcome only through the most liberal applications of fire and cold steel.

In addition to the primary stereotyping trends isolated in letters, another important genre of the same period tends to cut across stereotypic lines and might be perceived as generating a most heatedly emotional and decidedly anti-Indian popular response among readers: the so-called narratives of Indian captives. Perhaps the first manuscript of this school was published in 1682 by Mrs. Mary Rowlandson. Samples of her prose clearly meet the standards established above:

Now away we must go with those barbarous creatures, with our bodies wounded and bleeding, and our hearts no

less than our bodies...This was the dolefullest night that
ever my eyes saw. Oh, the roaring and singing and
dancing and yelling of those black creatures in the night,
which made the place a lively resemblance of hell.[5]

Such narratives were copiously cited as evidence by
such unabashed white supremacists as Increase Mather
in his 1684 epic, *Essay for the Recording of Illustrious
Providences.* Not to be outdone, brother Cotton joined in
with his *Magnalia Christi Americana* of 1702:

In fine, when the Children of the English Captives cried
at any time, so that they were not presently quieted, the
manner of the Indians was to dash out their brains
against a tree...they took the small children, and held em
under Water till they had near Drowned them...And the
Indians in their frolics would Whip and Beat the small
children, until they set em into grievous Outcries, and
then throw em to their amazed Mothers for them to quiet
em as well as they could.[6]

This "accounting" was followed by others such as
William Fleming's *Narrative of the sufferings and surpriz-
ing Deliverances of William and Elizabeth Fleming* in
1750 and the even more venomous (and very popular)
*French and Indian Cruelty Exemplified, in the Life and
Various Vicissitudes of Fortune,* of Peter Williamson in
1757:

From these few instances of savage cruelty, the deplor-
able situation of these defenceless inhabitants, and what
they hourly suffered in that part of the globe, must strike
the utmost horror to a human soul, and cause in every
breast the utmost detestation, not only against the authors of such tragic scenes, but against those who through
inattentions, or pusillanimous and erroneous principles,
suffered these savages at first, unrepelled, or even unmo-
lested, to commit such outrages and incredible depreda-
tions and murders.[7]

In themselves, each of the works produced by the writers covered in this section ostensibly has more to do with the non-fictional strains which have developed over the years in American literature than with the generic or popular term "literature." While the books and papers comprising historical archives are technically referred to (usually within scholarly circles) as "the literature," the generally understood and popularly held sense of the term refers quite specifically to material intentionally written and representative of fictive expression. The two modes are theoretically quite distinctive. Still, the allegedly non-fiction writing of the early English colonists noted above has had a large impact by creating the very conditions of stereotype and emotionalism from which later literary efforts sprang:

> From the initial poorly-informed reports on the Red Man emerged the bigoted and ethnocentric literary attitudes of pious but land-hungry Puritans. Soon were to follow the commercial and greatly fictional captivity narratives, and then the turn of the century "histories" of the Indian wars [never the "White," or "Settlers or Colonists" wars]...Perhaps the most tragic thing is that this was only the beginning.[8]

The Literary Version of Manifest Destiny

Perhaps the first American work which might appropriately be termed a novel (which, along with short stories, novellas, plays and poetry constitutes true literature in the popular conception) concerning American Indians was Charles Brockden Brown's 1799 release, *Edgar Huntley*. It was followed, in reasonably short order for the time, by two chapters "Traits of the Indian Character" and "Philip of Pokanoket." These were devoted to the extermination of the Narragansets during what the colonists called "King Philip's War" in Washington Irving's *Sketch Book*, dating from 1819. The latter absorbs the "noble savage" stereotype associated with Thomas Morton's earlier work:

> Even in his last refuge of desperation and dispair a sullen grandure gathers round his [Philip's] memory. We picture him to ourselves seated among his careworn followers, brooding in silence over his blasted fortunes and acquiring a savage sublimity from the wilderness of his lurking place. Defeated but not dismayed, crushed to earth but not humiliated, he seemed to grow more haughty beneath disaster and experience a fierce satisfaction in draining the last dregs of bitterness.[9]

Between 1823 and 1841, James Fenimore Cooper's novels—including *The Pioneers, The Last of the Mohicans, The Deerslayer, The Prairie* and *The Pathfinder*—had firmly established all of the stereotypes denoted above within the popular consciousness. Of course, Cooper had considerable help. During the same period, Chateaubriand's *Atala* appeared, as well as novels by William Gilmore Simms including *The Yamassee* and *Guy Rovers*. As well as novels, there were poems such as John Greenleaf Whittier's 1835 epic, *Mogg Megone* and, by 1855, Henry W. Longfellow's *The Song of Hiawatha, To the Driving Cloud* and *The Burial of Minnisink*. In a less pretentious vein, there was also during this general period the so-called "juvenile fiction" exemplified by Mayne Reid in *The Scalp Hunters* and *Desert Home*. The list is considerable.

The elements of this rapidly proliferating mass of creative output shared several features in common. For instance, none possessed the slightest concrete relationship to the actualities of native culture(s) they portrayed. Hence, each amounted to the imaginative invention of the authors, authors who by virtue of their medium were alien to the context (oral tradition) of which they presumed to write. It can be argued, and has,[10] that such prerogatives rest squarely within the realm of the fiction writer. While this may be true in an aesthetic sense, the practical application of the principle breaks down (for each of these works) on at least two levels:

- The justifying aesthetic rationale is itself an aspect of the European cultural context which generated the literate format at issue. Hence, utilizing aesthetic "freedom" as a justifying basis for the distortive literary manipulation of non-European cultural realities is merely a logically circular continuum. It may perhaps be reasonable that Europe is entitled (in the name of literature) to fabricate whole aspects of its own socio-cultural existence. However, the unilaterally extended proposition that Europeans are entitled to fabricate not only their own reality but also those of other cultures seems arrogant in the extreme, little more than a literary "Manifest Destiny."

- Regardless of the contradictions implied through application of purely European aesthetic values within a cross-cultural context, it must be held in mind that none of the authors in question operated in this abstract sense (such turf being generally reserved for their defenders). In each case, a more or less fictionally intended novel or poetic development was derived from the equally European (Anglo) but ostensibly non-fictive works cited in the previous section. Consequently, each later literary figure could lay claim to the "authenticity" of a firm grounding in the "historical record." That such history utterly ignored the indigenous oral accountings of the people/events thus portrayed, and did so in favor of the thoroughly alien literate record, serves to illustrate the self-contained dynamic through which literature dismisses anything beyond its pale (including the people being written

about). Again, the logic describes a perfect circle:
product and proof are one and the same.

The advent of the treatment of American Indians
within a formalized American fiction does not imply a
cessation or even a diminution of the "non-fictional" writing from which the fictional material grew. A most telling
example was the introduction of "Indian Religions" to the
readership of popular magazines during the 19th century.
In an 1884 essay published in *Atlantic Monthly,* writer
Charles Leland asserted that "...there is no proof of the
existence among our *[sic]* Indians of a belief in a Great
Spirit or in an infinite God before the coming of the
whites.[11] William Wassell, in an article in *Harper's
Monthly,* felt a factual sort of hope in the freeing of "pagan
savages" from "the sorcery and jugglery of weasoned med-
icine-men" by Christian missionaries who convinced them
of "simple teachings of the Bible."[12] In the same vein,
Amanda Miller celebrated the documentation of such
"civilizing" successes in an 1869 issue of *Overland
Monthly:*

> The contrast between the assemblage of hideously
> painted savages, whose countenances were rendered still
> the more revolting by their efforts to intensify their
> passions of hatred and revenge in their incantations of
> demonaltry, and the placid and devoted (Christian In-
> dian) congregation at Simcoe, was wonderful and delight-
> ful.[13]

By 1891, a serious scholar such as Alfred Riggs could
only conclude, on the basis of such a "factual" record, that
the Christian influence was leading the American Indian
to "a quickened conscience, a strengthened will, the power
of self-restraint...power to labor patiently, economy,
thrift...a new spiritual impulse, and a new revelation...and the customs of...a social order."[14] And there
were many other similar pieces in journals with titles such

as *Popular Science Monthly, North American Review, Nation, American Quarterly, Century, Scribner's Magazine, New Englander and Yale Review, Forum,* and others.[15] The conclusions of Alexander Whitaker discussed earlier were not only reiterated, but expanded upon.

It is relatively easy to perceive how, during the 19th century, any valid concept ever possessed by the English speaking population of North America as to Native Americans being peoples in their own right, peoples with entirely legitimate belief systems, values, knowledge and lifeways, had been lost in distortion presented through popular literature and pseudo-science. The stereotypes had assumed a documented authenticity in the public consciousness. Such a process cannot be viewed as meaningless distortion or justified under the guise of aesthetic freedom. For stereotyped and stereotyper alike, it becomes dehumanization and a tool justifying genocide.[16] As Russell Means recently stated:

> [W]ho seems most expert at dehumanizing other people? And why? Soldiers who have seen a lot of combat learn to do this to the enemy before going back into combat. Murderers do it before going out to murder. Nazi SS guards did it to concentration camp inmates. Cops do it. Corporation leaders do it to the workers they send into uranium mines and steel mills. Politicians do it to everyone in sight. And what the process has in common for each group doing the dehumanizing is that it makes it alright to kill and otherwise destroy other people. One of the Christian commandments says, "Thou shalt not kill," at least not humans, so the trick is to mentally convert the victims into non-humans. Then you can claim a violation of your own commandment as a virtue.[17]

Viewed in this way, treatment of the American Indian in the arena of American literature must be seen as part and parcel of the Anglo-American conquest of the North American continent. How else could general Euroamericans have been massively conditioned to accept,

on their behalf, a system or policy of non-stop expropriation and genocide of the native population throughout
U.S. history? The dehumanizing aspects of the stereotyping of American Indians in American literature may be
seen as an historical requirement of an imperial process.

The Course of Empire: From the Invasion of the Shock Troops to the Redefinition of Indigenous Culture

> The claim to a national culture in the past does not only
> rehabilitate that nation and serve as a justification for
> the hope of a future national culture. In the sphere of
> socioaffective equilibrium it is responsible for an impor-
> tant change in the native. Perhaps we have not suffi-
> ciently demonstrated that colonialism is not simply
> content to impose its rule upon the present and future of
> a dominated country. Colonialism is not merely satisfied
> with holding a people in its grip and emptying the
> native's brain of all form and content. By a kind of
> perverse logic, it turns to the past of an oppressed people,
> and distorts, disfigures and destroys it.
>
> —Frantz Fanon
> *The Wretched of the Earth*

The representation—indeed misrepresentation—is
a more accurate word, of indigenous people began virtually with the advent of English colonization of the Western
hemisphere. Within a relatively short period, styles of
exposition emerged which identified primary modes of
stereotype. These methods of stereotyping continue in
evolved formations today and must rightfully be viewed
as having their roots within the literary culture of England itself. This seems true on the basis of the sheer
falsity of colonial pronouncements concerning the indigenous American population. The pronouncements imply
that the notions involved were imported rather than lo-

cated upon arrival by the colonists, and reflect the prior existence of similar tendencies in "Mother England." Concerning this last:

> Whatever their practical intentions or purposes, the invaders did not confront the native peoples without certain preconceptions about their nature which help shape the way they pursued their goals. Conceptions of "savagery" that developed in the sixteenth and seventeenth centuries and became the common property of Western European culture constituted a distorting lens through which the early colonists assessed the potential and predicted the fate of the non-European peoples they encountered.[18]

The specific stereotypes of American Indians finally deployed in the New England colonies amount to elaboration and continuation of a stream of literary efforts already sanctioned by the Crown and its subjects. In practical terms, the established contours of this writing may be assessed as following a roughly "them vs. us" pathway:

> There were two crucial distinctions which allowed Europeans of the Renaissance and Reformation period to divide the human race into superior and inferior categories. One was between Christian and heathen and the other between "civil" and "savage."[19]

As we have seen, the primary stereotypes developed in the Americas did not vary from the established categories. Rather they represent merely the application of the prescribed generalities within a given context, that is, application to the indigenous populations within the territory of the New England colonies.

It is hardly an overstatement that the initial wave of any colonial invasion has been comprised of both the "cutting edge" and "hard core" of empire. These are the shock troops, arrogant, indoctrinated with the ideology of conquest, prepared to undergo hardship and sacrifice in order to actualize the ideal of their own inherent superiority to all that they encounter. Small wonder then that such "pioneers" would be prepared to bear false witness against those inhabitants of alien lands who would dare to stand in the way. A twofold purpose is served. First, in an immediate tactical sense, the overtly physical elimination and expropriation of indigenous peoples is the abrupt necessity of any preliminary colonization. It provides self-justification and even (in the hands of able propagandists) righteousness. The second purpose concerns a longer-term, strategic consideration: a less brutally doctrinaire segment of the "Mother Country" population ultimately must be attracted to the task of settling that which the invaders have conquered.

The latter point cannot be emphasized too strongly. Mere conquest is never the course of empire. Colonial warriors tend to realize their limitations, their own mortality. The achievement of mission can only be attained through the productive utilization of captured ground, the inevitable role of farmers, miners and merchants rather than soldiers. Hence, the literature of colonialism follows a course from the immediate self-glorifying accounts of first-wave assault troops, such as John Smith and Alexander Whitaker, to the salesmanship of Thomas Morton, and on to the longer-term restructuring of the past to serve present and future needs, at which Edward Johnson proved so adept. Things are never quite so clear cut in practice as they might be posed in theory. Smith blurred his efforts at self-justification into sales pitches concerning colonial real estate. Morton's advertisements of terrain contain residues of self-justification. Johnson reveals both aspects of concern within his historiography. But the emphases hold, in the main.

It is at this point a shift becomes evident. Immediate polemics fade into the background as tools for colonization. Now, historical recounting become feasible as an operant norm of literature, and the literary effort begins to proliferate within the colonial context. Understandably, this seems due to relaxation of initial tensions. The combat associated with the establishment of bridgeheads must end before significant writing can occur. In the Americas, this is evidenced in the work of the Mathers and others of the Puritan persuasion. Such material marks a shift. Earlier polemics accompanied the need to establish that settlement was in fact both possible and justifiable, that the colonies were viable entities for occupation by farmers as well as by "assault troops." The development of literature signals the emphasis upon the historical inevitability and moral correctness of colonial growth and perpetuation.

In inhabited areas, growth by one population segment is generally accommodated at the expense of another. And so it was in the Americas. The Puritan ideologues set the tone for a more or less continuous expansion of the English-speaking colonies, precipitating perpetual warfare with and expropriation of the various tribes encountered in the process. Yet, at this late date, John Smith had long since passed and, along with him, the cutting edge. The task now was to deploy the means to provoke and sanctify systematic warfare on the part of the settlement population itself. In this, the so-called captive narratives of Mary Rowlandson, William Fleming and others may be seen as having accrued a certain tactical utility.

At the onset of the 19th century, a new process had begun. Revolution had stripped England of its external colonies in the Americas and consolidation of the American nation-state had begun. The emphasis in arts and letters became that of creating the national heritage of the emerging state, a source of patriotism and pride within which history (unless wholly fabricated) played no part. Hence, the preoccupation with histories of the Americas during this period and the historical groundings provided to incipient American fiction. But, and there was never a

way to avoid this, the course of the European presence in
the hemisphere had always been intertwined with that of
the original inhabitants to the most intimate degree. The
construction of the U.S. national heritage in terms of
history therefore necessarily entailed the reconstruction
of American Indian history and reality to conform to the
desired image.

An obvious route achieve this end was to incorporate
preceding literature by English speakers (who constituted
the preponderant population of the new American state)
into the national heritage as the factual/perceptual basis
for both current and future literature. The rupture of
English colonization in North America really marked no
change in literary treatment of the American Indian. To
the contrary, it marked both the continuation and inten-
sification of practices initiated at the height of colonial
process. In both figurative and literal effect, the United
States merely supplanted England as the new preeminent
colonial power relative to Indians.

In Fanon's terms, the colonist who had metaphori-
cally stripped the native of his/her present through creation of a surrogate literary reality, defined to the
convenience of the colonizer, was now turning the meta-
phoric/mythic siege guns fully to the past. In this way, the
present for the native could be perpetually precluded
through the maintenance of this seamlessly constituted
surrogate reality as myth. Clearly too, any perpetual
"present" must encompass the future as well as the moment. The indigenous reality, the "national culture" of
Fanon's thesis, is thereby hopelessly trapped within the
definitional power of the oppressor, drifting endlessly in
lazy hermeneutic circles, stranded in a pastless/present-
less/futureless vacuum. The national identity of the colonizer is created and maintained through the usurpation
of the national identity of the colonized, a causal relationship.

The final conquest of the continental land mass by the United States absorbed the whole of the 19th century, a period which coincided with the formal creation of American literature. Region by region, tribe by tribe, indigenous cultures were overwhelmed and consigned to the reservation status marking the physical characteristics of U.S. internal colonialism. Throughout this era, an overarching theme in American writing, from the embryonic work of Charles Brockden Brown and Washington Irving to the late-century tracts of Charles Leland and Alfred Riggs, was the Indian. Or, rather, a certain image of the Indian which complemented the need of the nation's Euroamerican population to supplant the original inhabitants of the land.

Replacing Troops and Guns with Self-Colonization

In the late 19th century another shift occured in addition to that between the early polemics and the growth of literature. Where initial English colonial writings seemed primarily to be seriously concerned with the christian/heathen dichotomy, 19th century American literature gravitated more and more toward themes involving the civil versus savage juxtaposition. The trappings of quasi-missionary rhetoric were maintained in treatments such as that written by Amanda Miller, to be sure, but this is a blurring of distinctions of the same order as the overlapping of content evident between Smith, Whitaker and Morton in an earlier period. By the late 1800s, the original imperatives of missionarism, obvious enough in Puritan literature, had given way to a posture whereby Christianization simply marked a signification of the transition of the savage to civilized (non-obstructionist) status.

Another signification of the civilizing process was literacy itself, wherein a primary tool of the formulation and justification of European colonialism was offered up as a focus for attainment to the colonized. As the articulation of the Manifest Destiny doctrine underscored Euroamerica's assumed right to its concrete territorial ambitions, so too did articulation of aesthetic doctrine reserve unto the literate the right to interpret history and reality at will. In America, both theses were developed during the same period and progressed virtually in tandem. Both were designed to serve the population which invented them at the direct expense of others. But, while the most overt expressions of manifest destiny have become politically outmoded and have fallen into disrepute, the logic of literate aesthetic primacy has, if anything, become a dominant social norm.

The final absorption of the western United States into the national domain was accompanied by a constantly increasing public zeal to civilize the savage, or at least the popular conception of the savage. This latter is of considerable importance insofar as therein lies the primary function of literature within colonialism. The overwhelming preponderance of writing concerning the American Indian during the U.S. expansion was designed to create an image allowing conquest "for the Indians' own good," to effect "betterment" and "progress." The potential for a mass psychology of national guilt at its apparent policy of genocide and theft could be offset in no other conceivable fashion at that time. Further, the imposition of literacy and "education" can be perceived as the most effective means to inculcate in the Indians themselves a "correct" understanding (in future generations, at least) of the appropriateness of their physical and cultural demise. As has been noted in this connection:

Since schooling was brought to non-Europeans as a part of empire...it was integrated into an effort to bring indigenous peoples into imperial/colonial structures...After all, did not the European teacher and the school built on the European capitalist model transmit European values and norms and begin to transform traditional societies into "modern" ones...(?)[20]

At this juncture, a truly seamless model of colonialism made its appearance: The training of the colonized to colonize themselves. In this sense, hegemony over truth and knowledge replaces troops and guns finally as the relevant tool of colonization. Literature, always an important property of the European colonial process, assumed an increasingly important centrality to maintenance of the system. As Albert Memmi has observed:

> In order for the colonizer to be a complete master, it is not enough for him to be so in actual fact, but he must also believe in its (the colonial system's) legitimacy. In order for that legitimacy to be complete, it is not enough for the colonized to be a slave, he must also accept his role. The bond between the colonizer and the colonized is thus destructive and creative. It destroys and recreates the two partners in colonization into the colonizer and the colonized. One is disfigured into the oppressor, a partial, unpatriotic and treacherous being, worrying about his privileges and their defense; the other into an oppressed creature, whose development is broken and who compromises by his defeat.[21]

Such a view goes far towards answering the obvious questions concerning why, nearly a century after the conclusion of the primary U.S. territorial expansion, American literature still treats the Indian within its own desired framework. Witness the works of Carlos Castaneda, Ruth Beebe Hill and Cash Asher. In the same sense, it explains the nature of the support from publishers, a massive reading audience, and the academic community as a whole.

Removing the Last Vestiges of Literal and Figurative Threat

That which is cannot be admitted. That which will be must be converted by literate logic into that which cannot be. To this end, the publishers publish, the writers invent, the readers consume in as great a portion as may be provided, and the academics sanctify (over and over) the "last word" in true explanation as to where we've been, come and are going. None, or at least few, seem to act from outright malice; most are moved compulsively by internalized forces of fear (of retribution?), guilt and greed.

How then best to deploy the sophistry of literature within such a context? Certainly not in the crude polemical fashion of the Mathers and the Smiths. Those days passed with the need for blatant military suppression of tribal autonomy. No, direct attack is obsolete. In the post-holocaust era there is no viable ability to justify Sand Creek, the Washita and Wounded Knee. Rather, these are to be purged through a reconstitution of history as a series of tragic aberrations beginning and ending nowhere in time. The literal meaning of such events must at all costs be voided by sentiment and false nostalgia rather than treated as parts of an ongoing process. The literal is rendered tenuously figurative, and then dismissed altogether.

From there, reality can be reconstructed at will. Witness the contemporary obsession with establishing "authenticity." Ruth Beebe Hill requires the services of an aging Indian to verify her every word. Cash Asher requires another aging Indian to step forward and attest the truth of every word. Carlos Castenada relies upon a truly massive and sustained support from both the publishing and professional academic communities to validate his efforts. Schneebaum, Waldo, Lamb, Storm, all within the past fifteen years, receive considerable support from "reputable" publishers and from some of the most prestigious scholarly establishments in the country.[22]

It is not that they are "ordered" to say specific things about the Indian, although the ancient stereotypes are maintained (albeit in mutated form). Rather, it seems that the current goal of literature concerning American Indians is to create them, if not out of whole cloth, then from only the bare minimum of fact needed to give the resulting fiction the "ring of truth," to those Indians bound to colonialism as readily as to people of European heritage.

At the dawn of English colonization of the New World, Sir Walter Raleigh was able to write that the natives of Guiana, "have their eyes in their shoulders, and their mouths in the middle of their breasts." He was believed then by the English reading public, although his words assume proportions of absurdity today (as, one assumes, they must have to those in a position to know better at the time).

Things have come full circle on the literary front. Where, in the beginning, it was necessary to alter indigenous realities in order to assuage the invading colonial conscience, so it seems necessary today to alter these realities to assure the maintenance of empire. It seems to matter little what American Indians are converted into, as long as it is into other than what they are, have been and might become. Consigned to a mythical realm, they constitute no threat to the established order either figuratively (as matters of guilt and conscience) or literally (in terms of concrete opposition). That which is mythic in nature cannot be or has been murdered, expropriated and colonized in the "real world." The potential problem is solved through intellectual sleight of hand, aesthetic gimmickry and polemical discourse with specters. The objective is not art but absolution. As Vine Deloria, Jr. has observed in another context:

[T]herein lies the meaning of the whites fantasy about Indians—the problem of the Indian image. Underneath all the conflicting image of the Indian one fundamental truth emerges: the white man knows that he is alien and he knows that North America is Indian—and he will never let go of the Indian image because he thinks that by some clever manipulation he can achieve an authenticity which can never be his.[23]

In this sense at least, literature in America is and always has been part and parcel of the colonial process. In this sense too, it has always been that American literature constituted a confused netherworld wherein fictionalized journals met journalized fiction in a jumble of verbiage requisite only to the masking of a disavowed and painful reality.

Notes

1. Smith, John. *A Map of Virginia, with a description of the Country, the Commodities, People, Government and Religion* (1621) as cited in Halleck, Reuben Post, *History in American Literature* (New York, 1911), p. 18.

2. Whitaker, Alexander. *Good News from Virginia* as cited in Tyler, Moses Goit, *A History of American Literature, 1607-1765* (Ithaca, 1949), pp. 41-43.

3. Morton, Thomas. *New English Canaan* (1632) as cited in Washburn, Wilcomb E., ed., *The Indian and the White Man* (New York, 1965), pp. 35-38.

4. Johnson, Edward, *Wonder-Working Providence of Zions Savior in New England* (1654) as cited in Tyler, pp. 122-215.

5. Rowlandson, Mary. *The Sovereignty and Goodness of God Together With the Faithfulness of His Promise Displayed: Being a Narrative of the Captivity and Restoration of Mrs. Mary Rowlandson* (1682) as cited in Pearce, R.H., "Significance of the Captivity Narrative," *American Literature XIX* (March 1947), 1-20.

6. Mather, Cotton. *Magnalia Christi Americana* (1702), *Ibid.*, pp. 3-4, *The Reader's Encyclopedia of American Literature*, Max J.

Herzog, ed., New York, 1962; also cites another work closely related to the Mather opus, but bearing the even more unlikely title of *The Redeemed Captive Returning to Zion or a faithful history of Remarkable Occurrences in the Captivity and Deliverance of Mr. John Williams (Minister of the Gospel in Deerfield) who in the Desolation which befell the Plantation by the incursion of the French and Indians, was by them carried away, with his family and his neighborhood into Canada* (!!!) (1707).

7. Williamson, Peter. *French and Indian Cruelty Exemplified, in the Life and Various Vicissitudes of Fortune, of Peter Williamson* (1757) as cited in Pearce, pp. 7-8.

8. Beer, David F. "Anti-Indian Sentiment in Early Colonial Literature," *The Indian Historian*, Vol. 2, No. 1, San Francisco, Spring 1969, p. 48.

9. Irving, Washington. *Sketch Book* (1819), as cited in Ten Kate, C.F., "The Indian in American Literature" (1919), *Smithsonian Annual Reports*, 1921, reprinted in *The American Indian Reader: Literature*, American Indian Historical Society, San Francisco, 1973. Citation is from p. 189 of the latter volume.

10. See, as but one example, the subtle justification(s) advanced in Ten Kate.

11. Leland, Charles G. "The Edda Among the Algonquin Indians," *Atlantic Monthly*, LIV (August 1884), p. 223.

12. Wassell, William. "The Religion of the Sioux," *Harper's New Monthly Magazine*, LXXXIX (November, 1894), p. 945.

13. Miller, Amanda. "To Simcoe," *Overland Monthly*, III (August, 1869), p. 176.

14. Riggs, Alfred. "Some Difficulties of the Indian Problem," *New Englander and Yale Review*, LIV (April, 1891), p. 329.

15. A sampling of the essays and articles intended here is: Powell, John Westley. "Mythologic Philosophy I," *Popular Science Monthly*, XV (October 1879); Tripple, Eugene J. "Primitive Indian Tribes," *North American Review*, CI (July 1865); Schwatka, Frederick. "The Sun-Dance of the Sioux," *Century*, XVII (March 1890); Walsh, Herbert. "The Meaning of the Dakota Outbreak," *Scribner's Magazine*, IX (April 1891); Bourke, John G. "The Indian Messiah," *Nation* (December 4, 1890); Price, Hiram. "The Government and the Indians," *Forum*, X (February

1891); Parkman, Francis. "Indian Superstitions," *North American Review*, CIII (July 1866). As noted in the text, the listing could be continued *ad nauseum*.

16. The sense of the definition of dehumanization intended here is as simple as that offered by *The Merriam-Webster Dictionary* (New York, 1974): "...the divestiture of human qualities or personality..." Surely this is an apt summation of the fate experienced by the native in the literature covered so far.

17. Means, Russell. "Fighting Words on the Future of Mother Earth," *Mother Jones* (November 1980), 26-27.

18. Frederickson, George M. *White Supremacy: A Comparative Study in American and South African History* (Oxford University Press, 1981), p. 7.

19. *Ibid.*, pp. 7-8.

20. Carnoy, Martin. *Education as Cultural Imperialism* (David McKay and Co., 1974), p. 16.

21. Memmi, Albert. *Colonizer and Colonized* (Beacon Press, 1965), p. 89.

22. Some of the specific material intended within this observation includes Asher, Cash and Chief Red Fox, *The Memoirs of Chief Red Fox*, Fawcett Books, New York, 1972; Hill, Ruth Beebe, with Chunksa Yuha (Alonzo Blacksmith), *Hanta Yo: An American Saga*, Doubleday, New York, 1979; Storm, Hyemeyohsts, *Seven Arrows*, Ballantine Books, New York, 1972; Waldo, Anna Lee, *Sacajawea*, Avon Books, New York, 1978; Schneebaum, Tobias, *Keep the River on Your Right*, Grove Press, New York, 1970; as well as at least the first three books by Carlos Castaneda, the so-called "Castaneda Trilogy."

23. Deloria, Vine, Jr. "Foreword: American Fantasy," *The Pretend Indians: Images of Native Americans in the Movies*. Gretchen M. Bataille and Charles L. P. Silet, eds. (Iowa State University Press, 1980), p. xvi.

Carlos Castaneda

The Greatest Hoax
since Piltdown Man

Since the American public has already become accustomed to seeing the Jerome Rothenburg "translations," the poetry of "white shamans" such as Gary Snyder, Gene Fowler, Norman Moser, Barry Gifford, David Cloutier, to name a few, and other neo-romantic writers posing as Indians and/or Indian experts/spokesmen, such as Carlos Castaneda, Hyemeyohsts Storm, Tony Shearer, Doug Boyd, the Baha'i influenced "Indian" works of Naturegraph Publications, contemporary Indian writers are often discounted or ignored since they are not following or conforming to the molds created by these "experts."

—Geary Hobson
The Remembered Earth

In 1968, a book appeared on the American literary scene bearing the rather unlikely title, *The Teachings of Don Juan: A Yaqui Way of Knowledge.* Even less probable, on the surface at least, was that the publisher of this overnight bestseller was not a commercial publishing house, but the academically prestigious UCLA Press. In 1971, the successful author followed up with a sequel volume, *A Separate Reality: Further Conversations with Don Juan.* 1972 witnessed the release of *Journey to Ixtlan: The Lessons of Don Juan.*

In contrast to the initial book, the latter two were published through a commercial publisher, Simon and Schuster, perhaps because the author was preparing to submit his third manuscript under the title of *Sorcery: A Description of the World* to his UCLA doctoral committee as a dissertation shortly thereafter.[1] On the other hand, his motivation was perhaps more oriented toward Simon and Schuster's lucrative offer of releasing all three efforts as a "Don Juan Trilogy," a package set offered to those seeking initiation to the innermost secrets of American Indian spirituality. In any event, the literary transition from ostensibly serious anthropological writing, with its almost concomitant limited readership, to the mass market of Madison Avenue publishing seems to have presented our author with little demonstrable difficulty.

As a certified Ph.D. in anthropology, the writer went on to turn out *Tales of Power* in 1974, following up with *The Second Ring of Power* in 1977 and finally in 1981, *The Eagle's Gift;* all from Simon and Schuster. Along the way of his book publishing career, he also found time to undergird his professional academic stature with the publication of "The didactic uses of hallucinogenic plants: An examination of a system of teaching" in *Abstracts of the 67th Annual Meeting of the American Anthropological Association* (1968), and to add luster to his position within the lucrative cosmos of pop psychology with articles like "The Art of Dreaming" in *Psychology Today* (December 1977). By 1979, as Simon and Schuster was preparing to go to press with *The Art of Stalking,* which would have been the author's sixth book (had it been published, which—mysteriously enough—it was not), he had by various estimates grossed from $1 million to $3 million as a result of his literary efforts.[2]

In essence, the sequence of esoteric sagas at issue here revolve around the notion that, beginning sometime in 1963, a UCLA graduate student of anthropology ventured into the southern Sonora desert for purposes of meeting and understudying to an aging "Yaqui sorcerer" named Don Juan Matis. For the next five odd years he was allowed, on a more or less continuous basis, to take field notes in Spanish at a rather furious rate. At the end of this period, although still apprenticed to his master, he began to publish the fabulous results, albeit in edited and translated fashion. All of this, of course, seems at least superficially plausible, but there are certain problems involved which—beyond a certain point—begin to boggle the mind.

First, there seems to be some legitimate question as to the identity of the author. Carlos Cesár Salvadore Araña (Castaneda) claims to have been born in São Paulo, Brazil variously in 1931 or 1935. In actuality he was born in Cajamarca, Peru in 1925. He maintains his father was a professor of literature. The man seems actually to have been a goldsmith, according to a 1973 *Time* magazine article. He claims to have served as a U.S. Army paratrooper during the Korean conflict and that he was wounded (both testicles shot away). During that period, he was actually in Brazil, concerned with the incipient birth of an illegitimate daughter; there is no record of his ever serving in any unit or branch of the U.S. military (before, during or after Korea), much less that he was wounded.

He has also claimed the spelling of his father's family name to be the Portuguese "Aranha" rather than the Spanish "Araña" (Castaneda is actually his mother's family name). This is interesting in terms of his literary career in that, unlike the Spanish variant, the Portuguese word means "trickster" or "deceiver." Such word play seems entirely appropriate and is unlikely to have been unintentional, as we shall see.

Regardless of the intricacies of his personal history, several serious questions concerning the accuracy and general merit of Castaneda's writing should have been blatantly obvious, from the release of *The Teachings of Don Juan* onward. This is especially true within the scholarly community under whose mantle of "authenticity" and "scientific objectivity" his work was initially published. These questions center, not within the realm of specialized anthropological considerations concerning the author's supposed target group (the Yaqui), but on the sheer physicality Castaneda claims as the setting for his anthropological endeavors.

Bear in mind that the Castaneda chronicles theoretically occur in the southern Sonora desert, a region in which summer daylight temperatures all but invariably exceed 100° Fahrenheit, commonly go above 110°, and tend to prevail around the clock. Castaneda nonetheless rather flippantly referred his UCLA teachers and colleagues to such dates as "June 29," "July 24," and "August 19" as days when, under the tutelage of a veteran desert dweller who would have known better even if the urbanized Carlos had not, he "roamed for hours across the desert"[3] hunting quail and was so absorbed in the activity that "a whole day went by and [he] had not noticed the passage of time. [He] even forgot to eat lunch..."[4] He was also known to "stop around noon... to rest in an unshaded area."[5] As has been pointed out elsewhere, such activity would be virtually guaranteed to induce delirium, coma and death, yet Castaneda consistently asserts that he and don Juan performed such superhuman feats on a virtually incessant basis.[6]

Such "never-never land" descriptions of Sonoran summers are well matched by inaccurate descriptions of the Sonoran winters. Castaneda describes the generally frigid rains as "lukewarm" and refers to spending at least one night sleeping in them, in the open and unprotected.[7] Again, such activity would prove all but suicidal to even the heartiest native of the desert, never mind a slightly pudgy campus type such as the author.

Nor are climatic considerations the end of such obvious physical nonsense. Castaneda elsewhere refers to the desert as "crawling with mountain lions,"[8] a condition which directly contradicts the big cats' known predilection for acting as territorial loners (not to mention the fact that they've been very nearly exterminated over the past fifty years). He writes of being "charged" by an uncornered

puma,[9] another distinctly mythical mountain cat characteristic, but a trait he might well have confused with
readings concerning jaguars which, although currently
extinct in the region, did inhabit Sonora a few centuries
back. He also refers to taking refuge in a tree to escape
one particularly bloodthirsty beast.[10] This latter displays
a truly sublime ignorance of feline reality, insofar as
mountain cats are considerably more adept at tree climb-
ing than are humans. And on and on...

Nonetheless, *The Teachings of Don Juan* was immediately acclaimed as being destined for fame in the *New
York Times*. By May, 1971, reviewer Roger Jellinik was
proclaiming in the same mass circulation tabloid that
Castaneda's books represented an authentic accounting
of a "pre-logical form that is no-one-knows how old."[11] He
went on to say that no one could exaggerate the anthropological significance of Castaneda's work. By February
of 1972, the *Times* was running reviews such as that by
William Irving Thompson to the effect that Castaneda
was the first scholar to effectively integrate science with
the occult in an anthropologically valid sense.[12] October of
the same year saw Africa specialist Paul Riesman endorsing all of the first three don Juan books as "milestones in
[the] science of anthropology."[13]

Elsewhere, *Saturday Review* published a glowing
review by humanities professor Albert William Levi covering both *The Teachings of Don Juan* and *A Separate
Reality* in 1971.[14] This was followed in the same publication by a 1972 Joseph Kanon review saluting Castaneda
as one of the few "serious" current anthropological exper-
imenters in "reality perception and psychic phenomenon."[15] Both books received high approval in *Publishers
Weekly* the same year as being "consistent, luminous [and]
profoundly exciting."[16] A sampling of other quite favorable
reviews have appeared over the years in such widely
circulated publications as *Esquire* (1971 and 1975),
Harper's (1973 and 1974), *New Statesman* (1975), *Sunday*

Times (1975), *Cultural Information Service* (1976), and *CoEvolution Quarterly, Booklist* and *New Age* (all in 1977). With this degree of commercial hype, it is small wonder that by the spring of 1977 Simon and Schuster were reporting aggregate sales of nearly four million Castaneda books.[17]

It would, however, seem more than unfair to single out the commercial publishing industry as having arbitrarily established Castaneda's credentials as an "authentic" source of American Indian wisdom via the medium of Yaqui sorcerers. Considerable critical corroboration accrued, after all, from those who really should know about such matters. As was noted earlier, Castaneda was awarded a doctorate in anthropology from UCLA on the basis of his *Journey to Ixtlan* manuscript, already published, but conveniently retitled as a dissertation. His doctoral committee was hardly devoid of academic laurels, consisting of Philip Newman (the chair), Clement Meighan, Harold Garfinkle (of ethnomethodology fame), Kees Bolle, and Theodore Graves (later replaced by Robert Edgerton). The candidate's written examinations were administered by Newman, Meighan and Graves; Garfinkle and Bolle joined in for the orals. The award of the doctorate to Carlos Castaneda could hardly do less than validate the intrinsic legitimacy of his published work (three books at that point) as well as his "scholarly methodology."

Additionally, other generally credible academicians have tended to support Castaneda's work in print over the years. For example, Mary Douglas published an article in 1973 very much endorsing the first three don Juan books, at least in terms of Castaneda's "intellectual" approach to his subject matter.[18] She later published an expanded and revised version of this supportive argument as a chapter in one of her books (which are geared to a highly academic audience).[19] Similarly, Stan Wilke has gone to bat for both Castaneda and his "methods" on a number of occasions.[20]

And, to be sure, these more or less staid academics have
been joined by "new wave" theoreticians such as Theodore
Roszak who has championed Castaneda for having
brought out "...the ritualistic precision and pedagogical
discipline surrounding don Juan's teachings [which] re-
sound with generations of experiment, meditation and
philosophical systematization."[21]

As late as September 1981, the author encountered
a formal paper submitted to the *Journal of Ethnic Studies*
for prepublication reading and evaluation, which opted to
treat don Juan and, by extension, Castaneda, as wholly
authentic material and worthy of consideration alongside
the likes of Black Elk, Lame Deer, Handsome Lake and
Geronimo.[22] While little more need be said concerning the
degree of validation accorded Castaneda in academic circles, there is more.

Probably the strongest single endorsement of
Castaneda's anthropological and literary authenticity
came (and comes), not from the cloistered committees and
small journals of academic life, but from the highly visible
UCLA Press. It was, after all, the UCLA Press which not
only selected to publish Castaneda's initial manuscript,
but to publish it as legitimate research. Of course, on the
face of it, the press had its reasons. These come down in
no small part to the fact that *The Teachings of Don Juan*
was originally submitted to the director of the University
Press in late 1967 accompanied by strong support and
recommendations of four members of Castaneda's prominent (at UCLA, at least) doctoral committee. According to
the current director, James H. Clark (who did not hold
that position in the late '60s), the manuscript was turned
over to the press editorial committee, chaired by Walter
R. Goldschmidt, who also chaired the UCLA Department
of Anthropology. Goldschmidt was apparently the only
committee member to read the material prior to its acceptance as a serious piece of ethnography. Goldschmidt then

proceeded to write the foreword to the book, a rather singular endorsement.

It would seem, at this juncture, that the press had more than ample reason to publish. The catch, however, is that none of the recommending anthropologists (including Goldschmidt) possessed or even claimed to possess any particular expertise relative to Yaquis, sorcerers, or even general mestizo Mexican tribal lore. In addition, there were rather well qualified anthropologists on campus at the time who tended to express rather serious reservations concerning the integrity of Castaneda's field work, research and conclusions. They were emphatically not included in the prepublication deliberations. A classic example of this is Ralph Beals, one-time member of Castaneda's doctoral committee and Yaqui specialist, who withdrew from the degree-granting process when he became suspicious of his student's claims and pressed for the verbatim field notes Carlos claimed to be making; Castaneda, at that point, "simply disappeared."

In any event, the manuscript was passed along to a sponsoring editor, Robert Zachary, who oversaw its copyediting (which is more than can be said for the staff at Simon and Schuster, later on), designed and packaged the book, and established its promotional campaign. The latter had a decidedly "scholarly" flavor, exemplified by an advertisement placed on the back cover of *American Anthropologist* labeling the book "...nothing less than a revelation, [an] unprecedented...living document to the spirit,"[23] a drift which clearly led to assertions in academia that, "There is no question that Carlos Castaneda is an able anthropologist who has performed at a unique level of excellence in his field."[24]

The question really at issue here, aside from the raw mechanics of how publishing careers are handled by presses within U.S. citadels of higher learning, is really this: What sort of content were the preceding academic and commercial "heavies" opting to sell? What are they still selling, for that matter? What have a "Yaqui way of knowledge," "don Juan" and Carlos Castaneda to do with Yaquis—either in reality or as one might reasonably expect them to be presented through the filters of anthropological lensing? Or, what have any of the above to do with factual material of any sort?

In this connection, it seems proper that one first consider whether in fact the legendary don Juan, under whose careful instruction Carlos Castaneda allegedly became initiated to the innermost secrets of Yaquidom, exists or, indeed, ever existed. Normally, a question as fundamental as this could be readily and conclusively answered in the affirmative by a reputable anthropologist (or virtually any other variety of nonfiction writer). The existence of field notes might be counted on to provide at least partial verification. Similarly, tape recordings of interviews and/or simple conversation(s) would provide additional corroboration. Photographs are usually handy, and so on.

In Castaneda's case, however, things are not nearly so simple. To the contrary, he dispensed with such "hard" evidence as tape recordings and photographs out of hand through the assertion that don Juan categorically refused to allow use of either medium. This would, of course, leave several years' accumulation of field notes available for analysis.[25] On this matter, Castaneda seemingly concurred when such questions arose during the early 1970s, stating that he would gladly provide his written records for public scrutiny but that, sadly enough, such materials had been destroyed in a freak flooding of his basement.

As usual, the situation is superficially plausible but, upon closer examination, leaves unanswered rather natural questions as to why his doctoral committee had never been privy to the notes when determining the academic merit of Castaneda's research methodology. And what was the basis on which Castaneda launched his subsequent literary output (an additional three books to date, as well as an unpublished manuscript of some sort)?

But, if direct examination of Castaneda's field work breaks up on the shoals of natural catastrophe and the obstinacy of an aging Yaqui, indirect analysis remains entirely possible (and appropriate). Consider the linguistic implications of work such as that which Castaneda purports to have delivered. It seems reasonable enough to expect that, since the subject of study was theoretically a Yaqui immersed in a life-long pursuit of ancient Yaqui wisdom, he might be rather given to expressing himself in the Yaqui language. This would necessitate Castaneda being quite fluent in Yaqui (which he's never pretended to be) and would naturally have led to the bulk of his field notes having been jotted first in that language and then translated. Translation usually involves the encountering of certain words for which there are no translatable equivalents, particularly when one is dealing with esoteric or highly technical concepts (such as sorcery, for example). In practical terms, this generally results in the retention of the original specialized term or terms (with accompanying definition upon initial usage), or at least a citation of the original, peculiar, term within a translated text. Yet nowhere in the mass of Castaneda's published material does such practices seem pronounced and, as we shall see, in the few instances where Yaqui words appear, they seem diametrically opposed to conventional Yaqui usage.

Of course, Castaneda has always maintained that his mountainous field notes were compiled in Spanish, implying that this was the language of communication with don Juan. This, in combination with Castaneda's seemingly utter incomprehension of Yaqui, suggests that don Juan must not only have been exceedingly fluent in Spanish, but willing to translate virtually all of his most complex ideas into that language as an aid to his erstwhile interviewer/understudy. But even this tenuous proposition is significantly undercut when it is noted that the few hand-scrawled pages of Spanish notes Castaneda ever produced for examination[26] were noticeably tainted by his own Peruvian idiom rather than known Mexican word usages.[27] Either don Juan, the life-long Yaqui sorcerer, spent a considerable period of his life in Peru, or don Juan was an invention and Castaneda interviewed himself from time to time.

With this, it seems safe to assert that no anthropological source existed for Castaneda's material. Tangentially, of course, analytical means still exist which would allow for substantiation of the fact that a researcher at least conducted his or her field work in the field rather than in the library or through an active imagination. To some extent, the recounting of geographical particulars might accomplish this. But, as we have seen in his descriptions of activities in the desert, Castaneda failed this test in a singularly spectacular fashion. Again, the introduction of specific physical evidence, such as vegetal matter corroborating unorthodox assertions (or findings), might go far toward establishing credibility, in terms of context at least. This final criterion would seem tailored to Castaneda's repeated references to the smoking of hallucinogenic mushrooms with don Juan.[28]

Such evidence has indeed been requested by a nationally noted botanist, Dr. Gordon R. Wasson, a specialist in hallucinogens (who was particularly interested in Castaneda's "find" due to the fact that "smokable" mushrooms were—and are—unknown).[29] Although Castaneda agreed to provide samples to substantiate his case, he never did.[30] Much later, in an incident strikingly similar to his tragically destroyed field notes, he claimed that his solitary sample had been mishandled and "lost" by a UCLA laboratory assistant. The mushroom stories were finally dismissed as worthless nearly a decade after they were promoted by UCLA Press and the anthropology department as the greatest thing since sliced bread.[31]

Given the overall nature of the confluence of critical defects in Castaneda's supporting evidence, it seems reasonable to suggest that it is highly unlikely he did and experienced what he claimed. Insofar as don Juan Matis is integral to virtually all of Castaneda's claims, it is equally unlikely that the former exists or ever existed, at least in any Yaqui configuration (whether as a single individual or as an amalgamation of several individuals). In purest terms, it seems entirely likely that don Juan is and always has been the exclusive product of the over-active imagination of Carlos Castaneda, a product having literally nothing to do with Yaquis, American Indians and, in most instances, with reality of any sort.

This last statement may seem to be stretching the point a bit too far. Even given that Castaneda may well have invented the specifics of his field work, thus eliminating all aspects of authenticity from his accounts, he might still have utilized libraries and other resources to construct something of an accurate portrait of the inner mechanics of the Yaqui worldview. Hence, his work might still be marginally salvageable in the sense that it may be valid, even if inauthentic. In this connection, consider the following juxtaposition of quotations:

> My eyes were closed, and a large pool started to open up in front of them. I was able to see a red spot. I was aware of an unusual odor, and different parts of my body getting extremely warm, which felt extremely good.[32]

> What was very outstanding was the pungent odor of the water...I got very warm, and blood rushed to my ears. I saw a red spot in front of my eyes. "What would happen if I did not see red?" "You would see black." "What happens to those who see red?" "An effect of pleasure."[33]

The first quotation is a condensation of material published in *Psychedelic Review*. The second is from *The Teachings of Don Juan*. The first quotation predates the second; the journal in question was readily accessible in

the UCLA library in the late 1960s, and remains so today.
Of course, this could be purely coincidental, two authors
describing similar drug-induced experiences. Another
juxtaposition may prove helpful:

> The Human Aura is seen by the psychic observer as a
> luminous cloud, egg-shaped, streaked by fine lines like
> stiff bristles standing out in all directions.[34]

> A man looks like an egg of circulating fibers. And his arms
> and legs are like luminous bristles bursting out in all
> directions.[35]

This time the first quotation originates from an
obscure early 20th century text by a hack mystic called
Yogi Ramacharaka. The second is attributed to don Juan
by Castaneda. Coincidence begins to strain at this point,
but that is hardly the end of the matter. The echoes of
Sufism, Tantric Buddhism and the Hindu chakras perme-
ate the wisdom of don Juan. The matter could be charted
in much greater depth, and has been elsewhere.[36]
In 1968, Barbara Meyerhoff included the following
passage in her anthropology dissertation at UCLA: "We
were puzzled, but fell into our places at the end of the line
and found ourselves barely able to keep up, for the group
was nearly running." She was describing a peyote gathering among the Huichol Indians of Mexico. In 1972, fellow
UCLA anthropology student Carlos Castaneda, in a thoroughly resounding echo, stated that upon completion of a
gathering of mushrooms, don Juan was suddenly terrified
and—like the Huichols—left the gathering place very
rapidly. "I followed him," Castaneda wrote in *Journey to
Ixtlan*, "but...could not keep up...and he soon disappeared
into the darkness."[37] The same material was included in
the 1973 doctoral dissertation. Not only was Castaneda
"borrowing" his field notes from a broad variety of esoteric
library sources, but from other graduate students as well,

equally without attribution, but seemingly with the general blessings of the UCLA academic hierarchy.

But, if Castaneda is guilty of injecting a host of non-Yaqui characteristics into his elaborate profile of the "secrets of Yaquiness," what of his somewhat limited treatment of known Yaqui realities? For instance, he all but continuously refers to his fabulous smoking mushroom as "mescal," despite the fact that the term connotes an hallucinogenic cactus and derivative substance (mescaline) and, perhaps more popularly in Mexico, a cactus-flavored liquor (also literally, mescal).

Then there is the matter of his usage of the rightfully specialized term "sorcerer." As Ralph Beals has pointed out, the Spanish equivalent would be *brujo,* one who makes ones enemies sick with the help of the devil, an evil person.[38] Yet nowhere in any of his published material does Castaneda present evidence to the effect that don Juan engages in such practices. Indeed, he does not even allude to this. Clearly, the term is utterly misapplied. Nor would *curandero,* the Spanish term for one who heals the sick, be an appropriate description of the individual described by Castaneda. Even "shaman," that academic catch-all term for any non-European displaying spiritual propensities, fails to quite fit the portrait of don Juan that Castaneda conjures up.

We are left, at this point, with only the option of looking to that mystical magician of various American Indian cultures known as "the trickster," an elusive entity best defined by his lying and often cruel game-playing. As we have seen, this is precisely the term Castaneda used to describe himself, with the medium of a pun on his father's family name. Given the preceding observations, it seems hardly unwarranted to speculate that the true identity of don Juan might well be none other than Castaneda himself.

Such matters as these should have been readily detectable for the trained anthropologists who served such a crucial role in establishing Castaneda as a major figure in American letters. No less observable should have been Castaneda's treatment of two specifically Yaqui terms/concepts, "tonal" and "nagual." According to Adams and Rubel, clearly qualified Yaqui specialists, "The *tonal* is a companion animal or destiny...subject to stealing and specifically of concern in becoming ill."[39] This is a meaning of which Castaneda demonstrated awareness.[40] Yet he proceeded to employ this awareness to redefine the Yaqui conception via the "authenticating" medium of don Juan:

> The tonal is not an animal which guards a person...[it] is the social person...the organizer of the world...everything we know...everything that meets the eye...[it] begins at birth and ends at death...[it] is a creator which doesn't create a thing...[it] is but a reflection of that indiscribable unknown filled with order.[41]

In other words, Castaneda knowingly transformed a viable Yaqui concept into a tangent of psuedo-Eastern mysticism. Nor does *nagual* fare better. Again according to Adams and Rubel, as well as George Foster (another Yaqui expert), "The nagual is a special transformation of a man into an animal, and the term helps to define a witch."[42] Castaneda agrees,[43] only to dub the notion pure nonsense. The *nagual* is defined as:

> ...the part of us which we do not deal with at all...for which there is no description...[it] never ends...has no limit...is the only part of us we can create...is but a reflection of the indescribable void that contains everything.[44]

It would be hard to imagine a projection of Yaquiness more antithetical to Yaquiness than that put forth by Castaneda. He was, it may be fairly asserted, not unaware of the problems building up along this line. In fact, he began to disclaim the obvious as early as his second book: "So far I have made no attempt whatsoever to place don

Juan in a cultural milieu. The fact that he considers himself a Yaqui Indian does not mean that his knowledge of sorcery is known to or practiced by the Yaqui Indians in general."[45]

A neat polemical trick, that, intended to cut the ground from beneath the feet of potential critics. It was and is, however, categorically untrue. The subtitle of Castaneda's first book is, after all, "A Yaqui Way of Knowledge." A year after his disclaimer was published, a UCLA committee granted Castaneda a doctorate based on his assertion that he had conducted extensive field research into and had become expert on the subject of "Yaqui sorcery." As late as 1977, the *American Anthropologist* was still accepting Simon and Schuster's advertisements proclaiming both *The Teachings of Don Juan* and *A Separate Reality* as serious studies on "the religious practices of the Yaqui Indians."[46] And, even in 1978, the UCLA Press was still prepared to list *A Yaqui Way of Knowledge* as its "winner for 1968" under the general advertising line, "the last fifteen years have been good to us."[47]

There can be no question that such sustained and highly visible support from the academic world has served, in a very real sense, to entrench him as a bastion of knowledge peculiar to the Yaqui, a legitimation incurred at the direct expense of meaningful communication between Yaqui and non-Yaqui. For example, the 1971 edition of *Exploring Ways of Mankind* included a three page excerpt from *The Teachings of Don Juan* under the chapter heading, "A Yaqui Man of Knowledge." Walter Goldschmidt, who happened to edit the book, introduced the Castaneda material as indicative of how a Yaqui "shaman" led his apprentice down "the road of knowledge...of the Yaqui Indians."[48] The book remained in wide usage, its Castaneda section thus absorbed deeply into the undergraduate academic mainstream, until 1977.

As the Goldschmidt text was phasing out Castaneda, another book, entitled *Other Fields, Other Grasshoppers,*

by L.L. Langness made its debut before the same undergraduate audience. Under the chapter heading, "Listen to
the Lizards," ten pages of *The Teachings of Don Juan* are
excerpted as valid anthropological material because it
apprehends "the Yaqui view of reality" and explains "how
the Yaqui themselves understand knowledge."[49] In 1975,
the *English Journal* went so far as to prescribe *Journey
to Ixtlan* as an antidote to "fake Indian books."[50]

The whole of Castaneda's veneer of academic credibility feeds directly into reinforcement of a situation
which, reciprocally, serves to reinforce his scholarly pretensions. The don Juan books have been catalogued
through Library of Congress listings since their respective
release dates as 399.Y3 material, according to standard
notation. Translated, this breaks out as follows: 399 indicates "Indians of North America," .Y3 indicates "Tribes:
Yaqui." Further, all Castaneda books except *Journey to
Ixtlan* have been coded under the Dewey Decimal System
as 299.7; that is, as books concerning "Religions of North
American Indian Origin." This has led to subject heading
assignments such as "YAQUI INDIANS—RELIGION
AND MYTHOLOGY." Attribution also is indicated to one
"JUAN, DON, 1891 -" Hence, the Library of Congress
itself may be seen as solidly bolstering the authenticity of
Castaneda's entire fabrication.[51]

Ultimately, the trajectory through scholarship and
publishing traversed by Carlos Castaneda during a decade beginning in 1968 forces those who would examine
it to perceive a fraud of major proportions. As has been
stated elsewhere, "Don Juan may be the biggest hoax in
anthropology since the Piltdown Man." This is no idle
comparison. Richard DeMille has delineated a series of
parallels between Piltdown and don Juan. These include:

- Each was hailed as a giant step in science.

- Each combined disparate elements—Piltdown bones of ape and man, don Juan pre-literate and modern conceptual systems.

- Each could have been exposed at once by a competent, skeptical inquiry—into the shape of Piltdown's teeth, into the existence of Carlos's voluminous field notes.

- Each wasted the time or made fools of some trusting colleagues.

- Each was supported by a faction—Piltdown by British paleontologists, don Juan by anyone who thought publishing *The Teachings* or granting a doctorate to Castaneda would make merit for ethnomethodology or UCLA anthropology.

- Each was rendered more congenial by cultural bias—Piltdown for favoring intelligence and white superiority, don Juan for demonstrating that an anti-rationalist noble savage could reflect 1960s idealism back to dissident but regular consumers of electricity and Kool-Aid as though from an ancient culture.[52]

With so much said in so little space, it is perhaps most appropriate to allow DeMille to conclude this essay:

"[S]ome would dismiss the don Juan hoax as a moneymaking scheme or an administrative mix-up having nothing to do with the mainstream of anthropology (or literature: WC), but to do so is to forego valuable lessons. By facing up to the implications of frauds and hoaxes, and of their acceptance in quarters where people should know better, and of attempts to dismiss them once exposed, we can learn about the way science is conducted, [and] about the nature of sophisticated beliefs...among...people who are passionately committed to particular theories of how the world is put together."[53]

Notes

1. As listed in *Dissertation Abstracts International*, 1973, 33 (12 Part 1, Jun) 5625.B. UCLA Library call number: LD 791.9 A6 C275.

2, The $1 million figure accrues from Richard DeMille, author of *Castaneda's Journey: The Power and the Allegory*, Capra Press, Santa Barbara, CA, 1976. The higher figure is from Simon and Schuster by way of Castaneda's agent, Neil Brown.

3. Castaneda, Carlos, *Journey to Ixtlan: The Lessons of Don Juan*, Simon and Schuster, New York, 1972, p. 83.

4. *Ibid.*, p. 124.

5. *Ibid.*, p. 105.

6. Sebald, Hans, "Roasting Rabbits in Tulameria or the Lion, the Witch and the Horned Toad," in DeMille, Richard (ed.), *The Don Juan Papers: Further Castaneda Controversies*, Ross-Erikson Publishers, Santa Barbara, CA, 1980, p. 35.

7. Castaneda, Carlos, *Journey to Ixtlan, op. cit.*, p. 161.

8. *Ibid.*, pp. 144-151.

9. Castaneda, Carlos, *A Separate Reality: Further Conversation with Don Juan*, Simon and Schuster, New York, 1971, p. 186.

10. *Ibid.*, p. 296.

11. Jellinik, Roger, *New York Times*, May 14, 1971, p. 37. The second observed statement is from *New York Times*, October 14, 1971, p. 31.

12. Thompson, William Irving, *New York Times*, February 13, 1972, p. 26.

13. Riesman, Paul, "The Collaboration of Two Men and a Plant," *New York Times Book Review*, October 22, 1972, p. 7.

14. Levi, Albert William, *Saturday Review,* August 21, 1971, p. 25.

15. Kanon, Joseph, *Saturday Review,* November 11, 1972, pp. 67-69.

16. *Publishers Weekly:* favorable reviews appeared in 1968, 1969, 1971, 1972, 1974, 1976 and 1977; the cited remarks appeared in the latter.

17. DeMille, Richard, citing Michael Korda (of Simon and Schuster) in "Publishing the Factoids," *The Don Juan Papers, op. cit.,* p. 109.

18. Douglas, Mary, "Torn Between Two Realities," *The Times Higher Education Supplement,* No. 87, June 15, 1973, p. 13.

19. Douglas, Mary, "The Authenticity of Castaneda," *Implicit Meanings,* Routledge and Kegan Paul Publishers, London, 1975, pp. 193-200.

20. For example, Wilke has published supportive argumentation in reviews in *American Anthropologist,* August 1972 (pp. 921-922), March 1977 (pp. 84-91), December 1977 (p. 921) and (more indirectly) in June 1978 (pp. 363-364). He also published a similar review in *Anthropology and Humanist Quarterly,* June-September 1977 (pp. 12-18) and conducted a rather spirited defense of Castaneda at the 77th annual meeting of the American Anthropological Association in November 1978.

21. Roszak, Theodore, "A Sorcerer's Apprentice," *Nation,* February 1969, p. 185.

22. Lake, Robert G., Jr., "The Fourth Force: A Native American Perspective Concerning Transpersonal Development," unpublished manuscript currently submitted for readings/commentary.

23. *American Anthropologist,* June 1968.

24. Yablonski, Lewis, *The Los Angeles Times Book Review,* November 30, 1975, p. 24.

25. Castaneda was not necessarily content to restrict himself to claims of standard field notes. In an interview with Theodore Roszak entitled "Don Juan: The Sorcerer recorded as Tape Cassette #25021" and aired by station KPFA, Berkeley, CA in 1968, Castaneda maintained that one of his field practices was

the taking of copious mental notes while under the influence of hallucinogenic substances. He claimed these were later transcribed.

26. Wasson, Gordon R., *Economic Botany*, Vol. 27, No. 1, January-March 1973, pp. 151-152.

27. Preuss, Paul, "Does don Juan Live on Campus?" *Human Behavior*, Vol. 7, No. 11, November 1978, pp. 53-57. Preuss does not state this categorically; I infer it (WC).

28. DeMille, Richard, *Castaneda's Journey, op. cit.*, p. 167, Table I.

29. Letter, Gordon R. Wasson to Carlos Castaneda, dated August 26, 1968.

30. Letter, Carlos Castaneda to Gordon R. Wasson, dated September 6, 1968. It should be noted that Castaneda should have had ample opportunity to comply with his own agreement insofar as he has published accounts of at least six additional mushroom-smoking incidents after this date.

31. Ott, Jonathan and Jeremy Bigwood, *Teotanacatl: Hallucinogenic Mushrooms of North America*, Madrona, 1978, pp. 12 & 98.

32. The juxtaposition accrues, in slightly modified form, from DeMille, Richard, "The Shaman of Academe," *The Don Juan Papers, op. cit.*, p. 20.

33. *Ibid.*

34. Atkinson, William Walker (aka Yogi Ramacharaka), *Fourteen Lessons in Yogi Philosophy and Oriental Occultism*, Yogi Publication Society, New York, 1903.

35. Castaneda, Carlos, *The Second Ring of Power*, Simon and Schuster, New York, 1977, p. 87.

36. In addition to the DeMille books already cited, see the first essay in this book.

37. DeMille, Richard, "Validity is not Authenticity: Distinguishing Two Components of Truth," *The Don Juan Papers, op. cit.*, pp. 40-41.

38. Beals, Ralph, "Sonoran Fantasy or Coming of Age?" *American Anthropologist*, June 1978, p. 357.

39. Adams, Richard N. and Arthur J. Rubel, "Sickness and Social Relations," *Handbook of Middle American Indians*, 1973, p. 336.

40. Castaneda, Carlos, *Tales of Power*, Simon and Schuster, New York, 1974, p. 121. "The 'tonal'...was thought to be a kind of guardian spirit, usually an animal, that a child obtained at birth and with which he had intimate ties for the rest of his life."

41. Quotations are extracted from Ibid., pp. 122-125 and 270-271.

42. Adams and Rubel, *op. cit.*, p. 336. Also see Foster, George M., "Nagualism in Mexico and Guatemala," *Acta Americana*, Vol. 2, Nos. 1 & 2, January - June, 1944.

43. Castaneda, Carlos, *Tales of Power*, op. cit., p. 121: "Nagual...was the name given to the animal into which sorcerers could allegedly change themselves, or to the sorcerer who elicited such a transformation."

44. *Ibid.*, pp. 126, 141, 271. In *The Second Ring of Power*, Simon and Schuster, New York, 1977, Castaneda goes on to define nagual as "a person" (p. 69), "a substance" (p. 219), "a perception" (p. 220) and "a place" (p. 261).

45. Castaneda, Carlos, *Journey to Ixtlan*, op. cit., p. 8.

46. This was a full-page ad, guaranteed to attract attention in its scholarly format.

47. Full-page ad, *The New York Review of Books*, October 12, 1978, p. 15.

48. Goldschmidt, Walter, *Exploring Ways of Mankind*, 2nd edition, Holt, Rinehart and Winston, New York, 1971, pp. 187-190. 3rd edition, 1977.

49. Langness, L.L., *Other Fields, Other Grasshoppers: Readings in Cultural Anthropology*, Lippincott, New York, 1977, p. xi, 59.

50. Carlson, G. Robert, Tony Manna and Betty Lou Tucker, "Books for Young Adults 1974 Honor Roll Listing," *English Journal*, Vol. 64, No. 1, January 1975, pp. 112-115.

51. Berman, Stanford, "Cataloging Castaneda," *HLC Cataloging Bulletin*, September/October 1978, pp. 38-39.

52. DeMille, Richard, "Uclanthropus Piltdunides Castaneda," *The don Juan Papers*, op. cit., pp. 114-115.

53. *Ibid*, pp. 117-118.

Part II

Projecting White Values onto American Indian Culture

Ayn Rand and the Sioux

Tonto Revisited

There seems to be absolutely no limit to the strangeness white people want to attribute to Indians. There's no limit on the number of nuts who get rich masquerading as Indians, or Indian experts, or friends of the Indian, or whatever...No matter how absurd the story, and sometimes I think it's a case of "the more absurd the better," publishers and movie producers in America gobble it up for public consumption. And no matter how many times you prove what's being promoted as "truth" to be nothing more than a pack of lies, it just keeps going on. Today, we've got Carlos Castaneda, Chief Red Fox, Jamake Highwater, Ruth Beebe Hill and a whole bunch of others all becoming millionaires on the basis of out-and-out lies. And we've shown over and over again that they're lying through their teeth...It seems the only thing that white people in this country are interested in hearing is lies. Now, I don't know what you call that, but I call it insane.

—Janet McCloud
1987

I STAND AT THE CENTER AND THE LIGHT SHINES ALL AROUND ME. AND I KNOW THAT MY SPIRIT GLOWS MAKING THIS LIGHT. I COME INTO POWER WITH THE SUN FOR I AM THE SUN. I AM MY OWN LIGHT.

HERE AT THE CENTER I SEE THE MEANING OF ALL THINGS. AND NOW I KNOW THAT I AM THE MEANING, THE WHOLE MEANING.

THE FOUR DIRECTIONS COME TOGETHER IN ME. I AM THE CENTER AND EVERYTHING FLOWS FROM ME, RETURNS TO ME.

I AM THAT WHICH THEY CALL THE GREAT MYSTERY. I AM THAT WHICH EACH ONE CALLS WAKANTANKA BEFORE COMING HERE, BEFORE SEEING THE LIGHT.

I AM HERE AND SO I KNOW. HERE I KNOW EVERYTHING. HERE I KNOW MYSELF.

I AM THOUGHT AND WILL. NOTHING SITS ABOVE MY WILL.

I AM PRIDE AND JOY. AND NOTHING SITS ABOVE MY JOY.

I OWN MY LIFE, AND ONLY MINE. AND SO I APPRECIATE MY PERSON. AND SO SHALL MAKE PROPER USE OF MYSELF.

I STAND HERE IN THE LIGHT OF MY OWN PRESENCE AND I RECOGNIZE MY POWER.

I AM REASON. AND NOTHING SITS ABOVE MY CHOICE.

I AM TRUTH. AND SO I LIVE IN SPIRIT. AND SO I LIVE FOREVER.

I AM THE ONENESS OF THE WHOLE, AND WHATEVER HAPPENS, HAPPENS TO ME.

I AM AHBLEZA. I OWN THE EARTH.

So reads "Book Three: The Warrior 1819/20 to 1824/25," Chapter XXV (pages 605-606) of Ruth Beebe Hill's *Hanta Yo: An American Saga* (New York: Doubleday Publishers, 1979). The above is the chapter, the whole chapter, and nothing but the chapter. While it may seem an altogether short quotation to have composed the content of such a term, it says quite enough to be so designated. Within these few lines emerges an "insight" into the nature of traditional Lakota (western Sioux) lifeways which is so preposterous, so perverse in its pretensions, so vastly misleading as to speak volumes. That such postulations are ascribed as the secret revelations of a central Lakota leader (Ahbleza, a shirt wearer) gained during a central Lakota ceremony (the Sun Dance) gives this utter drivel an importance to the context of *Hanta Yo* which simply cannot be ignored. As has been said elsewhere—

If a Sioux Indian had the temerity to stand upright on the prairie and say something like that, he would be laughed right out of camp and the people would fear for their lives for such blasphemy.[1]

Nor need one become fixated with this single-page chapter within the totality of an 812-page work (excluding glossaries, charts, and whatnot). Chapter XXV of Book Three represents only the most crystalline statement of its kind. Elsewhere, Ms. Hill is quite prone to maintaining this "philosophical overview" through such passages as,

Maka kin le mitawa-I own the earth...Mika kin le mitawa, ce hibu welo...I own the earth, and so I come...I own the earth. Hanta yo, hanta yo. Clear the way, clear the way (page 502).

This babble is also attributed to the long-suffering Ahbleza during his single-handed routing of an attacking Crow war party, an overall performance he chalks up to his penetration of "Skan, existence; skan, existing and available, to the one, to the whole" (page 504). Nor is this latter merely a passing reference. Hill explains through Ahbleza that:

> I am I...Tuwa tuwe hoa he miya; I am I, really someone...I recognize the life-force. I identify this force as skan, something in movement. I am something in movement. I am skan. And with a body as proof (page 595).

This takes us once again to the Sun Dance, before which Ahbleza observes that,

> ...if I go-to-the-center and discover the great mystery, then nothing mysterious exists. And if I discover that which really exists, then I am the center and I, the reality (page 597).

How tidy; what hogwash. Ruth Beebe Hill insists that "Hanta Yo" is the unadulterated truth, at least in terms of the "Indian" definition of this concept: "The Indian definition of truth is what happens, and everything in this book happened."[2] Proceeding from the basis of such an assertion, she goes on in her introduction to the novel to explain that which happened:

> The American Indian, even before Columbus, was the remnant of a very old race in its final stage, a race that attained perhaps the highest level of individualism ever practiced...His view was never that of the altruist; he was a trader in spiritual values...he never answered to anyone but himself, never answered for anyone but himself. He conjugates the verb "think" in the first person singular only; he never presumes..."I" the sacred word; "I" and "you," if and when an affinity is determined. His was the language of the ego, cultivated in the premise by which he lived.

To this jumble, she offers still another series of unsupported assertions:

> The story is projected within the framework of Dakotah
> [*sic;* Dakota or eastern Sioux] philosophy, not something
> invented, not something put together from ethnological
> data catalogued and explained by persons outside the
> race and realm. It is a story Dakotah in description and
> discernment, Dakotah in precept and example, Dakotah
> in structure and style.

Thus, Hill specifically indicates that the philosophical ramblings occurring throughout her bulky manuscript
are gleaned directly from the Dakota. Yet one must logically wonder how it is that she manages to make her leap
beyond the ranks of those "persons outside the race and
realm." Certainly she is no Sioux. Her flawless elaboration
of "precept and example" has had modern Lakota scholars
from Vine Deloria, Jr., to Bea Medicine alternately furious
and in stitches since the book's release.[3]

Hill's reliance upon the accuracy of "Dakotah structure and style" as vouchsafed by one Chunksa Yuha (or
Alonzo Blacksmith, if one goes by the Santee rolls) is used
as justification for much of the book's content. Allegedly,
Hill and Chunksa Yuha spent fourteen years translating
the original manuscript (Hill claims to have spent a quarter century on *Hanta Yo)* into "archaic Dakotah"—in order
to remove pre-contact concepts, of course—then back into
English. The result seems to have more to do with archaic
English than anything else. At the very least the Dakota
manuscript is utterly unavailable to linguistic scholars
(which leads to a legitimate question as to its existence)
and, as has been pointed out elsewhere,[4] even the title
term, "hanta yo," does not conform to any known Sioux
usage; what Hill and Chunksa Yuha claim means "get out
of the way," simply means "move."

Mr. Blacksmith, for his part, seems to have caused
no small controversy back home at Santee—a place to
which he currently seems a bit hesitant to return—having
based his publishing credibility upon the youthful receipt
of training in cultural secrets by elders. His family and

tribe fail to recall any such instruction having occurred. The poor man's literal performance in the published material itself is reduced to a three-page introductory glorification of Ruth Beebe Hills efforts as savior of the sacred wisdom of the ancient Dakota. He ends with a fine example of the books overall adherence to "Dakotah [linguistic] structure and style": "I, Chunksa Yuha, grandson of Wapasa, say so, say so." One would at least hope he was well paid.

Yet, almost eerily, there is something familiar about this original revision of historical/cultural realities; not that it has much of anything to do with the Sioux. It is as though Hill had borrowed a character from the work of her long-time friend, Ayn Rand, adorned him in quill work and braids and cast him out into the reaches of South Dakota. Howard Roark meets H.G. Wells and—voila!—the "truth" of the anti-collectivistic, supremely individualist Sioux who practices the virtue of selfishness as a way of life is revealed. The philosophy expressed in *Hanta Yo* is pure indeed, but pure in terms of the doctrine of Ayn Rand.

The events depicted by Ruth Beebe Hill occurred only in the minds of a pathetically literate handful of Caucasian pseudo-intellectuals who cling to the failed philosophy of Ms. Rand. A philosophy which, like laissez-faire capitalism, has never known a place or time. It is as if Milton Friedman had set out to prove his beliefs by writing the "true" story of the Kiowas as small shopkeepers.

When all else fails, when the public just ain't buying *The Fountainhead* and *Atlas Shrugged* any longer, what better way to make a buck than to pass this same stale swill off on the heritage of Native America? There is, after all, a time-honored American tradition at stake: victims must be blamed for Euro-imports such as scalping, massacre, suicide, and drunkenness, all of which abound in *Hanta Yo*. Now the native can be saddled with the crypto-fascism of Ayn Rand as well. And, in the true stereotypical fashion of good Americana, it is the Lakota who must inevitably bear the brunt of cultural degradation both through being misrepresented in their own terms and through being projected as representatives of "Indians" (to use Ms. Hill's own terminology). Thus, the "epic" of *Hanta Yo* becomes merely the shabby mini-tragedy of the final decay of one of the grubbier peripheries of European thought; Tonto is revisited yet one more time.

If this were the end of the oddly familiar material evident in *Hanta Yo,* enough would have been said already. But, sadly, it is not. In her younger days, Ruth Beebe Hill had still another literary figure as a friend. This one, Mari Sandoz, held no great philosophical pretensions, but she did have a more than passing knowledge of the Lakota after 1750. And she wrote about that at some length. On a number of levels, Hill has lifted the story line from Sandoz' treatment of a real Oglala, Crazy Horse. However, Hill's "borrowing" from her friend's excellent work has not proceeded in direct fashion. She has cut the character of Crazy Horse into two distinct entities: 1) the warrior father, Olepi, and 2) the spiritual son, Ahbleza. This somewhat confuses the issue of her theft, but fails to hide it. It serves only to distort reality even further; no less a personage than Crazy Horse—a very important figure in Lakota tradition—becomes the Howard Roark of Ruth Beebe Hill's scheme. This, of course, is again rather contrary to the authors extravagant claims to authenticity.[5]

But it is precisely the question of authenticity which ultimately jerks *Hanta Yo* from the realm of the sublimely ridiculous into the realm of the dangerous. There is just enough of fact and reality mixed with the book's abundant absurdity to provide it with that certain "ring of truth" which its author desires. That such appearance is sheer illusion is irrelevant. It can seem a credible, if ponderous, treatment to those who are untutored in Siouian tradition—which, obviously, are most of us. Promoted by its publisher as the "Indian *Roots,*" accepted by prestigious anthropological institutions such as the Smithsonian,[6] and scheduled for production as a television mini-series by David Wolper Productions (producers of the highly successful *Roots* series), *Hanta Yo* seems destined to combine the worst aspects of the dime novel, Buffalo Bill's Wild West shows, and esoteric philosophy before a truly mass (and ultimately accepting?) audience. We are in the process of witnessing the sophisticated and relatively seamless re-stereotyping of Native America by a popular media ranging from Doubleday through Warner Brothers to ABC.

Thus, the closing of Ruth Beebe Hills introduction to *Hanta Yo* rightly must be treated more as something sinister than as merely humorously pretentious:

> [T]he author asks that the reader bring something to the reading process: a willingness to enter the Dakotah world uncritically, without vanity. In this way the story will return the reader to the spiritual source not only of the American Indian but to America itself.

This is not only insulting to the Sioux, it offers mind-warp to a whole nation.

Postscript

After a nearly four-year hiatus, during which the intensity of Native American criticism was allowed to subside, David Wolper Productions began production of its *Hanta Yo*-based television mini-series entitled *Mystic Warrior*. It was aired nationally as a four-part package by CBS. Says Vine Deloria, Jr.,

> The movie was even worse than the book, although I know that's hard to imagine. This is typical of the U.S. media. All they did was wait till the heat was off, and until they could find an Indian or two willing to endorse the authenticity of their fantasy—for money, no doubt— and then they just went ahead as if nothing were wrong. It's just one more example of what the white man likes to call acting 'in utmost good faith.'

Notes

1. Deloria, Vine J., "The Twisted World of *Hanta Yo,*" *Minority Notes*, Vol. 1, No. 1, Spring 1979.

2. Quoted in Newman, Joy, "*Hanta:* Insight into the Red Man's Roots or Just a Novel View of History?" *Tempo*, May 17, 1979.

3. Deloria, Vine Jr., "*Hanta Yo:* Super Hype," *CoEvolution Quarterly*, Vol. 5, No. 4, Fall 1979; Medicine, Bea, "*Hanta Yo:* A New Phenomenon," *The Indian Historian*, Vol. 12, No. 2, Spring 1979.

4. Medicine, *op. cit.*

5. See Sandoz, Mari, *Crazy Horse: Strange Man of the Oglalas*, University of Nebraska Press, Lincoln, 1961.

6. *Hanta Yo* was endorsed as authentic in the *Washington Post* by prominent Smithsonian historian Wilcomb Washburn during the spring of 1979.

7. Deloria, Vine Jr., letter to the author, May 1985.

Creek Mary's Blood

A Comparison to *Hanta Yo*

Native American women have been portrayed...in negative and stereotyped ways. After reviewing certain anthropological data, the distortions...become quite apparent. Few people realize the importance of women in Native American societies—past and present—and that their status was very different than that presented in these films (and literature)...Among both matrilineal and patrilineal tribes it has not been uncommon to find women warriors, statespeople, chiefs, religious leaders, medicine women...and some women controlled great amounts of economic and political power. They were not, as Euro-Americans imagine, merely chattel, servants to men, wives and mothers.

—Mary Oshana

"[I]t is precisely the question of authenticity which ultimately jerks *Hanta Yo* from the realm of the sublimely ridiculous into the realm of the dangerous. There is just enough of fact and reality mixed with the books abundant absurdity to provide it with that certain ring of truth which its author desires." It has been nearly two years since I wrote these lines in reference to what I consider to be one of the shoddier literary hoaxes ever to be foisted off on the legacy of the American Indian.[1] Today, it seems quite safe to assert that *Hanta Yo* has assumed its rightful position within the ranks of *The Memoirs of Chief Red Fox, Rolling Thunder, Seven Arrows, Sacajawea,* the collected works of Carlos Castaneda and the rest of America's vast constellation of phony literature on Indians.

Considering the hue and cry which surrounded that epic collaboration between Ruth Beebe Hill and Alonzo Blacksmith (aka "Chunksa Yuha"), a protest including such diverse American Indian spokespeople as Vine Deloria, Jr. and Bea Medicine[2] and with sufficient magnitude to squelch an incipient David Wolper television production of the screen rights, one might assume it would be a long time before another author or publisher dared such an obvious affront to the cultural and historical dignity of Indian people.

One might assume, but one would be wrong. Hardly had criticism of Doubleday's blatant *faux pas* in publishing *Hanta Yo* achieved a fever pitch, than Simon and Schuster joined the act with a "major new release" of its own: *Creek Mary's Blood* by Dee Brown (first hardcover edition in 1980; softcover Pocket follow-up in 1981). Sadly, every word of the opening quotation in this review essay would seem at least as appropriate to Dee Brown's product as it did to *Hanta Yo*. Each of the books in question is ostensibly representative of that peculiar genre of American letters, the historical novel. That is to say, each theoretically deals with historical realities through a filter of fictional interpretation. Put another way, the author of an historical novel is allowed the latitude to fabricate material which enhances generally known historical facts, renders the resultant treatment more popularly readable than most non-fictional history writing, and provides for the marketing of historical information across a broad public spectrum.

Validity and the Historical Novel

On the face of it, the historical novel thus possesses much by which it may be commended. As a generic characteristic of American literature, it may be perceived as offering a forum within which a public exposure to and understanding of historical issues can occur, albeit in less than academically pristine fashion. For example, the historical novelist is usually freed from his/her non-fiction historian counterparts' requirement for "absolute" documentation concerning all facts. There is, however, a major qualification to such freedom of action. This is simply that any work, novel or not, must adhere to the known historical realities in order to impart anything of true informational value. Fiction writers who claim the mantle of "historical novelist" may well claim literary license in inventing material to fill gaps within the historical record, particularly where such material relates to dialogue, character motivation, etc. But it seems rather beyond the pale of any "history" to utilize such license as a means to negate or reverse the facts themselves.

In the context of the historical novel, fact and fiction may reasonably be expected to merge into a "spirit of truth," so to speak. To do otherwise, an author willingly engages in mythologizing—or worse, to be sure—outright propagandism before a mass audience. The latter in particular is rather far from literary effort, at least by conventional standards. Contentions in defense of aesthetic latitude seem quite irrelevant in this instance, or at least moot. Both Ruth Beebe Hill and Dee Brown seem unquestionably to subscribe to such notions concerning the responsibility to truth, accuracy and authenticity concomitant to the writing of historical fiction.

For her part, Beebe Hill went so far as to assert the total and intrinsic validity of her book: "The Indian definition of truth is what happens, and everything in this book happened."[3] She allowed herself a certain degree of latitude concerning such trivia as people, places and things, insofar as she is not so much concerned with these as she is with the essence of the "archaic Dakotah" mind, philosophy, or—perhaps most aptly—worldview. But, as concerns this, the substance of her novel, she stated quite categorically in her introduction:

The story is projected within the framework of Dakotah philosophy, not something invented, not something put together from ethnological data catalogues and explained by persons outside the race and realm. It is a story Dakotah in description and discernment, Dakotah in precept and example, Dakotah in structure and style.

These are clearly not the mildest possible claims to historical authenticity and integrity. Certainly, the author felt the need to project an aura of absolute contextual validity within her role as a self-acknowledged fiction writer. Hill, of course, was a virtually unknown writer prior to the release of *Hanta Yo,* and had to assert her legitimacy. In so doing, however, she immediately exposed in clear terms the preposterous linguistic and conceptual basis from which she purported to define an historical epoch of Sioux consciousness.

Dee Brown, on the other hand, released his novel under somewhat different and perhaps murkier circumstances. He has refrained from making personal claims as to the validity and authenticity of the story portrayed in *Creek Mary's Blood.* To be sure, as is proudly emblazoned upon the book's cover, he is also author of *Bury My Heart At Wounded Knee* (Holt, Rinehart and Winston, 1970). Since release of that effort, he has been oft and loudly proclaimed as an historian of merit, particularly in matters concerning Indian/white relations. There is a certain reputation to be traded upon here, a reputation which greatly supplants the need in Hill's case for public posturing and assertions of legitimacy. Such are the facts of life and publishing.

But, the weight of Brown's credentials notwithstanding, what is the historical accuracy of the story woven as *Creek Mary's Blood,* a story popularly acclaimed as "Historical Fiction at its best" and "A dramatic record of the Indians proud strength and survival which vividly relives native American history"?[4] After all, unlike Ruth Beebe Hill's proclivity to dabble in historical thought processes,

Dee Brown opted to treat real people, places and events.
The relative merits of his effort, in terms of accuracy and
authenticity, should thus be much more immediately accessible than were hers. It is time to move to specifics.

Will the Real Creek Mary
Please Stand Up?

Let us consider the centerpiece and title character of
the book, Creek Mary herself. She was, after all, a real
woman with a real history, a factor which one assumes is
intended to lend instant credibility, in terms of historical
accuracy, to the novel. Brown could, of course, have chosen
to create a wholly fictional character as a means to describe the flow of historical events, constructed of a blend
of historical personalities and the pure needs of a fictional
narrative, rather than to write an account purporting to
convey the essence or spirit of a real human being. But he
chose the latter.

The author commences his tale by describing his
heroine as "Beloved Woman" of her generation of Creeks,
explains that her Creek name was Amayi, and asserts
that she once led a Creek war party against British troops
in the city of Savannah over a land dispute. Brown thus
reinforces the aura of surface authenticity his title implies, according to reliable historical sources.[5] Creek Mary
was in fact a ranking member of the matrilineal Creek
society of her day. Her name was Consaponaheeso rather
than Amayi, but she did lead the march on Savannah in
question, and it did concern a land dispute. Three of the
four primary facts asserted by Brown in initially establishing the identity of his title character are fundamentally correct. As concerns the fourth, this seems to center
more upon the perceived need to replace a word, the mere
pronunciation of which would be necessarily cumbersome
to the English-speaking tongue, rather than malicious

intent. There can be little doubt that Brown is concerned with Creek Mary in literal form at this point; a little known but very real historical identity is at issue.

From this rather auspicious beginning, the author proceeds to inform us that "Mary Amayi" was, in her youth, loved by a Danish trader who she spurned. The man went mad as a result of this rejection and was eventually lost to the swamps of Georgia which he'd entered in pursuit of his lost love. Perversely, given this sequence of events, Mary forever after wore a Danish coin embedded in a gorget at her throat. Equally unaccountably, she named her second son "Dane" in memory of her suicidal suitor. Brown goes on to explain that Mary's first born son, Opothle, was the product of her first marriage, a union with John Kingsley, an English trader whom "[s]he once loved...with all the passion in heart."[6] Use of the past tense in this connection was entirely appropriate insofar as we are further instructed that she took her child and left both Kingsley and his trading post in the dead of night because she had discovered "that at heart he was not a bad man...[b]ut he was tainted with the greed of his race, the urge to set men against men, an enemy of the natural world."[7]

This drama was supposedly played out shortly after the Savannah venture, a situation in which Brown has it that Mary acted as a militant advocate of Creek sovereignty and land rights. Her husband, she discovered to her dismay, was motivated during the expedition by a gross self-interest. At this point her Creek nationalism proved sufficient, given such mendacity as was displayed by John Kingsley, to provoke both her rather stealthy conclusion of her marriage and a lifetime's distrust of all things white. Needless to say, such an outlook precluded the entry of the novel's Creek Mary into further interludes of interracial marriage. To the contrary, so the novel has it, it launched her upon a course of championing a sort of early pan-Indianism which seems clearly to afford a female prefiguration of Tecumseh and the Prophet. At this juncture, serious distortions of the historical record have entered into Brown's epic. First, and perhaps not as trivial as it may seem at first glance, there is no indication in the literature that Mary ever entertained or rejected a Danish lover. Nor is there record of her having borne a son named in his memory. This, it could be argued, represents little more than an historically extraneous device through which the author seeks to enhance his narrative. If it were an isolated instance, such argumentation might be plausible enough. However, the same may not be contended relative to John Kingsley. The real Creek Mary's first husband was one John Musgrove, Jr., son of one of the primary British military commanders in the Carolinas during the first quarter of the 18th century. The couple did, in fact, operate a trading establishment on Georgia's Yamacraf Bluff. However, upon the birth of their first child (Opothle, by Brown's account), the couple abandoned this enterprise, relocating to South Carolina to live near Colonel Musgrove.[8] After the death of her first husband (she never left him), Mary was briefly married to a second Englishman, Jacob Matthews. What became of him is uncertain, but in 1749 she married the Reverend Thomas Bosomworth, a minister of the Church of England and chaplain to General James Edward Oglethorpe's Highland Regiment. The regiment's military purpose was to expropriate Creek lands in Georgia in the name of the Crown of England. This was Mary's third and final marriage; all were interracial.[9]

Ultimately, it was Bosomworth himself who was instrumental in persuading the Creeks to cede portions of their territory during Oglethorpe's tenure. However, he attempted to arrange such transfer of real estate to himself rather than to the Crown. President of the Georgia Trustees, William Stephens, somewhat naturally resisted such private endeavors, and it was in this context that the famed march on Savannah occurred. The gambit was for

Mary Musgrove-Matthews-Bosomworth to use her position within Creek society to interpose her tribesmen militarily between her husband's private and the Crown's official (competing) claims to the same Creek ground.[10]

The whole affair fell through when the Creek warrior leadership realized the dubious nature of events, renounced Mary, and dispersed. Stephens jailed the offending couple posthaste for a short period. They then reemerged, living out their respective lives working at expropriating Creek terrain on behalf of the British government.[11] This is a rather less pretty story than the one constructed by Brown. In fact, it is diametrically opposed. The situation which thus emerges under Brown's handling is that a truly significant, if somewhat obscure figure within Creek history, a figure roughly analogous to Benedict Arnold in U.S. history, is transformed into the equivalent of her nation's George Washington.

For anyone who wishes to assert that such crystalline role reversal is unimportant, much less true to the spirit of history, the implications of an Indian historian writing a fictional account in which Arnold plays out the role of a great patriot should speak for themselves. At best, any book offering such a rendering of history would be laughingly ignored. At worst, the offending writer would find his/her career maimed by public and scholarly reaction, assuming, of course, that said writer could locate a publisher willing to offer up such patent nonsense as historical fiction in the first place.

Why is it generally acceptable procedure for a historian to alter and, at times, actually reverse the facts of American Indian history, while it is unacceptable to depart from at least the spirit of the popular understanding of Euroamerican historical sequences? Why the double standard? The answer would seem much more closely associated with the propaganda potential inherent to the literary license aspects of writing historical fiction than to aesthetic questions of literary merit.

A Captive of Her Flesh

Such recasting of the known contours of Creek Mary's life are not necessarily the most offensive abuses which Brown willingly engages in. There is also the matter of material not found in any chronicle of the period, but which is introduced to define her personal character. Of course, such practice is well within the domain of any fiction, historical or otherwise. But the question of the sort of character Brown selects to articulate his fabricated Creek patriot seems rather important, given his reputation as one sympathetic to the Indian (another factor which lends credibility to his work—in liberal circles at any rate). Consider that, in Brown's story, Mary leaves John Kingsley in a fit of revulsion against the white race in its entirety. Her intended purpose is to rejoin the Creeks, resume her rightful role as a tribal political leader, and guide her people on the road of effective resistance to further European incursion. These are indeed noble thoughts, but what happens thereafter?

Creek Mary, the child of nature who leaves her husband due to his disharmony with the natural world, a woman born and raised in the forests of the Creek homeland, immediately becomes lost along a route she's taken many times. This scenario is so implausible on its face that one begins to cast about for the author's ulterior motive in introducing it. Such is not long in revealing itself. In her forlorn state, Mary becomes easy prey and is thereupon captured by a Cherokee named Long Warrior. He promptly carries her off to his village for purposes of indulging in the captor's right to carnal knowledge. Mary, for her part, will have none of it, despite having meekly allowed herself to be led up to the veritable bedroll. She claws Long Warrior's face and he humbly desists. He becomes bored with this no-win situtation rapidly enough and thereupon proceeds to escort his captive—with baby—back to the location of her capture. Presumably, she is thus free to resume her wayward journey back to her people. Far from jumping at the chance, Mary seizes the opportunity to feel the earth tremble and see the stars ignite in flaming splendor; she promptly seduces her would-be rapist. Mary is (of course) so taken with the abilities of her lover that she applies for permanent status in the Cherokee nation: for herself as a wife, for her son as a potential warrior. It is from this second marriage, Brown tells us, that her second son, Dane, was produced.

So what have we here? First, of course, we have a ranking female member of, and ostensible symbol of patriotism to the Creek people, whose personal commitments are so weak and/or confused that she voluntarily submits both herself and her son to a lifetime identity as Cherokees (a people for whom the Creeks lost no love during the period in question). And this, immediately after having overthrown her marital commitments as a means—specifically—of returning to her people. Whatever we may reasonably expect in terms of dedication, or even of human loyalty, in a figure proclaimed to be as central to major historical events as Brown's Creek Mary, this jumbled and neurotic display of self-identification is wide of the mark.

Some sort of motivation is in order through which the author can explain the behavioral spectacle exhibited by his leading lady. This, Brown provides. Mary, it seems, has been the victim of her lustful nature all along. By the time of her liaison with Long Warrior, it has already been related how she exhibited the casual habit of "bedding" the British General Oglethorpe in her younger days, despite the fact that "she felt no particular affection for him...and told her grandson that the great man was afflicted with bad teeth and a foul breath.[12] And then there is the matter of a somewhat mysterious but clearly intimate relationship she carries on for years with the Creek war leader, Menewa.

We end up with a portrayal of an exotic beauty whose sexual wiles are sufficiently developed to lure otherwise crafty Europeans into thrashing fatally about in the mire of Okefenokee while seeking the Holy Grail of her groin. We find a natural woman who is so inept in the woods that she must be "saved" by a rapist with whom she immediately engages in sexual teasing ("now you get it, now you don't") intended to bring about marriage. We discover a nymphomaniac creature who, when all else fails, may be found trading secrets of the flesh with an aging enemy possessed of rotting teeth and gums. Ah well, any roll in the hay is better than none...

Ultimately, Brown's caricature of this, by all accounts, marvelously complex woman reduces in print to a preoccupation with her skill and willingness to rely upon sex. This emblem of Creek leadership is not a person, but a creature constricted to the one-dimensional dialectic of her sexual prowess/physical charms, a truly "magnificent heroine"[13] within the conventional Euro-american tradition of stereotyping Native American women as genetically encoded prostitutes. All this seems to have much more to do with the Freudian fantasies of an aging white librarian/archivist than with history in whatever novel form. Stripped of its halo of "sympathetic" trappings, Brown's pornography (read: sexuality unredeemed by articulation of social reality, past or present) fulfills all the worst criteria of what has elsewhere been termed "the Pocahontas myth."[14] In sum, it is representative of a categorical fusion of racism and sexism.

Methodology and the Marketplace

Although the specific formation of fabrications applied by Brown to Creek Mary as an individual and as a symbol seem entirely unwarranted—and thus avoidable—under any circumstances, he would seem to have condemned himself to a realm of much broader distortion from the onset. This observation is intended in a purely structural sense as opposed to the contentual and, being structural, the problem was unavoidable within the scope of the project itself. Of course, this in itself leaves open the question of whether the project was worthy of being undertaken at all, but this possibility can be disregarded for the moment.

The methodology employed in the erection of the saga of *Creek Mary's Blood* was to seize upon a single individual and use her as a medium through which to explain the sweep of historical events over a given era and geographic area. It may have been that the original intent of Dee Brown was to write a shorter novel concerning his "find" in the obscure personage of Creek Mary, a subject heretofore not elaborated in a popular fiction. However, if this were originally the case, the scope of the work was altered dramatically. Rather than dealing specifically with the life and times of Mary Musgrove-Matthews-Bosomworth, a story which would seem of more than passing interest in its own right, Brown decided instead to concern himself with the overall theme of Indian displacement in the Southeast. Hence he was necessarily concerned with two subthemes; these he chose to represent through focus on two tribal groups. In essence:

- He concerned himself with the Creeks as representative of native resistance by virtue of the march on Savannah (erroneously, in terms of Creek interests) and the Red Stick War (accurately enough); and

- He concerned himself with the Cherokees as representative of removal by virtue of the nature of their juridical interactions with the Andrew Jackson administration and the intensity of their relocation experience (the "Trail of Tears").

Such a schema might well have worked had not the
author also clung to the notion that he might relate the
aggregate story through Creek Mary rather than retaining her as an interesting, though not overarching, figure.
The decision to utilize her in this way makes very good
commercial sense: a major novel based upon the exciting
tale of an indigenous woman leader of an oppressed group
by a significant contemporary historian is enough to line
up a substantial segment of the modern book-buying
market at the nation's cash registers. However, such a
decision immediately negated the potential of incorporating much, if any, reasonably accurate history into the
book.

The need to have this single woman central to the
recounting of the experiences of two distinctly different
peoples during two rather well demarcated periods goes
very far in explaining why Brown went to such absurd
lengths in altering Mary's true story. In short order, as we
have seen, she was contorted into shedding two marriages
she actually had, entering into one she never had (voluntarily, with a man of a traditionally opposing people),
distorting beyond recognition the only actual marriage
she was allowed to retain, and espousing a barrage of
views which run entirely counter to those she actually
held in real life. Naturally, the history concomitant to her
existence (and lack of it) suffers accordingly.

Assuming that temporal and chronological accuracy
hold some legitimate importance and function within any
history, be it fiction or not, consider the following. Creek
Mary was born in the year 1700. The Cherokee Trail of
Tears, which Brown has Mary accompanying, occurred
during the period 1828-35 (to use the most charitable
dating possible). The author indicates that she was an
elderly woman during this travail, but 130 years old.
Further, he indicates that she died in Oklahoma some
while after the end of the Cherokee removal. By the most

conservative estimation, she would have been 135, and more probably 140 at this point.

The solution Brown sought to this dilemma was to shroud his story in a deliberate haziness as concerns any sort of dating. But, perchance some avid reader were to look up the dates of salient historical events such as the march on Savannah and the Trail of Tears, a hedge against simple arithmetic was contrived. Rather than cast Mary at her true age at the time of the Savannah episode, he in effect altered her birth date, making her a young woman of about twenty at that time rather than in her early 50s, as was really the case.

This strategy of temporal tampering—strange practice for any historian—accomplished two major objectives. First, it allowed Brown to dabble about with the "color" aspects of his story while remaining true to his private fantasies, which seem to require youth rather than middle-age as a prerequisite of an object of lust. This is peculiarly a preoccupation of contemporary Euro-dominant conditioning, but that, in a way, is precisely the point. Second, deploying Mary as a young woman at the time of Savannah allowed Brown to make her live through all the events he wished her to participate in. The novel's contrived chronology would allow her to do what is claimed, and still die in Oklahoma at not more than 115 years of age. Hence, the impression conveyed in Brown's calculated distortion of temporal context is the superficial plausibility of a wildly improbable life span.

Once things have been arranged so that Mary can be located at the site or within the process of any major event in the Southeastern displacement process, it is a small matter for Brown to make her a central figure throughout. Not only does the novel's Mary lead the march on Savannah, but she champions the cause of Tecumseh's confederacy among the southern tribes, is involved as a confidant of the leadership during the Red Sticks War, is a leader in the circles of Cherokee resistance against

Jackson's anti-Indianism, and provides a traditionalist anchor to the people's flagging spirits along the trek to Oklahoma.

Now, in a sense, this may in itself seem a solid tribute to American Indian womanhood. Such, however, is not the case. In the first place, American Indian women are perfectly worthy of tribute without resort to contrived circumstances; their true accomplishments are long overdue for widespread telling. On the other hand, one must remember the nature of the character Brown created as Mary: an inept and weak person whose primary motivation at the gut level seems to be to satisfy sexual urges. Real people, after all, fulfilled the roles attributed to Creek Mary by Dee Brown. Each has his or her own story, relative importance within tribal history and tradition (both past and present) and, most importantly, a message to bring home. All of this has been supplanted by Brown's stereotypical Indian "princess" in his "splendid, beautiful, heartbreaking story!"[15] The message is thus entirely Brown's.

With the garb of sympathy removed, Brown's message comes down to this: That such a woman as the author describes could become the guiding force within not one, but two major native societies during what were perhaps the most important events of their respective histories bespeaks much as to the nature of the Indians' downfall. Creek Mary was not a successful political leader; she fails to win at politics throughout the whole book (perhaps because she must switch sides every fifteen pages in keeping with the demands of Brown's script). Neither is she a military leader. Her single foray into the field resulted in her warriors going home without her. Nor is it indicated anywhere in the book that she is a spiritual leader. Indeed, she is incapable even of fundamental human loyalty in many respects. With her in the proverbial driver's seat, even symbolically, the tribes are doomed to fail before they begin. Hence, they brought it on themselves, through faulty judgement if nothing else.

Truly, the "vast epic scope"[16] of *Creek Mary's Blood* "tells us much that we have not heard before."[17] In no small part, this must certainly be because so much of what we've not heard in this connection is simply untrue. But, who is to believe this? Certainly not a general reading public conditioned to accepting its view of history in such pulp packages. Certainly not major reviewers, whose "raves" have been quoted throughout this critique. Certainly not the high school pop history teachers, who already have begun to seize upon this book as required reading in their classes. Nor will the students to whom it is assigned. Ignorance can be overcome through education, or at least the provision of accurate information. Confronting false "knowledge" is another matter entirely. This seems particularly true when the basis for such belief is conveyed through the "unmatchable style" and "memorable power"[18] of such a highly visible and well credentialed historian as Dee Brown.

One must, in combating such an intellectual virus, all but inevitably be drawn into meaningless debates concerning the "author's ultimate intentions," "the permissible degree of artistic latitude involved" and hedges such as "the man's right to his opinion." Thus, the overcoming of ignorance becomes a polemical squabble over generally irrelevant (in terms of the issues at hand) abstract preoccupations. Such is the academic condition of life and letters.

Conclusion

It is time to cut through the twaddle. Dee Brown lied. He did so knowingly and in print. He did so in order, no doubt, to acquire the income of another best-seller as a prelude to his final years, a perfectly understandable motivation in a society which spurns its elders. But his is not a "victimless crime." The people historically misrepresented through the catapulting of his apparition of Creek Mary into the limelight of popular historical "knowledge" deserve far better remembrance than this. Their descendants have a right to see the truth of the events at issue and of their very heritage known, deserve better than consignment to yet another stereotyped oblivion in the public consciousness.

Nor is this the end of it. A country as permeated by the crippling twistedness of racism and sexism as the United States can ill afford another generation in which the same attitudes have been inculcated, no matter how "liberal" the form. What is needed now in America—and needed desperately—is an accurate understanding of humanity. Historical legitimacy can go far towards accommodating this need. Hence, the nation as a whole may be said to have suffered as a result of Brown's excursion into the sublime although—masochistically—it may delight in the nature of its pain. Finally, it may be said that history has suffered as a result of this charade. History, and all those—whether they are professional historians or pursue other avocations—who are concerned with it.

For his strange and self-indulgent amalgamation of fact and fantasy, we owe Dee Brown no vote of either confidence or gratitude. His mercenary trading upon past scholarly luster as a means to launch this travesty should earn him little other than academic scorn and the royalties accruing from his plunge into venality. But he should not be dismissed lightly as a "has-been" or "hack" historian. The very fact that he possessed such stature within the realm of historiography qualifies him as much more dangerous than Ruth Beebe Hill might ever have become. There is, I'm afraid, a lesson in that for all of us.

Notes

1. Churchill, Ward, "Ayn Rand and the Sioux—Tonto Revisited: Another Look at *Hanta Yo,*" *Lakota Eyapaha,* Vol. 4, No. 2, Pine Ridge, SD, 1980.

2. Deloria, Vine Jr., "The Twisted World of *Hanta Yo, Minority Notes,* Vol. 1, No. 1, University of Colorado at Boulder, 1980; Medicine, Bea, "*Hanta Yo:* A New Phenomenon," *The Indian Historian,* Vol. 12, No. 2, American Indian Historical Society, San Francisco, 1980.

3. Newman, Donna Joy, "Hanta: Insight to the Red Man's Roots or Just a Novel View of History?" Tempo, Los Angeles, May 17, 1979.

4. The quotations are taken from the jacket notes reprinted at the front of the Pocket Books edition of *Creek Mary's Blood.* The first is attributed to *Chicago Tribune Book World,* the second and third to the *ALA Booklist.*

5. Foreman, Caroline Thomas, *Indian Women Chiefs,* Hoffman Printing Company, Muskogee, Oklahoma, 1966.

6. Brown, Dee, *Creek Mary's Blood,* Pocket Books (Simon and Schuster), New York, 1981, p. 27.

7. *Ibid.*

8. Foreman, *op. cit.,* pp. 40-43.

9. *Ibid.*

10. *Ibid.,* p. 43.

11. Brown, *op. cit.,* p. 20.

12. *Ibid.* (jacket notes); attributed to *Publisher's Weekly.*

13. Bernstein, Alison, "Outgrowing Pocahontas: Toward a New History of American Indian Women," *Minority Notes,* Vol. 2, Nos. 1/2, University of Colorado at Boulder, 1981, pp. 3-31.

14. Brown, *op. cit.* (cover); attributed to Howard Fast, author of *The Immigrants.*

15. *Ibid.,* attributed to the *Chicago Sun Times.*

16. Brown, *op. cit.* (jacket notes); attributed to *Publisher's Weekly.*

17. *Ibid.;* the first quotation is attributed to the Pittsburg Press, the second to *Library Journal.*

Revolution
vs. Self-Determination

Roxanne Dunbar Ortiz's
Indians of the Americas

The future of the Sandinista revolution in Nicaragua is
more important to American Indians than [the Indians]
themselves.

—Vernon Bellecourt
1984

Roxanne Dunbar Ortiz, one of the more articulate
and prolific writers to have emerged from the ranks of
contemporary Native American activism, is back with a
new book. Her most ambitious effort to date, *Indians of
the Americas: Human Rights and Self-Determination* has
been published simultaneously by Praeger in North
America and Zed Press in England. Ordinarily, the release of Dunbar Ortiz's efforts has been the cause for some
degree of celebration among those concerned with American Indian issues. At least this has proven to be the case
with her earlier books: *The Great Sioux Nation: Sitting in
Judgment on America* (International Indian Treaty Coun-
cil/Moon Books, 1977), *Economic Development in American Indian Reservations* (University of New Mexico,
1979), *American Indian Energy Resources and Development* (UNM, 1980) and *Roots of Resistance: Land Tenure
in New Mexico, 1680-1980* (UCLA, 1980). Regardless of
specific deficiencies contained within these works, they
have been generally considered as offering a very positive
contribution to the literature.

Indians of the Americas, however, is cause for consternation. For the first time, Dunbar Ortiz seems to have engaged in a process of tailoring her factual treatment to conform to an *a priori* ideological prescription. As a result, her handling of both contemporary and historical data is undercut badly, even to the point of shoddiness in certain instances. Needless to say, her potentially commendable and very important analytical project tends to discredit itself along the way.

The book is structured into four primary parts. The first section, an extended introduction, purports to summarize the history of the Indians of the Americas from approximately 1500 through the present. Next comes a section handling the theoretical background of what, within marxist vernacular, is termed "the national question" from Tierra del Fuego to the Arctic Circle. The third section summarizes the history and status of the national question in North America, utilizing the experiences of the Diné (Navajo) and Lakota (Sioux) peoples as examples. The final section deals with areas south of the United States, and is evidently intended to pose an alternative to U.S. practice through elaboration of the Sandinista relationship to the Miskito (Dunbar Ortiz spells this "Miskitu" throughout the book) people in Nicaragua.

It is in this last connection that the problems inherent to Dunbar Ortiz's book become strongly apparent. It is evident she has made up her mind that the Sandinista government is a progressive hemispheric force relative to the heritage of overt imperialism and denial of indigenous sovereignty exhibited by the United States. One would, of course, be hard-pressed to disagree with such a pronouncement and, had matters ended there, all would be well. However, Dunbar Ortiz goes on to conclude that because the Sandinistas are relatively progressive overall, they *must* be essentially correct in their handling of issues concerning the sovereignty and autonomy of native peoples such as the Miskitos. She is, to be sure, willing to

cede that the young Sandinista government has stumbled
into certain (correctable) errors in its relations with Indians, although exactly what these errors have been is left
a mystery. On the other hand, she develops at length the
current and historical reasons why she holds that Miskito
insistence upon real sovereignty is impractical, even absurd. A considerable amount of data is deployed to support
her contentions in this regard, but the main points may
be summarized as follows:

- The post-contact history of the Miskitos and other
  groups indigenous to Nicaragua is such that traditional cultural forms have been distorted or lost;
  government in particular having been forced into
  conformity with European norms, and trea-
  ties/agreements made between Indians and non-Indians in Nicaragua historically either were never
  binding or have been eroded over time.

- The by-products of colonialist exploitation, especially under the United States/Somoza combination
  during the past 50 years, have served to so hopelessly disrupt traditional indigenous economies and
  the land base upon which they were predicated that
  any development of Miskito self-sufficiency is now
  unrealistic. Direct economic integration into the
  broader Nicaraguan state is, therefore, both necessary and humane.

- Under such circumstances, the Sandinista extension of coherent "cultural autonomy" programs
  (such as indigenous language literacy campaigns
  and arts and crafts projects) addresses what is
  really meant by "the national question" in the Nicaraguan context. Miskito and other indigenous na-

tional needs are met or will be met through existing
Sandinista policies.

• In any event, "Miskitia" is not really Miskito territory insofar as it is now shared by several other
  ethnic groups, including a preponderance of Ladi-
  nos, whose needs must be considered equally with
  those of the Miskito in any "just" resolution of the
  national question in Nicaragua.

• But for the armed intervention of the United States
  and its clients (e.g., the contras) in the northern
  areas of Nicaragua, a situation imposing a wartime
  way of life in the impact region, the national question would have long ago reached a resolution acceptable to all concerned parties in Nicaragua.

    There is an undeniably strong logic running through
this formulation. On the face of it, the apparent Miskito
resistance to good Sandinista intentions seems patently
nonsensical. The question thus becomes one of how to
account for the irrational behavior of virtually an entire
national/ethnic group. Dunbar Ortiz approaches this
issue somewhat obliquely, more by inference than by
outright statement or contention. Pointing to the example
of Steadman Fagoth Müller, a former leader of the indigenous (primarily Miskito) rights organization
MISURASATA who moved into the orbit of the CIA, she
is able—by implication—to tar the entire native sovereignty movement with the brush of U.S. sponsorship.
Voila! The riddle is solved: The CIA is manipulating and
employing the Miskitos as a reactionary guerilla army in
essentially the same way that it utilized the Hmong of
Laos during its "secret war" in that country during the
1960s and early '70s. Native organizations struggling for
national sovereignty are thus neatly converted into fun-

damental stumbling blocks to achieving indigenous sovereignty, at least within "progressive contexts" such as Nicaragua. Rather than being Miskito patriots, the MISURASATA activists are merely the dupes of North American imperialism.

Such a contorted analysis should not be dismissed out of hand. The netherworld of clandestine operations "handled" by the CIA in the Third World is replete with similarly convoluted examples of conflicted interest. Still, Dunbar Ortiz's clear lack of cited evidence in establishing the "fact" of CIA control over MISURASATA, especially in view of her abundant footnotes for every other major contention offered in the book, renders her line of reasoning suspect. When coupled to the fact that the Sandinista government itself elected to enter into negotiations with MISURASATA designed to resolve indigenous demands for sovereignty in a manner acceptable to the organization—and explicitly denied contentions of MISURASATA's alleged connections to the CIA in the bargain—the reasoning passes from suspect to implausible. Had there ever been tangible evidence that MISURASATA was a CIA front, it goes without saying the Sandinistas would never have set out to negotiate settlement of an "internal" Nicaraguan problem with the group.

An author, of course, has the right to speculate within even the most nonfictional of works (although, in nonfiction, it is surely reasonable that speculation be clearly delineated from fact). Similarly, authors have a right to be wrong in their speculations. So Dunbar Ortiz's little excursion into mud-slinging might be excusable on its face. Her "CIA connection" might also serve as a convenient means to lend otherwise "incomprehensible" MISURASATA demands for territorial integrity, political autonomy and political independence a dimension of rationality.

It is well to remember before accepting this analysis, however, that the incomprehensibility of MISURASATA's agenda is itself based upon Dunbar Ortiz's own assessment of the situation of the Miskito, and the quality of the data she brings to bear in making her case in this regard. It is equally important to note that the Sandinista willingness to treat the positions advanced by MISURASATA seriously suggest that they themselves operated under rather less rigid and negative understandings of the feasibility of real Miskitia sovereignty than those espoused by Dunbar Ortiz. While such facts hardly serve to abolish the validity of her observations, they do render her insights doubly suspect.

Here, it is interesting to contrast Dunbar Ortiz's handling of the national question in North America with her treatment of Nicaragua. As regards North America, for example, she rejects U.S. government assertions concerning the erosion of indigenous rights to real sovereignty and the binding nature of treaty relationships. In her analysis of the situation in Nicaragua, she neatly reverses her field, pointing out that the Sandinistas contested the legitimacy of past treaties with the Miskitos and other indigenous nations. And there is more:

- In North America, where Levis, pick-up trucks and fry bread have become virtual signifiers of "Indianness," she acknowledges that there has been a tremendous disruption of indigenous cultures, but (rightly) notes that it remains possible in many—or most—instances to maintain or recover the essential vitality of the traditional worldview (and to reconstitute societies based upon that worldview). In Nicaragua, where the Miskitos still live in relative sociocultural proximity to their traditional ways, she somehow discovers that cultural dislocation is beyond repair.

• In North America, where the Indian Reorganization Act of 1934 has saddled virtually every indigenous nation (including, to be sure, her two case
studies) with an externally imposed puppet regime,
Dunbar Ortiz can readily discover strategies
through which native self-government and self-determination might be realized. Among the Miskitos,
on the other hand, she contends that the imposition
of a "king" by the English has irretrievably destroyed the mechanisms of self-government.

• Within the Navajo Nation of North America, as a
case in point, an arid region which has been so
devastated by mineral extraction, uranium contamination and the drawing-down of water resources as to have been termed a "national sacrifice
area" by the U.S. government, Dunbar Ortiz believes she sees the possibility of establishing a viable, self-sufficient economy based upon traditional
modes such as sheepherding. In Miskitia, a semi-
tropical region with fertile soil more-or-less readily
reclaimable by virtue of ample rainfall (and with
the potential of ocean-derived protein within easy
reach), Dunbar Ortiz cannot discover a way by
which self-sufficiency is an attainable goal. It is
therefore "humane" for the Miskitos to be incorporated into the general Nicaraguan economy in precisely the ways she emphatically rejects when
undertaken by governments in North America.

• Creation of written forms of the Lakota and Diné
languages, arts and crafts programs and similar
activities undertaken by the government of the
United States in the name of the cultural advocacy
of American Indian interests have been often (and
quite correctly) dismissed by Dunbar Ortiz as con-

stituting tokenism and avoidance of the real issues. In her analysis of the Nicaraguan situation, she touts the extension of exactly similar programs by the Sandinistas as evidence not only of good intentions, but of active efforts to resolve what is really at issue.

- Within the Lakota Nation of North America, Dunbar Ortiz observes that the influx of non-Indians into Indian territory—the "checkerboarding" of reservations, etc.—has been a conscious part of U.S. policy designed to erode Lakota rights and to preclude just settlement of land disputes. This, she concludes, reasonably enough, is an unacceptable situation which must be reversed. In Nicaragua, on the other hand, she points to the presence of large numbers of non-Indians in Miskito territory as evidence that it is no longer really Miskito territory.

This series of complete contradictions of her own positions leaves Dunbar Ortiz in a conceptual position *vis à vis* the Miskitos which is not particularly different in its essentials from that expressed by the U.S. government's Bureau of Indian Affairs relative to North American Indians. This is, to say the least, an odd posture for a supposed radical advocate of Indian rights to adopt. Still, it is possible that the facts of the situation simply compelled Dunbar Ortiz to assume her stance where Miskitia is concerned. Certainly, the data she offers tends to support her case rather seamlessly, and reality *has* been known to refute mere logical consistency often enough. Here, however, we enter into an area of somewhat slippery ground: critical information, of both historical and current import relative to Nicaragua, is virtually inaccessible (and hence unknown) to the vast majority of the potential readers of *Indians of the Americas*. It being largely impossible to assess Dunbar Ortiz's Central American data base in its own right, we are left in a certain sense to assume out of faith that she has proceeded accurately and in a reasonably unbiased fashion to assemble the empirical support to her own very strained argument.

Perhaps the only means open to most of us in North America to achieve a sense of how Dunbar Ortiz has likely handled her factual material relative to the Miskito/Sandinista confrontation is to consider her handling of other, more known quantities, such as data pertaining to North America itself. As Dunbar Ortiz is a professional historian, it seems appropriate to begin with the manner in which she deals with historical facts. We need read no further than page six to find her stating in all seriousness that, in pre-contact Aztec society, "A religious cult came to dominate which *daily required human sacrifice of thousands of people* to the Sun God [emphasis added]." No citation is afforded this rather staggering assertion, a matter which is understandable given that it could only accrue from some of the most arcane, reactionary and long discredited sources imaginable (*e.g.,* Maurice Collen's *Cortez and Montezuma,* New York, 1954). The whole notion of a "theocratic holocaust" integral to Mexicano culture was, as is well known, fabricated as a means to contend that "the Aztecs were as bad as the *Conquistadores,"* and hence rationalize the nature of Spanish "progress" in Mexico.

Dunbar Ortiz's objective, of course, has nothing to do with reinforcing the pronouncements of the right-wing intelligentsia. Rather, this almost passing comment may be seen as an element designed to assist in setting the stage for validation of quite another vision of social progression which she herself advances later in the book. What is fundamentally at issue, however, is that what has been advanced as historical *fact* here is—regardless of ideological intent—quite nonsensical in purely arithmetical terms. To be as charitable as possible, and to accept "thousands" as indicative of only a bare minimum—that is, 2,000—then a daily sacrifice of human beings on the scale Dunbar Ortiz posits requires an annual consumption of some 730,000 lives for satiation of the Sun God alone. Based against an aggregate population of some 30 million, the total population Dunbar Ortiz assigns all of central Mexico in pre-contact times, such a population drain is a clear impossibility on any sort of sustained basis.

Elsewhere, the author plays equally fast and loose with her facts. For example, on page 151, she has the Navajo Grand Council being established in 1937, a full three years after the Indian Reorganization Act of 1934. In actuality, the Council was formed fifteen years earlier, in 1923, and served as a prototype for the council form of government imposed more broadly through the 1934 legislation. Or, on page 183, she makes a point of some sort by noting "the Pit River people's pride in killing the only U.S. Army General (Canby) ever killed in battle Custer was a Colonel, and only made a General posthumously..." Actually, and quite contrary to Dunbar Ortiz, 30-odd U.S. Generals were killed in battle during the American Civil War alone. The last known such fatality, Major General George W. Casey (commander of the 1st Air Cavalry Division in Vietnam), was killed on July 7, 1970. As concerns Custer, he was *never* a colonel, nor was his promotion really posthumous. At the time of his death at the Little Big Horn, he enjoyed the active duty rank of Lieutenant colonel (a step below colonel), and the brevet (equivalent of reserve) rank of Major General, attained as a field commander during the Civil War. In 1862, nearly a decade and a half prior to his death, Custer had become the youngest brigadier general ever to serve in the U.S. Army. This chronicle of errors concerning the North American historical record could be extended at length. The performance is odd (to say the least) for a professional historian such as Dunbar Ortiz.

The problem does not end in the historical arena, however, but extends into Dunbar Ortiz's contemporary factual understanding of indigenous circumstances in North America. For instance, on pages 169-70, Dunbar Ortiz has it that "In one attack by nearly 100 FBI agents on a small Indian compound on the Pine Ridge Reservation in June 1975, two FBI agents were killed. An important Indian leader, not present on this occasion, was charged with the murders." The Indian leader in question is, as Dunbar Ortiz goes on to note, Leonard Peltier, currently serving a double-life sentence for homicide in the federal maximum security facility in Leavenworth, Kansas. He was not, as Dunbar Ortiz implies, the only individual charged in the deaths of the two FBI agents (and they were not the only fatalities of the day; an AIM member named Joe Stuntz Killsright was also killed). To the contrary, three other Indians (Jimmy Eagle, Bob Robideau and Dino Butler) were also indicted, two of them (Robideau and Butler) ultimately tried and acquitted on grounds of self-defense. None of those charged, including Peltier, has ever denied being present at the scene of the fatalities, or engaging in the firefight in which the FBI men died. Rather, they have contended that the deaths did not constitute the crime of murder. Finally, nobody other than Roxanne Dunbar Ortiz has ever suggested that anywhere near 100 FBI agents participated in the attack on the Jumping Bull compound near Oglala, South Dakota. It is certain that the attack was initiated by the two dead agents, and that in the immediate aftermath some 15-20 additional agents arrived (albeit, supported by a much larger number of BIA police, GOON squad members and *ad hoc* groups of white vigilantes). Larger numbers of agents—over 200—arrived the following day.

Elsewhere, on page 148, Dunbar Ortiz observes that "16,000 Navajos would be uprooted" by current U.S. government plans to force relocation of traditional people from the so-called "Navajo-Hopi Joint Use Area" of Arizona (a ploy to clear the way for extraction of an estimated 24 billion tons of coal in the area). These are U.S. government figures, notoriously low and generally discredited. The most common figure advanced relative to the number of Navajos to be impacted in this scheme exceeds 10,000. The AIM activists resisting forced relocation, whose perspective Dunbar Ortiz purports to represent, operate from a figure of 13,500, nearly 10 percent of the Navajo Reservation's overall population and a figure lending substance to contentions of genocide. Again, the list of Dunbar Ortiz's factual errors could be extended to a considerable length, but the point should be made.

The author's inaccurate and misleading handling of data relative to North America is not restricted to sins of commission, however. There is ample evidence that she has consciously manipulated her information by omission as well, in order to achieve a certain desired "factual" effect. Consider, for example, her treatment of proponents of a "Fourth World" perspective in the second section of the book ("The National question in the Americas"). The Fourth World, or indigenist outlook, one which is attracting rapidly increasing numbers of native people recently, runs directly counter to Dunbar Ortiz's own tacit sympathy to socialist goals and objectives, and which she has attacked rather stridently in a published essay: "The Fourth World and Indigenism: Politics of Isolation," *Journal of Ethnic Studies,* 12:1, 1984. The entire theory is allowed approximately one page and two quotations in a theoretical section running a total of 44 pages. This should be contrasted to her devotion of approximately 10 pages to the lesser intellectual phenomenon of "Indigenous Socialism" and "Contemporary Socialist Thinking" in the same section. When one adds the clearly socialist cant displayed in other subheadings of the section, such as "The Significance of Ethnicity," the short change extended to indigenous theory *per se* becomes obvious; even count-

ing the four pages she devotes to "Pan Indianism" as being
clearly on the indigenist side of the equation.

The situation is aggravated greatly in that she
chooses to devote literally all her content on socialism to
the formulations of obscure (by North American standards) Mexican, Bolivian and Peruvian marxists such as
Hector Diaz-Polanco, Pablo Gonzalez Casanova and
Stefano Varese. The pronouncements of the various
schools of North American marxism are avoided altogether (which is probably a good idea, assuming one
wishes to put the best possible face on marxist thinking
relative to indigenous populations). More importantly,
Dunbar Ortiz omits all reference to the fast-developing
North American indigenous critique of marxist theory and
practice as represented by the widely distributed tracts of
John Mohawk and Russell Means, among others.

As concerns references in a broader sense, omission—even deception—shows through once again.
Throughout *Indians of the Americas,* Dunbar Ortiz pres-
ents an appearance of a scholarly approach to her subject
matter through the deployment of copious footnotes to
support her various observations and assertions. In total,
she utilizes 407 separate notes in the course of her exposition, a seemingly rigorous exercise in documentation.
Upon examination, however, one discovers that 46 of the
notes—approximately 10 percent—lead directly back to
Dunbar Ortiz's own essays, articles, books and translations. This is exclusive of another 8 percent devoted only
to amplification of points made in the text rather than
documentation and/or citation from *Indigenous World/El
Mundo Indigena,* which Dunbar Ortiz edits. Of the 124
notes Dunbar Ortiz uses to support her case in her final
section: "The Miskitu Nation in Revolutionary Nicaragua", fifteen accrue directly from the Sandinista Ministry
of Information and other government agencies, two simply elaborate Dunbar Ortiz's own sense of the Sandinistas'
good intentions at greater length than is allowable in the

text, and only two can be said to directly reflect MISURASATA data (by way of photocopies of documents and interviews).

In sum, it cannot be viewed as safe to assume that Dunbar Ortiz's thesis concerning the nature of the Miskito national question in Nicaragua is in any serious way validated by her presentation of "the facts." Her book at every turn confronts the reader with inaccurate and sloppy utilization of data, elimination of uncomfortable or contrary information, lopsided analysis and resort to unabashed self-promotion as a (or *the*) reigning current authority on all things Indian. From this, it may be taken as a given that the author's case has not been made and, insofar as she has obviously gone through some serious contortions to make things appear otherwise, one is led to wonder strongly whether it was ever even marginally tenable in the first place.

At the very best, Dunbar Ortiz, who might have proven one of the hemispheric Indian movement's strongest intellectual assets, has engaged in such a shoddy display of scholarship it is likely she has permanently discredited herself both academically and within movement ranks. In any event, it will be a long road back to her former position of stature. At worst, she has joined the all but endless list of brilliant or potentially brilliant intellectuals such as George Lukacs and Louis Althusser who have willingly sacrificed themselves to the doctrinal demands of marxism's leninist/stalinist tradition, forcing reality into conformance with "the party line." All of us—leftist, rightist, indigenist and "apolitical" alike—are badly in need of both real insight into the Miskito situation, and the sort of comprehensive overview and analysis Roxanne Dunbar Ortiz claimed to be publishing. She does each of us an extreme disservice by trading on her reputation as an Indian scholar and activist in order to intentionally misrepresent the situation.

Part III

History as Propaganda
of the Victors

It Did Happen Here

Sand Creek, Scholarship and the American Character

Nits make lice...Kill all, big and little...[And] damn any man who takes the side of the Indians.

—Colonel John M. Chivington
Commander, Colorado Volunteer Cavalry
1864

At a number of levels, the 1864 Sand Creek Massacre of Cheyenne and Arapahoe Indians in what was then called Colorado Territory has come to symbolize the manner in which Euroamerica "settled" the western United States. More than the comparable slaughters which ensued along the Washita River, Sappa Creek, Bear River, Wounded Knee and hundreds of other sites throughout the Plains and Great Basin regions, Sand Creek had everything necessary to commend it as an archetypal event: a white population, moved by gold fever, knowingly tramples upon legally binding treaty provisions by massively invading Indian country; the federal government, rather than attempting to honor its own existing treaty obligations to protect the Indians' solemnly guaranteed national borders, engineers a second—utterly fraudulent—instrument purporting to legitimate its citizens' illegal occupation of the Cheyenne-Arapaho homeland; a conspiratorial circle of merchants and politicians among the invaders glimpses the potential for vast personal wealth and power in liquidation of the "savages" and the resultant Colorado statehood this might make possible. A propaganda campaign to whip up a public blood lust

111

against the Indians is therefore initiated, a mostly phony "war" is conjured up, and special dispensation is secured from Washington, D.C. to create bodies of soldiers devoted exclusively to Indian killing.

The Indians, pushed to the wall, are divided as to whether they should fight back or simply surrender to the onrushing wave of national and cultural oblivion which threatens to engulf them. Either way, they are tremendously outgunned and beset by the murderous frenzy of an alien population bent upon their eradication as "a species." A large number of the Cheyennes and a few Arapahoes attempt to remain at peace with their opponents, allowing themselves to be mostly disarmed and immobilized in exchange for official assurances that they will be safe from attack so long as they remain at a location selected for them at Sand Creek, in southeastern Colorado. They live there quietly, under protection of a white flag flown above the lodge of their leader, Black Kettle, until the very moment of the preplanned attack which decimates them. No sparkling hero arrives to save the day at the last moment, and the matter is never "set right." A large though undetermined number of Indians, mostly women, children and old people, are killed and grotesquely mutilated. Those who survive are driven permanently from the territory, and the plotters' plans are largely consummated. Colorado duly becomes a state. Many of the conspirators prosper. Evil wins out, pure and simple.

Literature concerning the wanton butchery occurring at Sand Creek on November 29, 1864 began to emerge almost immediately. This was first the case in the pages of jingoist local tabloids like the *Rocky Mountain News*— where the massacre was heralded as a glorious event— and then in lengthy reports issued by three separate governmental commissions charged with investigating what exactly had happened. Each of these—*Massacre of Cheyennes* (U.S. Congress, 1865), *The Chivington Massa-*

cre (U.S. Congress, 1865) and *Sand Creek Massacre* (Sec-
retary of War, 1867)—concluded unequivocally that there
was no merit to the rationalizations advanced by those
responsible and that mass murder had indeed been perpetrated against the Cheyennes and Arapahoes. That
said, however, each report stopped well short of recommending any sort of criminal punishment for any of the
perpetrators, never mind abortion of the process of state
formation that had been set in motion by the killers'
collective misdeeds. To the contrary, the only tangible
consequence visited upon anyone who had played a major
role in the mini-Holocaust accrued to Colonel John Milton
Chivington, a former Methodist minister and overall commander of the troops (the 3rd and portions of the 1st
Colorado Volunteer Cavalry Regiments) who had done the
actual killing. "Disgraced" by the official findings,
Chivington was forced to abandon his previously promis-
ing political career in favor of other lines of work.

Since the immediate reports and investigations,
Sand Creek has found a ready place in recountings of
Euroamerica's takeover of the Great Plains, ranging in
tone, tenor and intent from Frank Hall's four-volume
History of the State of Colorado (Blakely, 1899), through
Frederick Jackson Turner's *The Significance of the Fron-
tier in American History* (Holt, 1947), to S.L.A. Marshall's
The Crimsoned Prairie (Scribner, 1972) and E.S. Connell's
Son of the Morning Star (North Point, 1984). Similarly, it
has been integral to those works seeking to chronicle the
effects of U.S. westward expansion upon the indigenous
people at issue. These include George Bird Grinnell's *The
Fighting Cheyennes* (Scribner, 1915) and *The Cheyenne
Indians* (Yale University, 1923), or J.H. Moore's *The Cheyenne Nation* (University of Nebraska, 1987). The massacre and its implications have also played central roles in
the biographies of certain of the non-Indian principles
involved. Edgar Carlisle MacMechen's *Life of Governor
John Evans, Second Territorial Governor of Colorado*

(Wahlgreen, 1924) and Reginald S. Craig's sympathetic study of Chivington, *The Fighting Parson* (Westernlore, 1959), spring immediately to mind in this regard—as do the autobiographical accounts of lesser players like Morse Coffin in his *The Battle of Sand Creek* (W.M. Morrison, 1965).

Biographers in particular have taken considerable liberties with the record, both factually and philosophically, in their quest either to completely vindicate and rehabilitate their subjects or, at least, to neutralize the genocidal negativity of their central figures' words and conduct. In this they are joined by writers focusing directly upon the massacre itself, notably Eugene F. Ware's *The Indian War of 1864* (Crane & Co., 1911) and William R. Dunn's *"I Stand by Sand Creek": A Defense of Colonel John M. Chivington and the Third Colorado Cavalry* (Old Army Press, 1985). Such lies, distortions and unabashed polemics on behalf of Sand Creek's perpetrators have together provided a convenient umbrella under which "more responsible" scholars have persistently sheltered. The unpleasantness inherent both in the specifics of Sand Creek itself, and in the far broader sweep of policy to which it was inextricably linked, has been avoided. The conventional academic wisdom thus has landed squarely on the comfortable proposition that, while the massacre was an undoubted "tragedy," its real meaning and place in American history remains somehow "unknowable" or "stubbornly mysterious" (in this vein, see Raymond G. Carey's "The Puzzle of Sand Creek" in *Colorado Magazine,* Vol. 41, No. 4, 1964, and Michael A. Sievers' "Shifting Sands of Sand Creek Historiography" in *Colorado Magazine,* Vol. 49, No. 2, 1972).

There have been, to be sure, efforts which have gone in decidedly different directions. Noteworthy in this regard, albeit to varying degrees, have been William H. Leckie's *The Military Conquest of the Southern Plains* (University of Oklahoma, 1963), Ralph K. Andrist's *The*

Long Death (Collier, 1964), Dee Brown's *Bury My Heart at Wounded Knee* (Holt, Rinehart and Winston, 1970), and John Selby's *The Conquest of the American West* (Rowman and Littlefield, 1976), each of which treats the massacre for what it was and attempts to situate it within an accurate contextual rendering of overall policy and public sentiment. Paramount among this genre is Stan Hoig's *The Sand Creek Massacre* (University of Oklahoma, 1961), an honest and meticulously researched volume which has stood for nearly thirty years as the definitive study for those pursuing a genuine understanding of the whole affair. Aside from the obligatory inclusion of Sand Creek in Father Peter Powell's works on the Cheyenne, there has been since the mid-70s, something of a hiatus in the generation of worthwhile material in this vein. It is thus interesting and important that a single six-month period in 1989-90 saw the release of two new books on the topic: David Svaldi's *Sand Creek and the Rhetoric of Extermination: A Case Study in Indian-White Relations* (University Press of America, 1989) and *Month of the Freezing Moon: The Sand Creek Massacre, November 1864* by Duane Schultz (St. Martin's, 1990).

Of these two new works, Schultz's book follows by far the more shopworn and predictable pattern. It is a standard history of the "who did what to whom" variety, tracing the by-now familiar progression of events leading up to, comprising and immediately following from the massacre itself. In this, it is accurate enough on the main points, although essentially duplicative of Hoig's earlier and much better written volume. Were this all that was involved, *Month of the Freezing Moon* would be nothing so much as a vaguely plagiaristic redundancy, more or less harmless despite its tendency to include easily avoidable errors of detail which serve to muddy rather than further clarify the record. A good example of this comes at page 135, where Schultz places Left Hand, a primary Arapaho leader, among those slain at Sand Creek. This myth, created by the glory seekers of the Colorado Volunteers, has been debunked long since by Hoig (p. 154) and Margaret Coel in her exhaustive biography of the supposed victim, *Chief Left Hand: Southern Arapaho* (University of Oklahoma, 1981), among others.

Schultz, however, goes much further, and this is where his work is transformed from being merely irrelevant into something truly malicious and objectionable. This comes with his adoption of the Euroamerican standard of "academic objectivity" which decreed that whenever one addresses the atrocities committed by the *status quo*, one is duty-bound to "balance one's view" by depicting some negativity embodied in its victims. This holds as an iron law of "responsible scholarship," even when counterbalancing information must be quite literally invented. Hence, while Schultz follows Hoig's lead in dissecting and refuting assorted untruths about specific Cheyenne actions manufactured by the perpetrators in order to justify of the massacre, he simultaneously embraces those same sources—or those like them (*e.g.:* Richens Lacy "Uncle Dick" Wooten)—as credible and valid when it comes to describing the broader dimensions of Indian character and behavior:

> [B]efore there were whites to rob and plunder and steal from, the [Indians] robbed and stole from each other. Before there were white men in the country to kill, they killed each other. Before there were white women and children to scalp and mutilate and torture, the Indians scalped and mutilated and tortured the women and children of the enemies of their own race. They made slaves of each other when there were no palefaces to be captured and sold or held for ransom, and before they commenced lying in ambush along the trails of the white man to murder unwary travelers, the Indians of one tribe would set the same sort of death traps for the Indians of another tribe (p. 16).

None of this is substantiated, or even substantiable. It instead flies directly in the face of most well researched and grounded contemporary understandings regarding how the Cheyennes did business in pre-contact times as well as the early contact period. Deployed in the otherwise "critical" (of the whites) and "sympathetic" (to the Indians) setting so carefully developed by the author, such disinformation serves a peculiarly effective propaganda function. The general reader is given to conclude that, while it's "a shame" the good citizens of Colorado were forced to comport themselves as they had, the intrinsic bestiality of their enemies led inevitably to this result. The inherently horrible nature of the victims themselves—*not* the fundamental nature of the process by which they were victimized—accounts for the nature of their fate. The process itself thereby becomes "necessary" and consequently beyond need of justification.

In this construction, Evans, Chivington and the others are indeed guilty, but only of "excesses," not of intent. This is to say, by definition, that they undertook a good thing (the conquest of native nations) and "pushed it too far" (using methods which were overly crude). The reader is then left to ponder whether even this might not be excusable—or at least "understandable" (which is to say, "forgivable")—"under the circumstances" or "in the heat of the fray." The techniques of presentation at issue here are hardly novel or unique to Schultz, having been well-refined since 1950 by various apologists for nazism seeking to vindicate the "core impulse" guiding the Waffen SS to its gruesome performance in eastern Europe during World War II. That the author of *Month of the Freezing Moon* might actually desire his revision of Hoig join the ranks of North American corollaries to such German endeavors would not seem especially out of character, in view of his earlier record of cranking out uniformly hyper-patriotic accounts of U.S. military prowess. His works include *Hero of Bataan: The Story of General Jonathan M.*

Wainwright (St. Martins, 1981), *Wake Island: The Heroic Gallant Fight* (Jove, 1985), *The Last Battle Station: The Story of the USS Houston* (St. Martins, 1986), and *The Doolittle Raid* (St. Martins, 1988).

David Svaldi's first book commands an altogether different assessment. Anchoring his analysis in the whole range of public pronouncements emerging in Colorado contemporaneously with the massacre, the author drives home the point that the will to exterminate Indians (*any* Indians, of *whatever* character) was a hegemonic force among the territory's settler population throughout the crucial period. There simply was no generalized dissent from the prevailing will—isolated figures like Edward Wynkoop and Silas Soule are rightly treated as exceptions to prove the rule—to be found until well after the fact. Meaning is assigned to the will to exterminate through reliance upon already established theoretical structures elaborated in William Stanton's *The Leopard's Spots: Attitudes Towards Race in America, 1815-1859* (University of Chicago, 1960), Murray Edelman's *Politics as Symbolic Action: Mass Arousal and Quiescence* (Markham, 1971), Reginald Horsman's *Race and Manifest Destiny* (Harvard University, 1981), and elsewhere.

Following the same sort of trajectory plotted by Richard Drinnon in his superb *Facing West: The Metaphysics of Indian Hating and Empire Building* (University of Minnesota, 1980), the analysis offered in *Sand Creek and the Rhetoric of Extermination* picks up the thread of Euroamerica's genocidal mentality in colonial New England during the mid-18th century, and carries it through to the My Lai Massacre in Vietnam more than 200 years later. Under such scrutiny, any notion that Sand Creek was an "aberration" is rapidly dispelled. Although U.S. citizens residing east of the Mississippi River widely condemned the massacre at the time, such condemnation fell uniformly short of demanding either criminal prosecution of the perpetrators or redress for surviving

victims. Why? Because the inhabitants of each state of the
union were uncomfortably aware that their own antecedents had, in the not-so-distant past, done precisely the
same thing to the indigenous people of their region.

No area within what are now the 48 contiguous
states of the United States is exempt from having produced its own historical variant of the Sand Creek phenomenon. The very existence of the United States in its
modern territorial and demographic configuration is con-
tingent upon this fact. Racially-oriented invasion, conquest, genocide and subsequent denial are all integral,
constantly recurring and thus defining features of the
Euroamerican make-up from the instant the first boat-
load of self-ordained colonists set foot in the "New World."
At base, nothing has changed for the better in this regard
up through the present moment. Nor will things be likely
to improve until such time as denial is supplanted by a
willingness to face such things squarely, without evasion
or equivocation. Towards this positive objective, David
Svaldi has performed a sterling service, joining the still
tiny group of Hoigs and Drinnons who strive to inject a
measure of accuracy into the popular consciousness of
what has transpired in North America since 1600.

This is by no means to say that *Sand Creek and the
Rhetoric of Extermination* is a perfect book. It suffers from
being written in a dry, overly-academic, almost disserta-
tion-like manner. It passes over numerous examples—
from Lord Jeffrey Amherst's use of bacteriological warfare
against Indians in 1763, to the slaughter of a million
"Moros" by U.S. forces in the Philippines at the end of the
19th century—which were deserving of mention and
would have provided further support of the author's thesis. Similarly, it would have been useful and instructive
had Svaldi devoted time and attention—even tran-
siently—to exploring of the rhetorical similarities (and
dissimilarities) between exterminationists in the United
States and those of the Third Reich. A sharper compre-

hension of that ugly relationship might well have emerged from such handling, strengthening our grasp of Svaldi's overall premises.

It is nonetheless apparent that the book accomplishes much in improving our posture of understanding about Sand Creek and its implications. It also lays a sound foundation for investigating the conceptual cross-currents between nazism and Euroamerican ideologies of exterminationism, as called for above. Perhaps this will be David Svaldi's next project. Be this as it may, *Sand Creek and the Rhetoric of Extermination* must be assessed as tangible proof that the whole truth of "the American experience" will eventually come out, despite the best efforts of those like Duane Schultz who would seek to block or confuse it. There is reason enough in this for us to give a certain hopeful applause.

That Day in Gordon

Deformation of History and the American Novel

I'll readily admit the importance of something called literary license in the writing of works of fiction. It is a necessary mechanism for filling gaps in the popular consciousness. But, like anything else, it extends just so far. Literary license is supposed to be a means to get at and complete the truth. When it is used knowingly and intentionally as a means of covering over the truth, or of standing it squarely on its head, "license" should be understood as more a function of propaganda than of literature. Unfortunately, this last is the situation which has pertained to almost all fiction writing—and supposed non-fiction writing, for that matter, about, American Indians since the first European set foot in this hemisphere.

—Jimmie Durham
1981

    With his recent novel, *That Day in Gordon,* Raymond H. Abbott pursues an excellent idea somewhat reminiscent of James Welch's in *The Death of Jim Lonely,* or even *Winter in the Blood.* It is a concept crying out for treatment at the hands of a skilled and sensitive writer. Too bad, then, that the author fumbles his way along, deploying a meat-axe where surgical instruments were required, passing completely over points in urgent need of development, and displaying a generally profound lack of understanding of virtually his entire subject matter. This is a truly classic case of insight and ability failing to match inspiration.

In substance, the book sets out to explore the inter-relationships between whites and Indians on and around the Rosebud and Pine Ridge Sioux Reservations in South Dakota. The main theme concern Indians and missionaries, Indians and area ranchers, Indians and local constabulary, and so forth. In a secondary sort of way, Indian/Indian themes are utilized to provide a certain explanatory scope: the various relationships within a "typical" contemporary Lakota family, the interactions between tribal members and their elected officials, etc. Abbott's somewhat limited cast of characters seems to have been mustered sheerly in order to establish this series of equations.

The first real reef struck by the reader in plying the routes of such an expository sea is the author's marked inadequacy in constructing viable dialogue. Not only does he appear to be unfamiliar with the slang and regional idiom which might have brought his project to life, but his ranchers, Indians and cops are forever uttering phrases like, "I am going—" and "we will think—" It's as if Abbott is completely unaware that everyday spoken English universally contracts from such formalism into the conventions of "I'm" and "we'll." The result, of course, is that the novel's characterizations—which should have been its most expressive vehicle—come off as entirely wooden and unbelievable.

This stems not only from the stilted speech of the protagonists, but from their lack of effective development as *people*. The novel's Indians are uniformly either hopeless drunks drifting dangerously through squalid lives of pointless desperation, or mere props, tossed in only as a way of posing some peripheral point. His ranchers lead similarly one-dimensional existences, wrong-thinking at times, but basically good, well-intentioned folks whose major interracial desire seems to be for their red-skinned neighbors finally to see the light, abandoning their silly and self-defeating "Indian-ness" in favor of the thrift, sobriety and—most of all—"dependability" required for bootstrapping into the good life of modern, white America. Nowhere does the author provide a fully-fleshed character whose personal evolution and formative experiences might allow the reader a possibility of appreciating how things have come to be as the book describes them.

It may be that Abbott felt he could transfer sufficient grounding and motivation to carry his actors through their plotline simply by offering hints of the context in which his fictitious events unfold. If so, it should be noted that such strategy—even when fully elaborated through historical and topical vignettes—has seldom proven successful in and of itself, although it seldom fails so spectacularly as it does in this case. Still, the author's gambits in context articulation are of considerable importance in analyzing the meaning of his book, if for no other reason than because they lay bare the nature of his own biases and misconceptions in relation to his chosen setting. In this regard, he is blatantly guilty of both sins of omission and of commission.

An example of the former may be readily found. He has situated the bulk of his drama around Gordon, Nebraska at a time (which may be taken as 1972) when large numbers of militant Indians (discernible as the American Indian Movement, AIM) led by "Boneshirt" (a rather transparent cover-name for Russell Means) are unaccountably threatening the tranquility of the area adjacent to the reservation and thereby "raising tensions." Mention is made that these marauding hordes are not only terrorizing small towns in Nebraska, but in South Dakota as well. The reader is left to understand this situation solely on the basis of repeated assertions, by white and Indian characters alike, that Boneshirt and his crowd are "loco."

It is impossible not to conclude that Abbott has deliberately failed to include mention of even the most obvious and well-documented facts here: AIM went to Gordon in strength during February 1972, not on some thuggish lark, but at the request of the relatives of an Oglala Lakota man named Raymond Yellow Thunder, who had been stripped naked in an American Legion hall by a group of local whites, tortured with lit cigarettes, beaten senseless and tossed into a car trunk to die of exposure. Two men were arrested in this ritual murder, but charged only with second-degree manslaughter. When they were released without bond, AIM was sent in to insist they be rejailed and charged with murder in the first degree. As Russell Means put it on the spot, "We came here today to put Gordon on the map, and if these two guys aren't brought up on murder charges, we're coming back to take this place *off* the map." The point was and is that the legal trivialization of the murder of Indians in off-reservation communities like Gordon—which has been going on for as long as such towns have existed—will no longer be allowed to go unremarked, or tolerated.

This is what had Nebraska whites "upset" during the span of Abbott's period piece, although you'd never suspect it from his handling. To the contrary, he seems to combine the Yellow Thunder matter with a similar murder occurring in South Dakota at about the same time— the stabbing death of Wesley Bad Heart Bull in Buffalo Gap (which led directly to the famed "Custer Courthouse Confrontation" between AIM and the state police when Bad Heart Bull's assailants were also charged with manslaughter)—and then runs the whole story in reverse; the author has his primary Indian character, Black Horse, stab the local sheriff to death. The sin of omission is thus neatly converted into a sin of commission in a clever exercise in victim-blaming.

Perhaps worse, in this connection is his single forthright foray, on pages 122-23, in elucidating exactly what he sees as being the crux of the matter issue:

> Land was the center of the controversy—The Indian had recently become much more conscious and protective of

his land base and the outside threats to it and that, in
turn, angered many whites who leased Indian lands and
ran cattle on the leased sections. These Indian lands,
reservation lands, came at an over-increasing price to
whites, which only made matters worse. But not only
were the Indians protecting what they already owned, or
was held in trust for them, they were clamoring for more
land. Trying to expand their holdings through court actions and treaty rights. Whites, on the other hand, had
lived for years with the hope that if not they, then at least
their children would live to see the day the reservation
system was dismantled and the land sold for what it
would bring and to the highest bidder. And they were
confident it would go to enterprising and hard-working
local whites who were about the only ones who put the
land to good use anyway. Now, however, the reverse was
a possibility—[and] as a consequence—there was a back-
lash from whites in the region.

So many substantial misrepresentations of fact are
bound up in this conceptual passage that it is difficult to
know where to begin in rebuttal. Certainly, there is nothing "recent" in Lakota preoccupation with the land. As is
extremely well known, the "Mother Earth" is absolutely
central to Lakota religion and worldview; it is known to
have been the fundamental impetus behind their waging
a century of defensive wars against white invasion; it was
the essential ingredient of the 1868 Fort Laramie Treaty,
by which Red Cloud reserved every square inch of the
territory of Abbott's concern for the Lakota, and *in perpe-
tuity*. The preservation of this same land base is what
caused these same Indians—during the late 19th century—to face starvation (*i.e.*, suspension of all rations)
rather than sign over title of the Black Hills to the United
States, and its recovery is what has kept them in court
throughout the whole of the 20th century. Clearly, AIM's
present slogan that "The Black Hills are not for Sale,"
coined after the U.S. Supreme Court acknowledged that

millions of acres had been taken illegally from the Lakota, has long and uninterrupted roots in Indian tradition.

For their part, the author's "enterprising and hard-working local whites" are aware of this, even if Abbott somehow is not, and that their use of the land—whether "good" or otherwise—accrues only from their forbearer's outright theft of it in defiance of both their supposed ethical/moral superiority and their own laws. That they now hold spurious deeds to the 90 percent of the 1868 Treaty Territory stripped from the Lakota since that document was ever-so-solemnly signed, is an accomplished, if unconscionable reality, as is the economic hegemony they've extended over even the residual 10 percent comprising the current Sioux Reservation Complex. They know, too, that the "ever-increasing prices" they must pay for all-but-exclusive use of the best of these reservation lands often amounts to no more than a doubling of the $1 per acre rate they pay through long-term leases engineered for them by the Bureau of Indian Affairs in its capacity as an executioner of the federal government's self-annointed "trust responsibility" over Indian property.

Unlike Abbott, the white ranchers and police of South Dakota and Nebraska know that, by and large, the Lakota have been left with no land base on which to support themselves, either spiritually or materially. Their assets have been systematically usurped as a generator of profits; their poverty and despair are accounted for almost entirely by non-Indian livelihoods and social structure. The lot of the Indian, in this case the Lakota people, is that of the abjectly colonized; created by area non-Indians, the colonizer. It is hardly a pleasant, pretty, or overly complicated situation. Rather, it is the stuff of guilt and rage, of naturally spiraling violence, festering repression and recipient insurrection. And *this* is why the resident whites are so bent upon seeing the reservation system dismantled and abolished.

Their's is not a desire borne of need for the land; they already have it. Nor is it a desire based upon a wish to save the tax dollars spent on Indian subsistence, as Abbott suggests on page 59. (The whites understand very well that such "rent" is quite meager when compared to the land garnered in exchange.) No, theirs is an obsessive, if usually sublimated need to rid themselves of the physical evidence of their collective misdeeds, to obliterate the nagging specter of human misery their way of life and scale of values has wrought, and to escape—finally and forever—the grim possibility that they may yet be called to account for what they have done to the Indian. At no level may they be at peace, or rest secure, until their victims have been made to disappear.

Obviously, a strong and useful book might have been erected upon such a factual and psychological foundation. The raw material could not be riper. Yet one is hard-pressed to imagine an author more perfectly ill-equipped than Raymond H. Abbott, both in his outlook and in his writerly attainments, to have attempted what was necessary. In the end, his clumsily-crafted tome belongs much more to the realm of crude propaganda than to the world of literature. If the editorial staff of Vanguard Press felt this manuscript was worthy of publication, they should consider another line of work.

Part IV

"Friends of the Indian"

"Friends of the Indian"

A Critical Appraisal of
Irredeemable America:
The Indian's Estate and Land Claims

> The white man made us many promises, but he kept only
> one. He promised to take our land, and he took it.
>
> —Red Cloud
> Oglala Lakota
> 1882

Land, as Red Cloud, Hugo Blanco and myriad others
have noted, is the absolutely essential issue defining
viable conceptions of Native America, whether in the past,
present or future. A deeply held sense of unity with
particular geographical contexts has provided, and continues to afford, the spiritual cement allowing cultural
cohesion across the entire spectrum of indigenous American societies. Contests for control of territory have also
been the fundamental basis of Indian/non-Indian interaction since the moment of first contact, and underlie the
virtually uninterrupted (and ongoing) pattern of genocide
suffered by American Indians over the past half-millen-
nium. It follows that the retention of any modicum of
Indian national and cultural integrity in coming decades
is a matter utterly and inextricably bound up with the
question of whether they will not only be able to maintain
their present residue of original land base, but—in many
cases—to expand upon it, recovering areas lost in earlier
expropriations. If Native America is to survive, the over-

riding historical trajectory marking this hemisphere since 1492 must be, in a word, reversed.

In many ways, the United States wields the most advanced and perfected of the internal colonialist systems by which settler-states throughout the Americas visit genocidal policies upon native peoples. In contrast, southerly U.S. client countries such as Paraguay, Brazil and Guatemala are engaged in physical liquidation procedures comparable to those largely discarded as obsolete by the United States after the Sand Creek, Washita and Wounded Knee massacres, approximately a century ago. As it is thus evident that the Latino client regimes both lag behind and take their cues from the nature and course of U.S. Indian policies, it is possible that favorable changes to these latter policies will cause all the rest to follow. The issue of Indian land rights within the United States can thereby be viewed as the crux of the question of Indian survival *per se*.

For this reason, it came as welcome and hopeful news a few years ago that Imre Sutton, a scholar of some repute in the field of North American cultural geography, was recruiting authors with an eye toward assembling an essay collection taking as its theme "the Indians' estate and land claims" in this country. Such an effort promised to render accessible to a broad readership an important body of factual and conceptual information, establishing a vital new tool of understanding for application to the Indians' perpetual struggle for dignity, a future, and the justice of regaining that which is and always has been theirs. The circumstances attending the book's publication were, to say the least, propitious.

And, in some ways, mostly within the realm of the narrowly factual, the project delivers. For example, in an essay somewhat misleadingly titled "Indian Claims and the American Conscience: A Brief History of the Indian Claims Commission," Harvey D. Rosenthal sets forth, quite succinctly, a rather comprehensive overview of the

origins, evolution and culmination of the bureaucratic
vehicle upon which the federal government sought to
"legally" quiet title to millions of acres removed from
Indian occupancy and control through a long-term process
of force and fraud. Michael J. Kaplan does a thoroughly
competent job of laying bare the contours of the imperially
arrogant logic which has gone into Euroamerica's belief
in its inherent "right" to unilaterally extinguish aboriginal title to land ("Issues in Land Claims: Aboriginal
Title"). Leonard A. Carlson unravels the officially-sanc-
tioned formulations by which the "dollar value" of expropriated Indian land is retroactively fixed for
"compensatory" purposes ("What Was It Worth? Economic
and Historical Aspects of Determining Awards in Indian
Land Claims Cases"). Similarly, several of the case studies presented in the volume, such as those by David J.
Wishart ("The Pawnee Claims Case, 1947-64"), Omer C.
Stuart ("The Shoshone Claims Case"), John F. Martin
("From Judgement to Restoration: The Havasupi Land
Claims Case"), David H. Getches ("Alternative Approaches to Land Claims: Alaska and Hawaii"), and Jack
Campisi ("The Trade and Intercourse Acts: Land Claims
on the Eastern Seaboard") contain considerable useful
material. Finally, the book's appendices include verbatim
reproductions of several handy documents, such as the
Indian Claims Commission Act of 1946 and the Pamunkey
Indian Act.

In moving beyond considerations of the mere recounting of ideas and events associated with various 20th
century federal mechanisms designed and intended to
legitimize past or present thefts of Indian land, however,
one encounters what might be described as, at best, a
vacuum. Although hundreds of pages are devoted to de-
lineating the intricacies of Euroamerican thought and
action regarding Indian land issues, *nowhere* is anything
remotely resembling an articulation of the *Indian* view of
the situation provided in its own right, or even as "bal-

ance." Such a lopsided handling of the subject matter is attributable, most obviously, to the fact that, of the fourteen contributors, only one writer identified as Indian is included. This is Roxanne Dunbar Ortiz who, on p. xxii, is listed as being of "Cheyenne descent." This is perhaps true, but it must also be borne in mind that Dunbar Ortiz has elsewhere maintained she "neither know[s] nor care[s]" whether she is Indian in any way at all, a situation which renders her participation in the current forum as an Indian tenuous at best.

In any event, the otherwise uniformly non-Indian roster of authors implicitly links Sutton's approach to that patronizing and subjectively racist Euroamerican intellectual tradition holding that "Friends of the Indian," preferably "Indian Experts," are always and by definition better qualified to speak on the Indians' behalf than are the Indians themselves. That the results of this "responsible scholarship" (to whom?) have historically proven to be extremely detrimental to Indian interests in the practical arena is beyond all reasonable doubt. For instance, it was precisely during the period when the "Friends" were in direct control of U.S. Indian policy formulation and implementation (roughly 1875-1925), that 100 million acres of reserved land was transferred from Indian control under the "civilizing" provisions of the Dawes Act and other equally helpful bits of federal legislation. Again, it was another great Friend, John Collier, who overcame tribal resistance to the supplanting of traditional Indian governmental forms through implementation of the Indian Reorganization Act of 1934, a matter which radically undercut the vestiges of sovereign autonomy within various extant federal Indian policies. Still, despite its obvious bankruptcy in terms of addressing "Indian needs," the perspective has yet to exhibit any lack of non-Indian academic adherents willing to queue up, forging careers for themselves in the manner of alchemists, endlessly repeating the same failed and costly (to Indians) experiment, ostensibly on the faith that their "good intentions" will ultimately cause things to work out just fine (again, for *whom* remains an unsolved query).

What is involved here is an essential problem in conceptualization. Although numerous "Friends of the Indian" have, over the years, been willing enough to point up various "difficulties" in U.S. policy—as Rosenthal, Kaplan and Carlson in particular do in the present volume—they have invariably retained a deep-seated belief in and alignment with that same policy's underlying assumptions and core postulations. Hence, they may mention (as Rosenthal does at p. 50, while describing the historical flow of policy) Chief Justice John Marshall's 1831 finding in *Cherokee Nation v. Georgia*. It unilaterally "accorded to the tribes the status of domestic dependent nations," without ever suggesting that the very notion of national quasi-sovereignty represents a blatant juridical oxymoron. This is a logical impossibility entirely analogous to the old joke about being "a little bit pregnant." Similarly, nowhere in the literature generated by the Friends is there so much as a hint that, given that the United States opted to enter into 371 separate treaties with Indian nations, the Marshall Doctrine might well be in complete contradiction to the Constitutional requirement (under Article I, Section 10) that the federal government enter into treaty relationships *only* with other *fully* sovereign entities.

Avoided with equal thoroughness by the Friends in their tacit adherence to the doctrine's premises is the nature of the "special status" accorded U.S. treaties with Indians. While the Friends, apparently without serious questioning, follow the federal government's official line that this relates exclusively to the fiduciary or "trust" responsibility exercised by the United States over subject Indian nations, the reality is that it derives from the fact that these treaty instruments are essentially the real estate documents through which Indians ceded large portions of what was already acknowledged to be their land, in exchange for formal international recognition of the borders of their national territories. This is the legal mechanism which allowed the United States to acquire title to its own land base while self-righteously and simultaneously renouncing prerogatives accruing from "conflict and conquest" (Rosenthal at p. 36). It follows that the United States cannot abrogate, or even unilaterally alter, the terms and provisions of its Indian treaties without at the same time voiding the legality of its title to its own territoriality. This, to be sure, is a circumstance which sharply differentiates Indian treaties from all others— mutual defense pacts and trade agreements, for example—and which bears an obvious potential to increase Indian leverage in contemporary land negotiations if pushed in appropriate arenas, such as the United Nations.

To take up such basic issues—as "irresponsible" Indians are apt to do—is to bring into question the whole structure of rationalization and logical convolution by which the U.S. internal colonial system perpetuates and legitimizes itself. For the Friends, whose primary historical objective in advancing "criticism" has been to become prominent and influential in federal policy circles rather than to actually reverse or dismantle the policies altogether, this is anathema. Consequently, Indians and Indian viewpoints must not only be excluded from their polite discourse, but polemical pickets must be permanently posted to both dismiss authentically Indian positions and extend apologia to the federal performance. One of the foremost practitioners of this somewhat specialized craft has been Wilcomb E. Washburn, a former army colonel and current Smithsonian historian whose main stock in trade of late has been to attack the "American Indian Movement radicals" who have been so presumptuous as to call things by their right names, publicly referring to "American 'colonialism,' 'imperialism,' and 'exploitation' [of Indians] at home." Others on Washburn's ideological hit list have been "deviant" scholars such as Deward E. Walker, Jr., and Allen P. Slickpoo, Sr., who have demonstrated the academic audacity to violate the Friend's strictest "canon of professionalism" by allowing Indians to speak for themselves—directly and uninterpreted—in the pages of their books.[1]

Sutton's inclusion of Washburn among his contributors is instructive, as is the placement of his essay, "Land Claims in the Mainstream," as the book's lead piece, setting the tenor for all that follows. Therein, we discover (at p. 26) that, "U.S. Indian policy is no longer repressive but supportive of Indian values and aspirations" (a condition which would undoubtedly surprise a number of Indians, such as the traditionalist David So Happy, imprisoned by the government during the 1980s for his expression of precisely such values and aspirations). Further (p. 27): "Virtually every country in the United Nations has a minority or aboriginal population with claims more compelling against its government than is any Indian claim against the United States Government." Such touting of the federal government's benevolence in reducing Indian landholdings to some 3 percent of their original scope, and Indian populations to outright vassalage, is accompanied by smug relegation of Indian politico-legal theorists like Russel Barsh (whose views clash emphatically with those of the Friends) to a domain "outside the real world" (p. 27). Washburn also offers a series of snide observations concerning the cases—he brackets the latter word in quotes, and cites himself as the ultimate authority on their merit—brought by such organizations as the Indian Law Resource Center and the International Indian Treaty Council. He then goes on to question the competency of *tribal*—rather than federal—courts to effectively administer justice on behalf of Indian constituencies (pp. 27-28).

As might be expected, it is necessary for Washburn to diverge from accuracy (and even truthfulness) in applying a veneer of "substantiation" to his outlook. This he accomplishes with a certain casual flair, as when (on p. 25) he offhandedly observes that, "In 1877 Congress passed an act (U.S. *Stat.* 254)...in effect, abrogating the [1868] Fort Laramie Treaty," a document upon which much of the contemporary Lakota claim to several million acres in and around the Black Hills is based. That he knew this to be categorically untrue is amply borne out by his discussion (also on p. 25) of the 1876 Lakota "agreement" to this act, coerced from them by the government for the expressed purpose of *not* abrogating the treaty in question. That the treaty remains very much in effect is also a matter implicit in a 1980 Supreme Court writ of *certiorari* to the U.S. Court of Claims, also noted by Washburn (p. 26) without his ever spelling out the obvious implications.

Clearly, with Friends of this order coming to their "assistance," Indians in the United States haven't a chance of survival. Unfortunately, Washburn is hardly the only, and not necessarily the worst, offender in Sutton's collection. For example, the work of the late Ralph L. Beals, whose essay "The Anthropologist as Expert Witness: Illustrations from the California Land Claim Case" is apparently intended as some sort of exemplar, perhaps may be best assessed via the observation that he was a participant in the "quiet title" travesty about which he writes—and which is still being openly resisted by many California Indians—as a witness for the *government* (i.e., as an "expert" called in to "credibly" minimize the Indians' entitlement even to monetary compensation for their stolen land).

Still, even in such company, it is left to Roxanne Dunbar Ortiz, the only professed radical on Sutton's roster, to pen the most potentially damaging material. After observing, accurately enough (at p. 252), that U.S. "laws and practices" effectively preclude resolution of Indian land rights issues within domestic courts, she proceeds (at p. 260) to endorse the 1960 United Nations General Assembly Resolution 1541, a position forged to counter Belgian assertions that "tribal peoples" had as much right to national sovereignty, recognized territoriality and sociopolitical autonomy as anyone else within the newly decolonized Congo. The outcome of this tactical expedient has been the legitimation of the denial of these rights to such peoples the world over, especially within decolonizing ("revolutionary" or "progressive") states for nearly 30 years. Accepting such a principle as having ever been valid and appropriate to codification in international law can serve only to foreclose international as well as domestic avenues of recourse for American Indians.

Although Dunbar Ortiz is quick to point out (p. 261) that U.N. Resolution 1541 "seriously and adversely affects [the] political goals" of Indian organizations, she goes on in the very next sentence to assert that "no authentic liberation movement would need to confront this legalistic issue." This seeming paradox was probably best explained by Washburn when he noted elsewhere: "Some scholars, like Roxanne Dunbar Ortiz, have unhesitatingly opted to support [Nicaragua's Sandinista government] against the [Miskito, Sumu and Rama] Indians."[2] In other words, for Dunbar Ortiz, Indian struggles for land and other rights are less than authentic, at least in comparison to the rights of the marxist states which appear to claim her first loyalty.

Small wonder, then, that Sutton chose the major title *Irredeemable America*—a caption he attributes (at p. xviii) to Dunbar Ortiz—to describe the thrust of his collection. Left to the "poignant...commentary on reality" offered by this volume, one could do little but conclude, in the final analysis, that not only is the Indian cause a hopeless one, but that there is somehow a real justice to the situation. The federal government itself could have done little better (and perhaps not so well) in representing its interests and position of denying the fundamentals of Indian land rights than has this assembly of Friends. The book thus offers a striking example of the near-seamlessness of "ideological confluence" prevailing between the U.S. political *status quo* and "respectable" academic circles, so often remarked upon by Noam Chomsky, Edward S. Herman, and others.

The circumstances which generated the need for *Irredeemable America* cried out for the strongest possible challenge to the assumptions of U.S. Indian policy. Insofar as the body of work contained in the book often goes in quite the opposite direction, the project must be assessed as a failure, and a profoundly reactionary one at that. American Indians—and those who would seek to truly support them—remain desperately in need of what Sutton's collection *might* have been. He and several of his contributors should be heartily ashamed of their performance.

Notes

1. Washburn, Wilcomb E., "Distinguishing History from Moral Philosophy and Public Advocacy," in Calvin Martin, ed., *The American Indian and the Problem of History*, Oxford University Press, New York, pp. 95-6.

2. *Ibid.*, p. 95.

Interpreting
the American Indian

A Critique of Michael Castro's
Apologia for Poetic Racism

> Repression works like a shadow, clouding memory and
> sometimes even to blind, and when it is on a national
> scale, it is just not good...It was a national quest, dictated
> by economic motives. Europe was hungry for raw mate-
> rial, and America was abundant forest, rivers, land.
>
> —Simon J. Ortiz
> *From Sand Creek*

The relationship between indigenous realities and
their interpretation by external observers, particularly by
those who profess sympathy or even commonality with the
native, has always been an important consideration for
indigenous activists and thinkers. This is especially true
in countries such as Australia, New Zealand, South Africa
and virtually all the nations of the Americas, places where
the form assumed by 19th century European imperialism
was that of the "settler-state." In such areas, colonization
meant that the natives were subsumed within or permanently subordinated to a "replacement population" imported from the colonizing country, as opposed to the more
classic model of colonialism where the mother country
merely dispatched military and administrative cadres to
occupy and manage its new "possession."

It is a given in any colonial situation that the colonizing power presumes that its culture is inherently superior to that of the colonized. Hence, it assumes the right,

the obligation and "civilizing mission"—the "white man's burden," as it were—to explain this to its subjects, rendering the colonized ever more accommodating to the "natural condition" of their domination by the colonial master, ever more compliant to the inevitability of material exploitation by the colonizer. This has been the clear purpose, historically of the interpretation of indigenous cultures by their conquerors. Still, within the structure of such a schema, there remains a clear distinction between the colonizer and the colonized, a more or less pure "them/us" dichotomy allowing ongoing cultural integrity (albeit in diluted form) to both parties.

Within the context of advanced settler-state colonization, however, things become rather more complex and confusing. Here, members of the dominant culture are unable to retain their sense of distance and separation from that which they dominate. Instead, over a period of generations, they increasingly develop direct ties to the "new land" and, consequently, exhibit an ever-increasing tendency to proclaim themselves "natives." This, of course, equates to a quite literal negation of the very essence and existence of those who are truly indigenous to the colonized locales. The famed anti-colonialist psychiatrist Frantz Fanon has termed this process "the final liquidation, indeed the digestion of the native." What is at issue in this instance is thus not simply systematic resource expropriation, with all the concomitant human misery that implies, but genocide. It is genocide of an extremely sophisticated type, to be sure, but it is genocide nonetheless.

As Albert Memmi, a noted literary figure of the Algerian revolution, has observed, this process of genocide assumes the form of an appropriation of the identity of the colonized by the colonizer. Stripped of the particularities of its identity, the colonized people ultimately dissolves and is absorbed whole by the corpus of a newly homogenized "master culture." Insofar as such a process is primarily intellectual rather than physical, interpretation of indigenous sensibilities and worldview for consumption by the non-indigenous constitutes a key element. Interpretation in this sense bespeaks not the repression of indigenous cultures prevalent under classical colonial conditions, but the repackaging and even promotion of native perspectives to facilitate their incorporation into the dominant culture. This, in turn, empowers the non-native to begin to view him/herself as a new hybrid embodying "the best of both worlds."

Psychically, the process tends to be self-validating, justified at a certain level by a desire to ease the degree of tension and discord between colonizer and colonized. Hence, the leading practitioners of identity appropriation are often motivated by sincere empathy and a genuine will to open viable channels of communication between oppressor and oppressed. The very real power dynamics of colonialism, however, preclude even the best and most sensitive of such efforts from doing other than reinforcing and enhancing the structure of domination at play.

In the United States, where settler-state colonialism is currently most developed, the desired "fusion" of indigenous realities (albeit in often grossly distorted configuration) with the dominant consciousness is generally accommodated by the mass media, what Theodor Adorno labeled "the culture industry," and which is intended as an expression to cover all genuinely popular communications formats from television to mass-distributed reading material. As such, it might seem more appropriately the topic for sociological consideration than for literary criticism. However, as Walter Benjamin long ago pointed out in his *Illuminations,* the content and methods of the culture industry itself are mediated and tempered by more rarified artistic forms: literature, dance, the plastic arts, drama, music and—perhaps most allegorically of all—poetry. A concrete linkage between the arts and the much more overtly propagandistic functions of the mass media can neither be truthfully denied nor rightly ignored.

Michael Castro, in his recent book *Interpreting the American Indian,* takes up the important question of the appropriation of indigenous identity by non-Indian poets in the 20th-century United States. In this, the first attempt at an overall and coherently formulated study of the subject, he is confronted with a situation rife with opportunity for exploration and development of in-depth analysis of that which is discovered. The book could well have been a landmark. Unfortunately, the author fails to achieve a particularly satisfactory posture, either as an explorer or as an analyst.

The book starts well enough. In his all-too-brief introductory section, Castro offers an overview of the evolution of Indian thematics in American literature, taking pains in the limited space he allows himself to bring out the relationship between the literary examples he employs and the phases of colonial development with which they correspond (*e.g.,* his citation of Melville on page xv linking "the brutish savage stereotype" to "the genocidal hand of government, as it cleared the way to America's manifest destiny"). A similar sort of promise is extended in the quotation with which he opts to lead his first chapter, a passage from Mary Austin's *American Rhythm,* in which the poet neatly encapsulates the pathos of identity appropriation by stating, "…when I say that I am not, have never been, nor offered myself, as an authority on things Amerindian, *I do not wish to have it understood that I may not, at times, have succeeded in being an Indian* [emphasis added]." As if to demonstrate compellingly that Austin's defiance was not a peculiar or isolated phenomenon within the context of his study, but rather represent sentiments integral to an accelerating pattern of appropriative progression, Castro leads his second chapter with the observation from William Carlos

Williams' *In the American Grain* that, "I do believe the average American to be an Indian..."

Between these astute selections of telling quotations, however, the author falls flat. Rather than following his own lead in examining the meaning of such postulations within the broader historical socioeconomic context (which, after all, has been reasonably well chronicled), he chooses to treat each biographically and aesthetically, as the manifestation of the individuated consciousness of its author. That such an idealized understanding of artistic creation, particularly that of the 20th century European/Euroamerican variety, has for some time been exposed as nonsensical goes without saying. One need not demand emulation of Arnold Hauser to expect art to be situated in social circumstance by any serious historian or critic.

Castro at least tacitly acknowledges such problems, and the necessity of locating his subjects somewhere beyond the immediate confines of their individual consciousness, when he takes the trouble of attempting to define them in terms of emergent trends in American literature. Such a method holds the possibility of providing a plausible, if superficial, closure while avoiding the obvious political volatility of coming to grips with broader contextual matters. But even at this level Castro sidesteps substance and meaning. Rather than building a nuanced examination of the range of poets topically mining the veins of "Indian-ness" during the decades he purports to investigate, the author resorts to compiling representative lists of materials published during various decades. Hence, he often reduces himself from the level of aesthetic criticism to that of vulgar journalism. Simultaneously, he opens up legitimate questions of whether he was, in fact, even conversant enough with his topic to presume to write a book.

Throughout a reading of *Interpreting the American Indian,* one is struck by the failure to examine the work of secondary or tertiary poets within the genre or of reference to contemporaneous criticism and the like. Nowhere is this thin treatment more in evidence than the single (final) chapter Castro devotes to consideration of Native American poetry. Very important voices, such as those of Peter Blue Cloud, Wendy Rose and Joy Harjo are included only by virtue of their mention in a list. Others, such as Mary Tall Mountain, William Oandasan and Linda Hogan do not appear at all. Nor is there so much as a reference to critical efforts such as Karl Kroeber's *Studies in American Indian Literature* project at Columbia University, an effort which is both rather influential and relatively well known. While such a listing of defects might be extended at length, these examples should speak for themselves.

To the extent that Castro's handling yields any explanatory power at all, it is of a clearly evasive and apologetic sort. While ignoring the more significant implications of the positions and utterances of his various protagonists (it is as if the 19th-century Indian policies he brings out in his introduction mysteriously disappear in the 20th), he seems forever in search of ways to mitigate them, to render them sympathetically and to tidy up the ugliness of the colonial ramifications of their poetics. The result is an "I'm OK, you're OK" sort of sentimentality.

Thus, to pick but one example, the author is able to indicate in his chapter on Gary Snyder that the poet has fashioned a career on the basis of excursions into other people's cultures, always to return as a primary medium of expression for that culture (first he fancied himself an articulator of the inner visions of Japanese Zen Buddhism and then won a Pulitzer elaborating an "American Indian" perspective on North America), yet without ever drawing a conclusion on what this peculiar state of affairs might mean. Of course, it is noted that Snyder has been (justly) criticized for having "borrowed" a bit too freely from other cultures without having come to grips with the meaning of his own heritage, but Castro then lets the thought die as if it is too uncomfortable a revelation to be dealt with further. The treatment of Snyder is therefore left quite vacuously to hinge upon the man's undeniably great technical skills in the poetic craft.

All in all, Michael Castro's book can only be viewed as a failed promise. It is abundantly lacking in analytical force, and is far too scanty to suggest itself as a survey text. The portraits it offers of given poets and their psychic relationships to American Indians (real or imagined) are much too narrowly "balanced" to offer real insight into their individual motivations and characters.[1] There are no thematics, beyond the title concept, tying the book together which would even seem particularly appropriate for future development elsewhere. Castro's effort might more aptly have been dubbed "interpreting the interpreters" in a sympathetic light. Still, by going to press with his title, the author has at least called attention to a hitherto unexplored subject. That he follows with a thoroughly inadequate text serves to demonstrate compellingly how very much work must be done before we have an articulation/understanding corresponding to the title. For showing us all graphically how not to accomplish this, we all owe Michael Castro a back-handed thanks.

Notes

1. There are, it seems to me, two exceptions to this last. In the cases of John Neihardt and Jerome Rothenburg, Castro may rightly be said to have accomplished an adequate treatment of their aesthetic implications at least.

Beyond Ethnicity

Werner Sollors'
Deepest Avatar of Racism

[Q]uite suddenly, with little comment or ceremony,
ethnicity is a ubiquitous presence.

—Ronald Cohen

The question of "ethnicity" has long been one of the
more perplexing challenges confronting students of American literature. Issues begin with controversy over proper
definition of the term itself, and extend into concerns as
to who might be viewed legitimately as an ethnic writer,
the influence of ethnic-specific work on the evolution of
the American writing tradition, and the impact of such
influence upon the whole of American letters today. Serious debate centers even on who might be said to be
qualified to evaluate the increasingly complex situation.
The result, of course, is an incredible intellectual muddle.

Now comes Werner Sollors, a literary scholar of no
small repute, offering to inject order and clarity into the
confusion. Tellingly titled *Beyond Ethnicity*, Sollors'
sweeping new study draws immediately upon its subtitle,
"Consent and Descent in American Culture" posting a
potentially powerful analytical method hinging on the
interaction of what its author describes as streams of
"consent" (subjectively chosen group identification) and
"descent" (objectively "born" or inherited identification)
common to all elements of ethnic differentiation in American culture. Further, to obtain the desired depth of insight into the facts and functions of ethnicity in writing,
he rejects mere topical scrutiny, choosing instead to apply

149

his dialectical mechanism of examination across the historical spectrum of appropriate literatures, from the output of colonial times through the present. Such an exploratory paradigm, inherently nuanced and comprehensive as it appears, promises much in terms of unraveling the primary characteristics marking the various pools of literary ethnicity prevailing in America. It also holds out the prospect of a coherent explanation of the individuated thrusts of these pools in tempering, defining and sometimes merging with what has come to be seen as an ethnically pluralistic American literature. From such a rich and multi-faceted handling of the subject matter, a range of accurate and incisive conclusions might reasonably be expected to be reached.

The "Confusing Category" of Race

Having so aptly prescribed a methodological approach to the problem he purports to treat, however, Sollors promptly busies himself with a dramatic undercutting of its innate utility. Early in the text, while attempting to counter what he believes to be M.G. Smith's "erroneous" proposition that "race [is] a special 'objective' category that cannot be meaningfully discussed under the heading 'ethnicity'" (p. 36), Sollors aligns himself with Harold Abramson's argument that, while "race is the most salient ethnic factor, it is still only one of the larger cultural and historical phenomenon [sic] of ethnicity" (p. 36). This would have been all well and good had Sollors not then proceeded to gut Abramson's "most salient ethnic factor" for his own purposes, reducing it to being just "one aspect of ethnicity" (p. 39), with no special emphasis at all.

The author attempts to defend his marginalization of the issue of race by professing concern with hypotheticals such as, "...in the complicated ethnic scene today, are Cuban immigrants or Japanese-American races or ethnic groups?" (pp. 38-39). The contradiction is strikingly evident: Such "either/or" dichotomies are precisely in line with the very Smith postulation Sollors had already categorically rejected, rather than Abramson's "both at once, with emphasis on race" formulation which he clearly claims to "have sided with" (p. 36). Utilization of the latter principle would, to be sure, have destroyed the author's superficially ambiguous straw man *a priori.*

Nonetheless, he insists upon having it both ways as an expedient to concluding that, "I think it most helpful not to be confused by the heavily charged term 'race'..." (p. 39), and thereupon drops the entire concept of racial differentiation as a factor of ethnicity. At this point, both the theses and content of *Beyond Ethnicity* have been forced drastically out of sync with its auspicious beginnings. Still, the situation might have been salvaged, at least to some extent. At one level, all of this abstract playing of both ends against the middle could be considered as no more than a somewhat deceptive and exceedingly sloppy way of circumscribing the scope of what Sollors had determined to be an overly ambitious project. This would be true if he followed up by matching his self-imposed methodological constraints by restricting subsequent practical considerations to the play of ethnic factors within a given racial group. And, indeed, in some ways it seems he sets out to follow such a course of *post hoc* consistency by erecting a "typology of ethnicity" for the New World based entirely upon tenets of biblical interpretation, with reference to the European migration (likened, of course, to the Jewish exodus from Egypt). Puritan New England, which Sollors follows Hans Kohn in describing as "the first example of modern nationalism" (p. 56), thus quickly becomes his benchmark of "ethnicization" or "ethnification" (terms borrowed from Andrew Greeley; p. 57).

He goes on to lay out the polarities of discussion as residing in, on the one hand, the "melting pot thesis" posited in 1909 in an Israel Zangwill play of the same title and, on the other hand, later opposing contentions which surfaced in such sociological works as Glazer and Moynihan's *Beyond the Melting Pot* (1963) and Michael Novak's *The Rise of the Unmeltable Ethnics* (1975). In this contestation, Sollors sets forth his affinity with the Zangwillian notion, ultimately assigning modern American ethnic distinctions status as a semiological preoccupation, *i.e.:* signifying the continuation of socially useful codes of symbology rather than the living of concrete daily realities. As he puts it on page 35, "modern ethnic identification works by external symbols rather than by continual activities which make demands upon people who define themselves as 'ethnic.' " Or, on page 39:

> I propose that for purposes of investigating group formation, inversion, boundary construction and social distancing, myths of origins and fusions, cultural markers and empty symbols, we may be better served, in the long run, by the vocabulary of kinship and cultural codes than by the cultural baggage that the word "ethnicity" contains.

In the main, Sollors attempts to accomplish a proof for this proposition within the remainder of his text by undertaking a relatively systematic analysis of the thematics of succeeding generations of European immigrants, from roughly the point of the English invasion of North America onward. As promised during its methodological exposition, the study's exemplary selections include not only such pillars of literary effort in prerevolutionary New England as Cotton Mather and Michel-Guillaume-Jean de Crevecoeur (aka: J. Hector St. Joan), but their late 20th-century successors such as Jack Kerouac and Norman Mailer. This temporal gamut is amply fleshed out with other luminaries as diverse as Ralph Waldo Emerson, Henry David Thoreau, James Fenimore Cooper, Harriet Beecher Stowe, Mark Twain, Vachel Lindsay, Francis Parkman and even Woody Allen. Various strains of Euroamerican (*i.e.* caucasian) literary ethnicity are accorded their interactive moment(s), some at considerable length, as with the deployment of Ludwig Lewishohn (German [and Jewish] American), John Brougham (Irish American), Ole E. Rolvaag (Norwegian American), Mary Antin (Russian [and Jewish] American), Mario Puzo and Emanuel Carnevali (Italian American), Abraham Cahan and Horace M. Kallen (Jewish American) and so on. Attention is also paid to argumentation as to whether writers such as Carl Sandburg, Eugene O'Neill, Nelson Algren, Nathanael West and Vladimir Nabokov should rightly be considered figures of ethnic literature at all. In summation, Sollors concludes that the functionality of ethnicity in American writing rests on what might be paradoxically called "the homogeneity of heterogenous existence." As he himself puts it, "Embracing a regional or group identity in voluntary defiance (as in Faulkner's 'I don't hate it, I don't hate it!') allows Americans to steer a Roycean middle course between ancient narrowness and vulgar monotony. By creating new, not traditionally anchored, group identities and by authenticating them, they may represent individuality and American identity at the same time" (pp. 206-207). Further, "...popular contrasts with the ethnically homogeneous and hierarchically structured old worlds are often melodramatically overdrawn" (p. 260).

In other words, according to Sollors, the melting pot has done its work to the point where America, the land of ethnic diversity, has become as ethnically homogeneous as the old world, at least at the practical level. Ethnicity now serves the social function of allowing the expression of creative individuality as "[f]reedom from the fetters of descent was achieved while other forms of descent were literally thought of as deserving fetters... Enough ethnic distinctions have emerged in the United States to put the theory of old world survival to rest" (p. 260). In this vein, "The language of consent and descent has been flexibly adapted to the most divergent kinds of ends and has amazingly helped to create a sense of Americanness among the heterogenous inhabitants of this country...[t]he ways in which stories have helped to create the rites and rituals which can impart to the diverse population of the United States a shared sense of destiny are impressive" (p. 259).

At this juncture, it seems appropriate to suggest that Sollors has produced a viable, if not necessarily definitive analysis of the "mainstream" experience in America, at least as apprehended within its literary tradition. He spells out compellingly how a seemingly disparate array of European migrations were able to resettle to this hemisphere and transcend their initial particularities, becoming in the end an overarching racially/culturally identified "we" or "us," regardless of residual and often contrived "ethnical" proclivities. Had this been all there was to it, despite early difficulties in theoretical formulation and a marked tendency toward an overblown language of universalization, *Beyond Ethnicity* might safely be considered a generally successful, useful and informative book. Matters, however, are not so simple.

The Real "Melting Pot"

The problem which prevents such a positive assessment begins when, on page 11, Sollors notes that there are certain recalcitrants abroad in the land who have "seldom fully appreciated their texts in the context of the newer theories of ethnicity [*e.g.*, the author's own conception of consent-dominated ethnic identification]." On the same page, he goes on to observe that, rather than "understanding their texts as [semiotic] codes for a socialization into ethnic groups and into America, readers have overemphasized and exaggerated the (frequently exoticized) ethnic particularities of the works [of nonwhites]...belief is widespread among critics who stress descent at the expense of consent [again, mainly non-whites] that only biological insiders can understand and explicate the literature of race and ethnicity." One can almost feel the author recoiling in horror as he concludes this passage by recounting how Richard Gilman has even "suggested a general moratorium on white critics [such as Sollors] reviewing black writers." He sets out to counter, and there follows the long and convoluted polemical ending in his determination that it is "most helpful" to utterly eliminate the "confusing" category of race from the analytical lexicon.

This decision to ignore questions of the functionality of racial designations in America was not, however, coupled to a corresponding restraint in dealing with multi-racial authors and literatures. To the contrary, having smugly stashed away the essential force and motivation of many (or most) non-white writers, Sollors consistently engages himself throughout the remainder of his book in trotting out carefully selected references to and quotations of them. Severed intentionally and completely from the sociocultural consciousness which generated them, these quotations/citations are interwoven at will by the author with the overwhelmingly more extensive material he has gleaned from Euroamerican sources. In each instance, the non-white selections are used in such a way as to appear directly subordinate to the "broader" Euroamerican literary context Sollors is describing, and, in this way, are utilized as mere tokens, props by which the author reinforces his major goal of establishing the primacy of consent in contemporary ethnic identification.

He is rather astute in his choices of those he abuses in this way, deploying as he does representatives from each non-white racial group and including at least mention of writers typically considered as "radicals" on the issue of race. Those descended from the various Asian ethnicities will find passing references to Frank Chin (Chinese-American), and Hisaye Yamamoto (Japanese-American), as well as brief quotation from the verse of

Diana Chang (Chinese-American). Chicanos are included by virtue of mention accorded Gaspar Perez de Villagra, Luis Valdez and Richard Rodriguez, while a brief synopsis is provided concerning the work of Jose Garcia Villa. Native Americans will find the names (no more) of N. Scott Momaday (Kiowa), Leslie Marmon Silko (Laguna) and Hyemeyohsts Storm (ersatz Cheyenne) on page 254.

Blacks—on whose literature and circumstances Sollors, head of the Afro-American Studies Department at Harvard University, apparently considers himself an expert—receive relatively heavy exposure in the form of mention or quotation from Frederick Douglass, Booker T. Washington, Jean Toomer, Richard Wright, James Weldon Johnson, Phyllis Wheatley, Amiri Baraka/LeRoi Jones, Nat Turner, Malcolm X, Elija Muhammad, Martin Robison Delaney, Marcus Garvey, and Ishmael Reed, among others. Nevertheless, it must be said that, among blacks, only the work of W.E.B. DuBois is afforded even a pretense of in-depth examination.

The object of this somewhat elaborate exercise in orchestration is to manipulate into apparent existence a circumstance wherein everyone—white and non-white alike—fits into what Sollors wishes to project as a single, holistic "American" socio-cultural matrix based upon a mutuality of consent among all concerned. Hence, there can be no attempt in *Beyond Ethnicity* to come to grips with even the most fundamentally obvious multi-racial questions, such as how an American black (or any other non-white) is supposed to transcend his/her inherited, genetic, racial darkness (*i.e.*, the determinate factor of his/her "descent") in order to "consent" to join the racially exclusivist white ethnic mainstream of the United States.

Such concerns are the purview of "archaic" theories of ethnicity, Sollors implies; he is occupied with meatier issues such as "[h]ow an Italian-American academic picks up an Afro-American militant gesture and uses it for his own purposes" (p. 14). Besides, to seriously address such

matters would tend to disturb the teleological tidiness of
the author's purposeful extrapolation of Euroamerican
realities to cover everybody else, and so he blocks with one
of his yanked-from-context quotations (this one a tired
banality from Nathan Huggins): "Contrary to what one
might suspect, an Afro-American and the grandson of a
Polish immigrant will be able to take more for granted
among themselves than the former could with a Nigerian
or the latter with a Warsaw worker" (pp. 13-14).

"Interpretations"

Perhaps as telling as the misappropriation of non-
white literature in which Sollors engages, is the literature
which he excludes while developing subject matter entirely relevant to it. For example, although the issue is
mentioned on page eight, the author doesn't bother to
articulate exactly how he validates his novel idea that the
ethos of consensual ethnic merging evidenced by Europe's
voluntary transplants to America would, or even could, be
shared by those American Indians whose lands and lives
the newcomers usurped (and continue to usurp). Rather,
he falls back on Michael Novak's inane suggestion that,
"Given a grandparent or two, one chooses to shape one's
life by one history rather than another" before blithely
launching into a drawn-out process of having Euroamerican writers speak for the Indian.

A total of 146 pages and two full chapters—"Roman-
tic Love, Arranged Marriage and Indian Melancholy" and
"Interlude: From Indian to Urban"—are devoted to Euroamerican "interpretation" of the meaning of "Indian-
ness" in the American melting pot, all without a single
Native American voice being heard. The implications of
this sort of handling present themselves most clearly
when, on pages 132-133, Sollors purports to decipher the
differences between American inter-ethnic humor and,
say, German anti-Jewish or Turkish anti-Armenian jokes.

The distinction, he claims, is that the latter two examples "served to support genocidal policies," and the reader is left to ponder what—precisely—an at least 75 percent reduction in American Indian population during the 19th century signifies, if not genocide. Similarly, there is no explanation as to why the author is unable to detect a whiff of the same aroma in U.S. slave and segregation policies. One is left wondering: is Sollors implying that American inter-ethnic humor never supports genocidal policies, or is he implying that no such policies exist to be supported by this humor?

Both crucial breaches of dialectical method—the deliberate miscasting of non-white writing within antithetical contexts, and its deliberate exclusion from contexts which were made to concern it—were, of course, perfectly avoidable on their face. This does not hold, however, given the predetermined conclusions and consequent structure of discourse Sollors set out to achieve. Had the real weight of Amiri Baraka's or Ishmael Reed's writing been set loose inside the author's carefully controlled study, the result could only have been a more-than-metaphoric undoing of his thesis of the dominance of ethnic consent. The same could be said for any number of black literary figures—Alice Walker, Manning Marable, Maya Angelou, Toni Morrison, Melvin Van Peebles, Erika Huggins, Eldridge Cleaver, Angela Davis and Bobby Seale among them—made conspicuous by their very absence from the pages of *Beyond Ethnicity*.

By the same token, had Leslie Marmon Silko been allowed off the leash which extended only as long as her name, she could have communicated a sense of otherness so profound as to completely unhinge Sollors' neatly crafted illusion of consensual ethnic interchange with Euroamerica. Inclusion of Vine Deloria, Jr.'s *God Is Red* (1973), or even his subsequent *Metaphysics of Modern Existence* (1979) would have broken beyond all repair the idea of a hegemonic Judeo-Christian ideal (*i.e.*, Puritanism) governing the evolution of American ethnicity along cross-racial lines. Allowing other prominent Indian literary voices—such as those of James Welch, Simon J. Ortiz, Wendy Rose, John Trudell and Joy Harjo—to be heard would simply have completed the overall job of demolition. Ultimately, then, the author had no real alternative but to play his hand the way he did.

Because of this, *Beyond Ethnicity* must stand as far worse than a failed promise. Its underlying premises were never tenable, its real trajectory never so much explanatory as deliberately obfuscatory. Whatever real utility it might have yielded in terms of a better understanding of ethnic interplay in Euroamerica is lost in its devious insistence upon having that particular cultural milieu exercise a domination which even Sollors describes as being "expressed in the power to define" (p. 193) everyone else's reality. At bottom, then, this is an extremely deceitful book and dangerous, not so much for the wildly Eurocentric perspective it exhibits, as for its gloss of rationality, balance and academic objectivity.

The Deepest Avatar of Racism

In the end, we are left to speculate as to why a scholar of Werner Sollors' undeniable abilities should have reduced himself to such a level as this, maiming beyond all redemption what might otherwise have stood as a solid and respectable little study. For what purpose does he go to such lengths in attempting to deny descent differentiations which even his own illustrations often tacitly conjure up? To what end does he persist in a peculiar form of intellectual masochism, pretending to miss points which even academic amateurs will find easy and all but self-evident? Why does he insist upon repeatedly trying to slam round pegs into square holes? The answer, perhaps, rests in the tenderness with which he reacted to Richard

Gilman's suggested critical moratorium, and Sollors' subsequent observation that:

> This attitude is quite common in ethnic studies today. It is based on the assumption that experience is first and foremost ethnic. Critics should practice cultural relativism and stick to their own turfs (based, of course, on descent), since an unbridgeable gap separates Americans of different ethnic backgrounds and most especially all white Anglo-Saxon Protestants (acronymically known as WASP) from all non-WASPs. (p. 12)

This is much more than a casual point or one observation among many. A nerve has been struck here, and struck hard. Sollors is himself a WASP (*i.e.*, of Germanic Anglo-Saxon Protestant descent) who has fashioned himself an academic career upon the enterprise of purporting to define and explain non-WASPs—most especially non-whites—to themselves. To this degree at least, he is functioning well within one of the most hallowed institutional corridors of the WASPishly-conceived "white man's burden." Assertions, such as Gilman's, that non-whites may be well-nigh better prepared and able to explain things for themselves seem, not unnaturally, to appear both personally threatening to Sollors and deeply subversive to his sense of the established propriety of things.

In any event, his defensive reaction to this perceived unruliness presently pervading ethnic studies, has been to emit the cry of the wounded WASP, scurrying to restore a certain ethnocentric order to the situation. This is first and always to demonstrate (*i.e.*, reassert) the inherent preeminence of WASP culture in America, mythologically lodged as it is in Puritan New England. Secondly, it must be shown that all subsequent migrations from Europe to the New World first revolved around this culturally integral mass and then were gradually allowed to merge with it. And finally, "proof" must be offered that all non-white groups in the United States are currently in the same sort of orbit previously experienced by, say, the Irish, and are seeking admission to the ethnic *status quo*.

Once this scenario for intercultural/interracial historiography and aesthetics has been rendered viable— "by any means necessary," to use a quotation from Huey P. Newton as Sollors might have, had he bothered—the situation is saved. The author, as a WASP insider, is in the ideal position to rejoin Gilmanesque upstarts with the observation that, not only is he as qualified to review non-white writing as any non-white critic, he is more so, given that he is already what they are aspiring to become. Sollors must be experiencing a truly sublime satisfaction in having been able to lick his psychic wounds in such fashion, putting his antagonists "in their place" so publicly. This is no doubt all the more true, given that the publisher of his atavistic excursion is no less than Oxford University Press, that cidatel of academic excellence into whose pages so few dissident thinkers "of color" have managed to find their way.

In the final analysis, however, it will be for naught. It is difficult to conceive of a book which could have done more to reinforce the basis for the attitudes Sollors decries than his own. He has greatly strengthened rather than diminished the credibility of those he sees as opponents. The ultimate irony, moreover, is not to be found at this level, but rather in the observation of the French philosopher Jean Baudrillard that:

> The deepest avatar of racism is to think that an error about [other] societies is politically or theoretically less serious than a misinterpretation of our own world. Just as a people who oppresses another cannot be free, so a culture that is mistaken about another must be mistaken about itself. (1975, 32-33)

The bottom line is that Werner Sollors misunderstands nothing so much as he misunderstands the WASP...and himself.

Sources

Abramson, Harold J., *Ethnic Diversity in Catholic America*, New York, London: John Wiley, 1973.

Baudrillard, John, *The Mirror of Production*, St. Louis, MO: TELOS Press, 1975.

Cohen, Ronald, "Ethnicity: Problems and Focus in Anthropology," *Annual Review of Anthropology*, Vol. 7 (1978), p. 379-403 (quote from p. 379).

Deloria, Vine, Jr., *God Is Red*, New York: Delta Books, 1973.

Deloria, Vine, Jr., *Metaphysics of Modern Existence*, New York: Harper and Row, 1979.

Glazer, Nathan and Daniel Patrick Moynihan, *Beyond the Melting Pot: The Negroes, Puerto Ricans, Jews, Italians and Irish of New York City*, Cambridge: MIT Press, 1963.

Greeley, Andrew M., *Ethnicity in the United States: A Preliminary Reconnaissance*, New York, London: John Wiley, 1974.

Huggins, Nathan I., "Afro-American National Character and Community," *Center Magazine* (July/August 1974), pp. 51-66.

Kohn, Hans, *The Ideal of Nationalism*, New York: Macmillan, 1945.

Novak, Michael, *The Rise of the Unmeltable Ethnics: Politics and Culture in the Seventies*, New York: Macmillan, 1975.

Smith, M.G., "Ethnicity and Ethnic Groups in America: The View From Harvard," *Ethnic and Racial Studies* 5 (1982), pp. 1-22.

Zangwill, Israel, *The Melting Pot*, New York: MacMillan, 1909 (Arno Press edition, 1975).

The New Racism

A Critique of James A. Clifton's
The Invented Indian

Here come the anthros,
Better hide your past away.
Here come the anthros,
On another holiday.

—Floyd Westerman
Here Come the Anthros

In a lecture delivered at the University of Colorado's Boulder campus in 1987, black liberation movement leader Kwame Turé (Stokely Carmichael) observed that, "In the struggles of the 1960s, we confronted a defining characteristic of American life which was as old as the republic itself. This was a racism which stood proud and defiant, which strutted its stuff in hoods and robes by the light of burning crosses, a racism that ruled through Jim Crow, backed up by the lyncher's rope. We confronted this racism and, it's fair to say, we defeated it in open battle. The evidence of this is that by the 1970s we witnessed racism in retreat and disarray. For the first time in American history, racism was forced to become a whimpering thing, scurrying timidly from shadow to shadow, slinking about the recesses of white consciousness." He then proceeded to describe what happened next:

> Here, we made a fundamental error. Having succeeded in driving racism underground, we became comfortable and complacent, falsely believing this hidden creature was dead or dying. Instead of going forward and driving our stake through the heart of the monster, we relaxed

163

and enjoyed ourselves, allowing racism time and space in which to recover from its wounds, to regroup, refit and reenter the fray. And so now it is back, vibrantly resurgent, having analyzed and digested the lessons of its temporary losses in the '60s. Consequently, it is a new and far more sophisticated form of racism which we must confront in the '80s...Racism today, and this will undoubtedly be the case throughout the '90s, no longer travels the road of Lester Maddox, Bull Connor and the Ku Klux Klan. Where the old racism was overt, frankly announcing its hatred and opposition to all peoples of color, the new racism smiles and insists it is our friend. Where the old racism ruled through physical violence, racism in its new form asserts its dominance through sheer mendacity. Racism has become covert in its expression, hiding behind a mask of calm and reason. The key to understanding racism today is that it inevitably parades itself about, cloaked in the garb of anti-racism. It is therefore far more dangerous, powerful, and difficult to combat than ever before.

The book at hand fits neatly into such an assessment. *The Invented Indian: Cultural Fictions and Government Policies* (Transaction Books, New York, 1990), a collection of essays assembled and edited by the University of Wisconsin anthropologist James A. Clifton, purportedly seeks, according to its jacket notes, to help American Indians by utilizing "passion, wit and sound scholarship" in order to inject a "healthy dose of realism" into both popular and academic non-Indian understandings of them.[1] This is a noble purpose, since only through such realism, the debunking of myths and stereotypes, and the correction of more "scientifically" erroneous information can relations between culturally distinct peoples be bettered. This is especially true in situations such as Indians and Euroamericans now find themselves, where one group has come to dominate completely the other. Unfortunately, the jacket blurbs lie. The function of *The Invented Indian* is to attempt a repeal of virtually every

glimmer of truth about Native America which has
emerged since 1970, reasserting in their stead the full
range of reactionary fables long advanced by proponents
of the white supremacist colonialism in which Indians are
presently engulfed.

Setting the Stage

The tone of what will follow is established by Clifton
himself on the first page of his introduction, "Memoir,
Exegesis," in a passage where he acknowledges a personal
lack of interest in "Indians *per se.*"[2] As he explains it in
the next several paragraphs, he got into the Indian business as a student, by accident, and only because of the
splendid opportunity to engage in clinical observation of
a process of radical "social transformation" afforded by the
government-mandated termination and dissolution of the
Klamath Nation during the 1950s. One is left with the
queasy feeling the editor/author's view is that indigenous
societies exist only to serve as a series of "valuable case
studies" edifying the curiosities of "skilled researchers,"
such as himself. Generous whiffs of the aromatic mentality described by Robert Jay Lifton in *The Nazi Doctors*
drift through more than a few of Clifton's initial passages.[3]

Nor do things improve thereafter. Throughout the
introduction and in the book's first chapter—"The Indian
Story: A Cultural Fiction," also written by the editor—it
is argued, in effect, that acknowledging anything positive
in the native past is an entirely wrongheaded proposition.[4]
This is so, he argues on the basis of no substantiation
whatever, because no genuine Indian accomplishments
have ever "really" been substantiated. Stripped of its
psuedo-academic trappings, however, Clifton's position is
entirely political, a matter he tacitly admits when he
announces that what is at issue in his book is not mere
"scholarly truth," but "deadly serious twentieth century
business."[5]

Reduced to simplest form, his thesis is that recognizing pre-contact indigenous attainments contributes to unseemly measures of pride and hope for the future on the part of modern Indians, a combination which retards their necessary and inevitable disappearance as culturally identifiable human groups. The rightful role of scholarship, he implies, is to assist in the process of cultural genocide, perfecting a Euro-specific hegemony designed to exclude American Indians from history and, ultimately, from existence itself. Noting that the approaching quincentennial of Columbus's arrival in the Americas provides a perfect arena for such counterproductive activities, Clifton announces that the intended function of *The Invented Indian* itself is to help restrain the general public from being "bamboozled," by such unhelpful sentiments as guilt or remorse into assisting native peoples in bettering their current lot.[6] 1992, it is suggested, instead should be the year in which "the vanishing native" finally vanishes, once and for all.

A major impediment to realization of this lofty goal, the editor makes clear, has been that far too many Indians and "sympathetic" non-Indians have been allowed lately to present their case. While gratuitously dismissing as "unfounded" such learned and widely respected material as the works of Vine Deloria, Jr., Francis Jennings' *The Invasion of America,* Russell Thornton's *American Indian Holocaust and Survival,* Steven Cornell's *Return of the Native,* William Axtell's *The Invasion Within,* Dee Brown's *Bury My Heart at Wounded Knee,* Jack Weatherford's *Indian Givers,* and other "volumes…draped with footnotes, statistical tables, and flow charts,"[7] Clifton demonstrates his own near-perfect ignorance of such subject matter by predicting that his conclusions will by attacked by such "Red McCarthyite" publications as *The Indian Historian,* a scholarly journal which has been defunct for approximately ten years.[8]

Predictably, the antidote Clifton selects as appropriate to counteract the severe problems he sees streaming from contemporary American Indian studies, is adoption of the methodological approach advocated by Werner Sollors in his guidebook to the new racist intellectualism, *Beyond Ethnicity*.[9] This is to say that all work done about Indians by Indians—or by non-Indians, but with which Indians are known to agree—should, no matter what its presentation or documentation, be disregarded out of hand as "partisan...intellectual atrocities."[10] "Sound scholarship" requires that all such material be (re)interpreted by "responsible" Euroamerican academics who, above all else, embody the necessary "distance" and "objectivity" necessary to arrive at "realistic" determinations about any people of color (by the same fallacy, of course, this would mean only people of color possess the neutrality and perspective needed to analyze and assess Euroamerica, but this point seems never to have dawned on either Sollors or Clifton).

The Invented Indian is thus composed, exclusively and intentionally, of articles authored by non-Indians, most of them eager to go on record as "rethinking" one or another positive characteristic attributed to native people. Most of them appear to be motivated primarily by a desire to engage in public one-upsmanship with colleagues who they perceive as having snubbed them professionally at one time or another. Four of the contributors, including Clifton himself, are rather candid about having personal axes to grind with Indians in general. In several cases, they seem to have been further commended to the editor by nothing so much as their complete and utter incompetence to address the topics assigned them.

Charlatans and Shams

For instance, there is Temple University anthropologist Elizabeth Tooker, an alleged "leading authority on the culture and history of Northern Iroquoians."[11] Her essay, "The United States Constitution and the Iroquois League," supposedly refutes the "myth" that the Six Nations Haudenosaunee confederacy was a model of governance which significantly influenced the thinking of the founding fathers in the process of their conceiving the U.S. republic.[12] Tooker has spent several years vociferously repeating her theme in every possible forum, and has actively attacked the credibility of scholars such as Donald Grinde and Bruce Johansen, the results of whose research have reached opposite conclusions.[13] Yet, when questioned closely on the matter at a recent academic conference, this "expert" was forced to admit not only that she had ignored all Iroquois source material while forming her thesis, but that she is quite unfamiliar with the relevant papers of John Adams, Thomas Jefferson, Benjamin Franklin, Tom Paine, and others among the U.S. founders themselves.[14]

Tooker is joined in her endeavor by Leland McDonald, a University of Victoria anthropologist who confesses to spending much of his own research time "refreshing [his] soul bird-watching or observing the fauna of tidepools."[15] This would, of course, be commendable for someone working in ornithology or marine biology, but McDonald's project—elaborated in a piece titled "Liberty, Justice, Fraternity: Was the Indian Really Egalitarian?"—is to deny the generally-recognized democratic content, not only of the Haudenosaunee, but of other indigenous North American societies as well.[16] In so doing, he not only rejects detailed information tendered not only by native people themselves, but by such notable non-Indian scholars as Lewis Henry Morgan and Franz Boas. Tellingly, he approaches the Herculean task of overturn-

ing a cornerstone of his discipline on the basis of a paucity
of personal field work and a total of 21 end notes, nine of
them lacking any citation whatsoever.

Then there is University of Colorado Religious Studies Professor Sam Gill, a self-annointed authority on
native spirituality. In *The Invented Indian,* he contends
that a core concept of many indigenous traditions, the
sense of earth as feminine entity—did not exist until
Europeans came along to teach it. His essay, "Mother
Earth: An American Myth," is a capsulized recycling of his
earlier *Mother Earth: An American Story,* a book already
exposed as one of the shoddier historiographical exercises
in living memory.[17] At least one of Gill's supposed sources
for his Mother Earth thesis has gone on record calling him
an out-and-out liar, while others have said as much in less
public fashion.[18]

Next, we are treated to a pontification by David
Henige, whose credentials to address an American Indian
technical topic consist of being a bibliographer in *African*
Studies at the University of Wisconsin. In his "Their
Numbers Become Thick: Native American Historical Demography as Expiation," Henige claims to refute the
arithmetic of such researchers as Lesley B. Simpson,
Sherburne F. Cook, Woodrow Borah, Carl O. Sauer and
Henry Dobyns, whom he dubs collectively as "High Count-
ers."[19] Although he never quite gets around to giving his
own estimate of the pre-contact native population of North
America, one is left to conclude that he seeks to negate
any estimates going beyond the initial "conservative" pro-
jections advanced by James Mooney and Alfred L. Kroeber—whose own methodological abuses are by this point
notorious, a matter about which Henige remains conspic-
uously silent—during the first half of this century.[20] Suspicions that this revision of American Indian population
estimates is a goal of *The Invented Indian* are reinforced
by in the form of a smug assertion, advanced without so
much as a pretense of support, by French sociologist

Jean-Jacques Simard in his essay, "Ghosts and Shadows: The Reduction of North American Natives": "The [less than two million] people today enumerated as Indian and Inuit in the United States and Canada now total about the same as the estimated [by Mooney and Kroeber] population of the continent when Columbus arrived."[21]

Insights and Obfuscations

The question of indigenous agriculture is also raised. In this connection, an essay is deployed by the late Lynn Ceci, an anthropologist whose undistinguished career seems to have consisted primarily of furiously questioning whether Indians ever engaged in *any* sort of human enterprise. In the course of her lengthy tenure at SUNY, the author developed into an able if tedious tactician, as her posthumous contribution to the present volume readily indicates. Unable to deny the obvious altogether, Ceci's "Squanto and the Pilgrims: On Planting Corn 'in the manner of the Indians'" instead belabors the weighty question of whether native planters along the eastern seaboard really used fish as fertilizer in the way described by early European colonists.[22] The idea appears to be if the author can establish that this bit of Americana is incorrect, at least in part, then the whole notion that many Indian peoples were essentially farmers rather than "hunter-gatherers" can be drawn into question. As with most things, the process of deconstructing reality proceeds one step at a time.

Ceci's effort is accompanied by an even more trivial piece by Carol I. Mason who, like Clifton, is a University of Wisconsin anthropologist. In "A Small Sweet Something: Maple Sugaring in the New World," Mason fails even in her own terms to disprove that Indians utilized this substance (along with honey and other sweets) as an integral dietary component in precontact times, or that they passed along knowledge of it to the first European explorers: "[H]ow can independent testing procedures verify or not verify the conclusions drawn from the documents?...The promise of archaeological verification for problems of this kind is too often still but a promise."[23] Nonetheless, she goes on to conclude authoritatively that, "The Indian as aboriginal sugar maker is a projection of the state of dietary affairs in seventeenth-century England, a clearly ethnocentric interpretation of what constitutes an appropriate human diet."[24]

Another article mining the veins of banality, albeit with a non-agricultural focus, is "Pride and Prejudice: The Pocahontas Myth and the Pamunkey" by Christian F. Feest, a University of Vienna anthropologist who doubles as curator of North and Middle American collections at the Museum für Völkerkunde in the same city.[25] Feest's first essay—his second contribution to this volume will be addressed below—is not so much offensive as it is irrelevant, showing as it does that a given indigenous people has undergone culture change over the past three centuries, and that the nature of this change has included incorporation of aspects of other cultures with which it has interacted. The intent may have been to demonstrate that the Pamunkey are no longer "really Indian" from a perspective which defines "Indianness" as looking and acting exactly as might have in 1607. But all that is ultimately accomplished is to show that native North American cultures are neither static nor less adaptable than any other.

Perhaps ironically, *The Invented Indian* does contain three relatively good articles, written by Alice B. Kehoe, Richard de Mille, and Christian F. Feest, respectively. In "Primal Gaia: Primitivists and Plastic Medicine Men," Kehoe, an anthropologist at Marquette University, does an excellent job of illuminating the fraudulent nature of "New Age Indianists" of both the genetically Indian (*i.e.,* Vincent "Sun Bear" LaDuke, "Rolling Thunder," Dhyani Ywahoo, Hyemeyohsts Storm and Wallace Black Elk) and of the non-Indian (*i.e.*, Adolf "Hungry Wolf" Gutohrlein, J. "Jamake Highwater" Marks, Gary Snyder, Hilda Neihardt Petri, "John Redtail Freesoul," Lynn Andrews and José Arguelles) varieties.[26] A major problem with her piece, however, is that it is largely redundant, merely echoing public denunciations of these same individuals and practices advanced by native organizations as prominent and diverse as the North American Circle of Elders, American Indian Movement, National Indian Youth Council, and Northwest Indian Women's Circle, beginning at least as early as 1980.[27] The author not only fails to acknowledge or reference the positions already adopted by indigenous traditionalists, she attributes the term "plastic medicine men" to "an Austrian Friends-of-the-Indian group" when it actually originated in the Colorado AIM chapter.[28] The resulting impression conveyed is that Indians typically support ersatz shamanism, while it is left to smart white folks like herself to save the day by seeing through it.

Far and away the most honest and accurate item included in *The Invented Indian* is "Validity is Not Authenticity: Distinguishing Two Components of Truth," a reprint of an essay written by non-academician Richard de Mille for his earlier *The Don Juan Papers*.[29] The author vigorously disassembles the various lies about the Yaqui and other indigenous peoples injected into both the scholarly and popular arenas by Carlos Aranja (aka Carlos Castaneda), whom de Mille accurately describes elsewhere as being "the greatest anthropological hoax since Piltdown Man."[30] To his great credit, de Mille makes it absolutely clear that the Castaneda problem is a specifically Eurocentric rather than Native American phenomenon, and spends the bulk of his time analyzing the ways in which the discipline of anthropology churns out what might be best described as "disinformation specialists." Taken most broadly, his is a message that many of the contributors to the present volume would do well to heed in the context of their own misbegotten twistings of reality.

Feest, too, does an at least adequate job in his second essay, "Europe's Indians," in which he unmasks the spurious foundations of Old World conceptions of Indianness elaborated by hack writers such as Karl May.[31] Taken together, these last three pieces might have formed the basis for a useful and informative book. Unfortunately, given the setting in which they have been published, they serve now more as a brush with which to tar genuine indigenous spiritual traditions than as a means of exposing the assorted phonies preying upon these traditions. They are simply insufficient in themselves to offset the thrust of the rest of the collection.

The Real Agenda

The thrust of the book is all the more clear when one considers the cluster of essays which comprise the core of *The Invented Indian,* laying bare the sort of bedrock issues which prompted editor Clifton to collect and publish it. Put bluntly, this central material aims to delgitimize any Indian land claims (or reserved land rights, for that matter), efforts to assert control over their own affairs, or attempts to speak the truth of what is being done to them. The package is presented as being "of benefit" to Indians insofar as their acceptance of it might foster "improved interracial relations." The rest of the volume may be assessed as orchestrated more or less to provide "background," adding an appearance of academic credibility to this more nuts-and-bolts body of highly-politicized verbiage.

Leading the pack in this regard is Allan van Gestel, an attorney whose main qualification as a contributor is having unsuccessfully defended non-Indian interests against the 1985 Oneida Land Claim in New York State. Titling his essay "When Fictions Take Hostages," the

author asserts that individual non-Indian property owners within Indian land claim areas are victimized, both by
having their titles clouded during litigation, and by facing
potential eviction from their homes whenever Indians
win.[32] The individuals at risk, he declares (accurately
enough), are largely innocent of personal wrongdoing, and
thus should not be made to bear the burden of redressing
indigenous peoples' grievances. Indians' persistence in
filing suits to recover lands taken from them in contraven-
tion of both U.S. and international law is, he contends,
tantamount to taking these bystanders "hostage" in order
to force state or federal governments to restore lands they
probably would not otherwise cede.[33] It is incumbent upon
Indians, he argues, to cease such provocative endeavors
lest the rage of the hostages eventually vent itself upon
their captors.[34] No mention is made of the possibility that
the Euroamerican governments might bear a certain responsibility to resolve the problem by ending their blanket
refusal to return territory they demonstrably—and often
admittedly—took from indigenous people through other
than legal means.

Although he claims juridical expertise, van Gestel
inverts the entire tradition of English common law, on
which U.S. codes are based, by suggesting that non-Indians holding deeds within Indian treaty areas are somehow inherently entitled to keep the property—no matter
if it can be shown to be stolen—simply by virtue of having
"acted in good faith" in acquiring it. In this, he is obviously
playing to a crowd of non-Indians who seek peace of mind
in their property investments, rather than following legal
logic. The latter holds clearly and as a matter of fundamental principle that stolen property must be returned to
its rightful owners wherever these can be found. Those
who receive stolen property are *never* entitled to keep it,
even though they may have had no participation in or
knowledge of the theft, and may even have honestly pur-
chased the property from the thief or thieves. Such per-

sons *are* entitled to be compensated for their losses by the
thieves, in this case the government, *not* the Indians.
Were he truly concerned with promoting interracial harmony based on sound legal posture, van Gestel might
advocate that Indians and non-Indians unite in a common
effort to bring the government in line with its own laws.
Instead, he strives to affix blame where it doesn't belong,
set one group of victims against the other, and allow the
only guilty parties in the whole mix to walk away unpun-
ished.

Apparently aware of the intrinsic irrationality of the
stance he's assumed, the author hurriedly scuttles to the
task of amending it. This is done by asserting that Indians
possess no legitimate standing from which to press claims
that anything, including land, was ever stolen from them.
Native peoples were never, he says, "'distinct, independent, political communities' qualified to exercise powers
of self-governance and having other prerogatives by virtue
of their...sovereignty." In fact, they weren't even "tribes,"
in his view.[35] Exactly what he thinks the indigenous form
of socio-political existence was (herds? packs? coveys?
gaggles?) is left unstated as he plunges ahead, decreeing
that the "notion of an Indian 'tribe' or 'nation' is a...fiction"
contrived by Euroamerican jurists and politicians to allow
them to go about acquiring legal title to much of North
America through an orderly process of bilateral and mul-
tilateral treaty negotiations with indigenous groups.[36]
Now that the desired acreage has been obtained, including
most of that reserved by Indians for themselves as part of
the treaty process, the "fiction" has outlived its usefulness
and should be discarded without further ado. Indians
would thus become what van Gestel insists they always
were—non-entities—and non-entities, to be sure, have no
legal standing. Hence, no thieves, no stolen property, and
no problem.

Leaving aside the peculiar readings of history with
which he accompanies his theories, the author has delib-

erately avoided several other salient issues. First, and most important, there is the fact that *all* nations—not least that renegade republic known as the United States—as well as the sovereignty thereof, are "legal fictions" in the sense van Gestel employs the term. Indigenous nations are no different than any other in this respect. Moreover, behind his careful abstractions there are real human beings who have, for the benefit of others, been dispossessed of the real land which is their real birthright. They experience real loss and feel real pain as a result. They are collectively entitled to, but have been systematically denied, very real human rights of collective self-determination.

Second, the United States Constitution is quite clear in its first article, requiring that treaty relationships be entered into by the federal government *only* with other fully sovereign national entities. This means, whether van Gestel likes it or not, that each time the Senate ratified a treaty with an Indian people, as it did at least 371 times, it simultaneously bestowed formal U.S. recognition of the other party as a sovereign nation in the most unequivocal legal sense.

Third, neither the Constitution, nor international custom and convention, allow for the United States to legally "unrecognize" a nation that is already recognized. To the contrary, any such action would likely violate the "crimes against the peace" provisions of the Nuremburg Principles—formulated by the United States itself—and a number of other elements of international law.

Fourth, the legitimacy of U.S. title to its territorality within the 48 contiguous states derives exclusively—the U.S. having officially renounced rights of conquest by 1790—from the treaty agreements reciprocally guaranteeing specific territoralities to signatory indigenous nations. Abrogation of the treaties would nullify U.S. title to all territory within its main land mass, with ownership reverting entirely to the original inhabitants under the Doctrine of Discovery.

Fifth, and conclusively, the entire cynically manipulative approach van Gestel suggests as appropriate for U.S. participation in treaty relations is quite literally Hitlerian in both its mode and its moral content. The magnitude of malicious falsity involved in his reasoning is staggering. It is plainly not justice he seeks, but *lebensraum*. That, and a rationalization leading to some psychic consolidation of a white supremacist empire. Thankfully, he is in no position to implement his malignant vision.

Additional Polemics

Still, he is hardly alone in his crypto-fascist sentiments, as witnessed by the submission of Stephen E. Feraca, a deeply embittered non-Indian employee of the Bureau of Indian Affairs who went into retirement as quickly as possible after that agency began to exercise Indian hiring preferences. In his essay, "Inside the BIA: Or, 'We're Getting Rid of All These Honkies,'" the author first paints what can only be an intentionally misleading portrait of how insensitively and with what steel-trap efficiency the Bureau served the interests of native people in the days before "they" came aboard in large numbers.[37] In order to do this, of course, he must ignore the BIA's characteristic penchant for using its "trust" control over Indian affairs to force the long-term, low-cost leasing of every possible acre of reservation land to non-Indian interests. Similarly, he fails to mention the Bureau's chronic pattern of negotiating mining contracts—which typically lacked even minimal safety and land reclamation provisions, and which seldom pay the BIA's indigenous "wards" more than 15 percent of market rate on extracted minerals—with major corporations desiring to operate on reservation lands. And again, he is silent concerning the large numbers of Indian women involuntarily sterilized while availing themselves of Bureau-co-ordinated "health services."

The reasons for Feraca's neglect of the facts is quite simple. His purpose is to bemoan—through a lengthy stream of personal anecdotes in which no names are named, and which rely upon a grand total of two end notes for substantiation—the "reverse racism" of Indian prefer-ence policies,[38] and the subsequent "severe damage" to the BIA's beneficent programming.[39] In a perverse way, he is correct. Indian preference is a a belated, and rather insuf-ficient, response to more than a century of unremitting "whites only" policies which have excluded Indian partic-ipation from all meaningful participation in decisionmak-ing. Further, whatever else may be said of the congregation of native bureaucrats ("apples" is their con-ventional descriptor) now haunting the Bureau's hallowed halls, they *have* made headway in halting or at least curtailing some of the BIA's worst practices. In a nutshell, then, Feraca's sour grapes reduce to nothing other than a demand that, "in fairness," Indian affairs should be re-turned to its historical status as a medium of white careerism, and service as an instrument through which the absolute, unhampered non-Indian control over resid-ual native land, lives and resources may be extended.

The icing is put on the cake by the late John A. Price, yet another in the seemingly unending roster of anthro-pologists contributing to *The Invented Indian*. Described as "an authority on the native peoples of Canada, and on advocacy groups and development programs concerning them," the author devotes much of his article—entitled "Ethnic Advocacy Groups Versus Propaganda: Canada's Indian Support Groups"—to explaining how "preferen-tially" indigenous peoples are treated under Canadian law.[40] As an example, he observes that "Indians are ex-empt from federal and provincial taxation on reserve land, personal property on reserve land, and income derived while working on reserve land." Such a situation, he says, is unfair "to the citizenry at large."[41] Worse, Price contends, it stems from "new interpretations of old treaties," never mentioning that these new interpretations represent a substantial diminishment of the native rights that original indigenous signatories intended the treaties to secure.[42]

The author then moves on to considering the "ungrateful" response of indigenous people and their supporters to various aspects of Canadian Indian policy. Taking a series of block quotes drawn from several publications, each of which provides a cogent assessment of the topic it treats, he dismisses them as part of "an implicit political strategy, which is propagandistic in design and execution."[43] His method of analysis in arriving at this conclusion is not so much faulty as inexplicable. For instance, he offers the following illustration of commentary on Canada's dual standard of justice:

> In one highly publicized case, Donald Marshall, a Micmac wrongly served eleven years in prison for murder before the White man, Roy Ehsanz, who committed the crime, confessed, and Marshall was released. "In contrast to Marshall's life sentence for second degree murder, Ehsanz got one year for manslaughter."[44]

Price makes no claim that this is untrue. To the contrary, he seems to accept the veracity of what is said. Hence, it becomes apparent that what he really seeks is to categorize *any* native criticism of the *status quo,* no matter how well founded, as "propaganda." Following this definition, the only non-propagandistic observations Indians and their supporters can make—and thus the only legitimate "advocacy" posture open to them—would be those which, no matter how inaccurately, serve to support and endorse official conduct. That adhering to such "standards" would place native people in the role of actively seeking their own demise is precisely the point.

The articles prepared by van Gestel, Feraca and Price ultimately form a tidy triad: 1) *any* recognition of indigenous land rights in North America is "unfair to the broader population"; 2) *any* genuine Indian control over their own affairs is "racist" and therefore "unfair to non-Indians"; and 3) *any* native comment or complaint concerning losses of basic rights and resources may be dismissed *a priori* as mere "political gimmickry." To these might be added a fourth element, representing most of the rest of the book, holding that any historical/anthropological interpretations of fact leading to conclusions that American Indians ever comported themselves as *bona fide* human beings—readings which might serve to make the main three premises seem unconscionable—are "grossly inaccurate." The theoretical stage for a "final solution of the Indian problem" is thus amply set.

Conclusion

"Propaganda," says Price on the first page of his essay, "typically uses stereotyping for political or commercial ends. The presentations are too biased, too selective to tell the whole truth. Emotional appeals may be substituted for a fully reasoned, balanced analysis of issues. One result is that even honest, ethical, and reasoned [positions which go in the same direction] become tainted by association with the propaganda of fanatic proponents of any cause...Such problems occur when advocates abandon fundamental principles of serious research...[presenting] only that evidence and information which supports the position they are endorsing."[45] All in all, this observation may be accepted as an adequate depiction of his own material and much of the rest of the book.

James Clifton has assembled an odyssey into historical revisionism, not in the admirable sense originally connoted by the work of Alice and Staughton Lynd, Howard Zinn and others, but in the more recent and thor-

oughly squalid sense exemplified by those like Arthur
Butz who seek to "debunk the myth" that the Third Reich
perpetrated genocide against the Jews and Gypsies.[46] It is
bad enough that we have such minds festering within
contemporary society. The problem is made far worse by
the willingness of supposedly reputable publishers to
present such pseudo-scholarship in the guise of legitimate
academic exposition. If there is any utility at all to the
release of *The Invented Indian,* it lies in the open self-identification of a whole cast of North American neo-Nazis.
Now we know beyond any reasonable doubt where they
stand. All those involved should be accorded the degree of
disgust they have so richly earned.

Notes

1. Clifton, James A., *The Invented Indian: Cultural Fictions and
Government Policies,* Transaction Books, New Brunswick, NJ,
1990.

2. The introduction spans pages 1-28.

3. Lifton, Robert Jay, *The Nazi Doctors: Medical Killing and the
Psychology of Genocide,* Basic Books, New York, 1986.

4. Clifton's essay falls at pp. 29-48.

5. *Ibid.,* p. 26.

6. *Ibid.,* p. 27.

7. *Ibid.,* p. 41. The books at issue are Jennings, Francis, *The
Invasion of America: Indians, Colonialism, and the Cant of
Conquest* (University of North Carolina Press, Chapel Hill,
1975); Thornton, Russell, *American Indian Holocaust and Sur-
vival: A Population History Since 1492* (University of Oklahoma
Press, Norman, OK, 1988); Cornell, Steven, *Return of the Native:
American Indian Political Resurgence* (Oxford University Press,
New York, 1987); Axtell, William, *The Invasion Within: The
Contest of Cultures in Colonial North America* (Oxford Univer-
sity Press, New York, 1985); Brown, Dee, *Bury My Heart at
Wounded Knee: An Indian History of the American West* (Holt,
Rinehart and Winston, New York, 1971); and Weatherford, Jack,
Indian Givers: How the Indians of the Americas Transformed the

World (Crown Publishers, New York, 1988). Clifton also seems to take particular exception to Deloria's *Custer Died For Your Sins: An Indian Manifesto* (Macmillan, New York, 1969) and *God Is Red* (Grossett and Dunlap, New York, 1973).

8. Clifton, *op. cit.*, p. 26.

9. Sollors, Werner, *Beyond Ethnicity: Descent and Consent in American Literature*, Oxford University Press, New York, 1985.

10. Clifton, op. *cit.*, p. 41.

11. *Ibid.*, p. 378.

12. Tooker's essay appears at pp. 107-28.

13. Tooker is particularly unctuous about Grinde's *The Iroquois and the Founding of the American Nation* (Indian Historian Press, San Francisco, 1977) and Johansen's *Forgotten Founders* (Gambit Publishers, Ipswich, CT, 1982), as well as Barriero, Jose (ed.), *Indian Roots of American Democracy (Northeast Indian Quarterly*, Cornell University, Ithaca, NY, 1988). Her polemics seem designed, at least in part, as an attempt to block publication of Grinde's and Johansen's *Exemplar of Liberty* (UCLA, 1990).

14. For detailed analysis, see Grinde, Donald, Jr., "The Iroquois Political Concept and the Genesis of the American Government: Further Research and Contentions," *Northeast Indian Quarterly*, Vol. 6, No. 4, Winter 1989.

15. Clifton, *op. cit.*, p. 376.

16. McDonald's essay appears at pp. 145-67.

17. Gill's essay falls at pp. 129-44. The book in question was published by the University of Chicago Press in 1987. For criticism, see the feature section edited by M. Annette Jaimes and devoted primarily to Gill in *Bloomsbury Review*, Summer 1988.

18. See Jaimes' interview with Russell Means in *Bloomsbury*, *op. cit.*

19. Henige's essay may be found at pp. 169-91. His title is a play upon Dobyns, Henry F., *Their Numbers Become Thinned: Native American Population Dynamics in Eastern North America* (University of Tennessee Press, Nashville, 1983). He focuses his attack upon Cook, Sherburne F., and Leslie B. Simpson, "The

Population of Central Mexico in the Sixteenth Century" (*Ibero-Americana*, No. 31, University of California Press, Berkeley, 1948); Borah, Woodrow W., "The Historical Demography of Aboriginal and Colonial America: An Attempt at Perspective" (in William E. Denevan, (ed.), *The Native Population of the Americas in 1492*, University of Wisconsin Press, Madison, 1976); and Borah's "America as Model: The Demographic Impact of European Expansion Upon the Non-European World" (in *Actos y Memorias del XXXV Congreso International de Americanistas*, Instituto Nacional de Anthropologia, Mexico City, 1964).

20. Henige seems especially attracted to Mooney's estimates, published as *The Aboriginal Population of America North of Mexico* (John R. Swanton [ed.], *Smithsonian Miscellaneous Collections*, LXXX, No. 7, Washington, D.C., 1928), and Kroeber's subsequent downward revision published in his *Cultural and Natural Areas of Native North America* (University of California Publications in American Archeology and Ethnology, XXXVIII, Berkeley and Los Angeles, 1939). The demographies of both men are definitively exposed as fraudulent in Jennings, *op. cit.*, pp. 16-31.

21. Ceci's essay falls at pp. 333-69 of Clifton, *op. cit.*, the quote at pp. 340-1.

22. *Ibid.*, pp. 71-9.

23. Mason's essay may be found at pp. 91-105, the quote at p. 103.

24. *Ibid.*

25. Feest's essay appears at pp. 49-70.

26. Kehoe's essay may be found at pp. 193-209.

27. Texts of these denunciations are reproduced in Churchill, Ward (ed.), *Critical Issues in Native North America*, Volume II, International Work Group on Indigenous Affairs, Copenhagen Denmark, 1991.

28. *Ibid.*, p. 199.

29. De Mille's essay appears at pp. 227-54. It is reprinted from *The Don Juan Papers: Further Castaneda Controversies*, Wadsworth Publishers, Belmont, CA, 1990.

30. The description is taken from De Mille, Richard, *Castaneda's Journey: The Power and the Allegory,* Capra Press, Santa Barbara, CA, 1976.

31. Feest's second essay comes at pp. 313-32.

32. Van Gestel's essay is at pp. 291-312.

33. *Ibid.,* p. 298.

34. *Ibid.,* p. 294.

35. *Ibid.,* pp. 300-2.

36. *Ibid.,* p. 300.

37. Feraca's essay falls at pp. 271-90.

38. *Ibid.,* p. 281.

39. *Ibid.,* p. 286

40. Price's essay may be found at pp. 255-70, the description of his pedigree at p. 378.

41. *Ibid.,* pp. 260-1.

42. *Ibid.,* p. 259.

43. *Ibid.,* p. 269.

44. *Ibid.*

45. *Ibid.,* p. 255.

46. See, for example, Butz, Arthur D., *The Hoax of the Twentieth Century: The Case Against the Presumed Extermination of European Jewry,* Institute for Historical Review, Torrance, CA, 1977.

Part V

Culture Vultures: Genocide with "Good Intentions"

A Little Matter of Genocide

Sam Gill's *Mother Earth,* Colonialism and the Expropriation of Indigenous Spiritual Tradition in Academia

> They came for our land, for what grew or could be grown on it, for the resources in it, and for our clean air and pure water. They stole these things from us, and in the taking they also stole our free ways and the best of our leaders, killed in battle or assassinated. And now, after all that, they've come for the very last of our possessions; now they want our pride, our history, our spiritual traditions. They want to rewrite and remake these things, to claim them for themselves. The lies and thefts just never end.
>
> —Margo Thunderbird
> 1988

The exploitation and appropriation of Native American spiritual traditions is nothing new. In many ways the process began the moment the first of Columbus's wayward seamen washed up on a Caribbean beach, returning home with wondrous tales of *los Indios.* And it has been functioning in increasingly concerted fashion, under rationales ranging from the crassly commercial to the purely academic, ever since. Over the past two decades, the ranks of those queueing up to cash in on the lucre and luster of "American Indian Religious Studies" have come to include a number of "New Age" luminaries reinforced by a significant portion of the university elite.

The classic example of this has been Carlos Castaneda (aka Carlos Aranja), whose well-stewed borrowings from Timothy Leary, the Yogi Ramacharaka, and Barbara Meyeroff were blended with a liberal dose of his own turgid fantasies, packaged as a "Yaqui way of knowledge," resulting in not only a lengthy string of best-sellers but a Ph.D. in anthropology from UCLA. So lacking was/is the base of real knowledge concerning things Indian within academia that it took nearly a decade for Castaneda to be apprehended as "the greatest anthropological hoax since Piltdown Man." One still encounters abundant instances of *The Teachings of Don Juan* and *Journey to Ixtlan* being used in courses and cited (apparently in all seriousness) in ostensibly scholarly works as offering "insight" into American Indian thought and spiritual practice.

Then there is "Dr. Jamake Highwater," an alleged Cherokee/Blackfeet from either Montana or Canada (the story varies from time to time), born by his own accounts in various different years. In an earlier incarnation (*circa* the late '60s), this same individual appeared as "J. Marks," a non-Indian modern dance promoter in the San Francisco area whose main literary claim to fame was as the author of an "authorized biography" of rock star Mick Jagger. Small wonder that the many later texts of "Dr. Highwater" on Native American spirituality and the nature of "the primal mind" bear more than passing resemblance to both the lore of Greek myths and the insights of hip-pop idiom *à la Rolling Stone* magazine. Still, Highwater's material consistently turns up as required reading in undergraduate courses and referenced in supposedly scholarly fora. The man has also received more than one hefty grant to translate his literary ramblings into "educational" PBS film productions.

Then again, there is Ruth Beebe Hill whose epic pot-boiler novel, *Hanta Yo,* set certain sales records during the late '70s while depicting the collectivist spirituality of the 19th-century Lakota as a living prefiguration of her friend Ayn Rand's grossly individualistic crypto-fascism. In the face of near-universal howls of outrage from the contemporary Lakota community, Hill resorted to "validating" her postulations by retaining the services of a single aging and impoverished Sioux man, Alonzo Blacksmith (aka "Chunksa Yuha") to attest to the book's "authenticity." Before dropping once again into well-deserved obscurity, Blacksmith intoned—allegedly in a "dialect" unknown to Siouxian linguistics—that what Hill had written was true because "I, Chunksa Yuha, say so, say so." This ludicrous performance was sufficient to allow a range of professors to argue that the controversy [was] really just "a matter of opinion" because "*all* Indians are not in agreement as to the inaccuracy of *Hanta Yo.*" Such pronouncements virtually ensured that sales would remain brisk in supermarkets and college book stores, and that producer David Wolper would convert it into a t.v. mini-series entitled *Mystic Warrior* during the mid-'80s.

And, as if all this were not enough, we are currently treated to the spectacle of Lynn Andrews, an air-head "feminist" yuppie who once wrangled herself a weekend in the company of a pair of elderly Indian women of indistinct tribal origin. In her version of events, they had apparently been waiting their entire lives for just such an opportunity to unburden themselves of every innermost secret of their people's spiritual knowledge. They immediately acquainted her with such previously unknown "facts" as the presence of kachinas in the Arctic Circle and the power of "Jaguar Women," charged her with serving as their "messenger," and sent her forth to write a series of books so outlandish in their pretensions as to make Castaneda seem a model of propriety by comparison. Predictably, the Andrews books have begun to penetrate the "popular literature" curriculum of academe.

To round out the picture, beyond the roster of such heavy-hitters circle a host of also-rans extending from "Chief Red Fox" and "Nino Cochise" (real names and ethnicities unknown) to Hyemeyohsts Storm, David Seals and scores of others, each of whom has made a significant recent contribution (for profit) to the misrepresentation and appropriation of indigenous spirituality, and most of whom have been tendered some measure of credibility by the "certified scholars" of American universities. So pervasive are these "scholars" that scarcely an Indian in the United States has not been confronted by some hippie-like apparition wishing to teach crystal-healing methods to Navajo grandmothers, claiming to be a pipe-carrier reincarnated from a 17th century Cheyenne warrior, and with an assumed "Indian name" such as "Beautiful Painted Arrow" or "Chief Piercing Eyes." Needless to say, this circumstance has in turn spawned a whole new clot of hucksters such as "Sun Bear" (Vincent LaDuke, a Chippewa) who—along with his non-Indian consort *cum* business manager, Wabun (Marlise James)—has been able to make himself rather wealthy over the past few years by forming (on the basis of suitable "membership fees") what he calls "the Bear Tribe," and the selling of ersatz sweat lodge and medicine wheel ceremonies to anyone who wants to play Indian for a day and can afford the price of admission.

As the Sioux scholar Vine Deloria, Jr., put it in 1982,

> the realities of Indian belief and existence have become so misunderstood and distorted at this point that when a real Indian stands up and speaks the truth at any given moment, he or she is not only unlikely to be believed, but will probably be publicly contradicted and 'corrected' by the citation of some non-Indian and totally inaccurate "expert." Moreover, young Indians in universities are now being trained to view themselves and their cultures in the terms prescribed by such experts *rather than* in the traditional terms of the tribal elders. The process automatically sets the members of Indian communities at odds with one another, while outsiders run around picking up the pieces for themselves. In this way, the experts are perfecting a system of self-validation in which all semblance of honesty and accuracy are lost. This is not

only a travesty of scholarship, but it is absolutely devastating to Indian societies.

Pam Colorado, an Oneida academic working in Canada, goes further:

The process is ultimately intended to supplant Indians, even in areas of their own customs and spirituality. In the end, non-Indians will have complete power to define what is and is not Indian, even for Indians. We are talking here about an absolute ideological/conceptual subordination of Indian people in addition to the total physical subordination they already experience. When this happens, the last vestiges of real Indian society and Indian rights will disappear. Non-Indians will then "own" our heritage and ideas as thoroughly as they now claim to own our land and resources.

A Little Matter of Genocide

Those who engage in such activities usually claim to do so not for the fame and fortune (real or potential) involved, but for loftier motives. Many of Castaneda's defenders, for example, have argued that despite his blatant misrepresentation of Yaqui culture, his books nonetheless articulate valid spiritual principles, the "higher truth value" of which simply transcend such "petty criticism" as demanding at least minimal adherence to facts. Similar themes have been sounded with regard to Highwater, Andrews, and others. Within academia proper, such thinking has led to the emergence of a whole new pseudo-discipline, "ethnomethodology," in which inconvenient realities can be simply disregarded and allegorical "truth" is habitually substituted for conventional data. Harold Garfinkle, a founder of ethnomethodology at UCLA, has contended that such an approach represents "the pursuit of knowledge in its purest form."

At another level, the poet Gary Snyder, who has won literary awards for writing poetry in which he pretends to see the world through the eyes of an American Indian "shaman," has framed things more clearly: "Spirituality is not something which can be 'owned' like a car or a house," says Snyder. "Spiritual knowledge belongs to all humanity equally. Given the state of the world today, we all have not only the right but the obligation to pursue all forms of spiritual insight, and at every possible level. In this sense, it seems to me that I have as much right to pursue and articulate the belief systems developed by Native Americans as they do, and arguments to the contrary strike me as absurd in the extreme."

Indeed, the expression of such proprietary interest in native spiritual tradition is hardly confined to Snyder. For instance, at a 1986 benefit concert staged to raise funds to support the efforts of traditional Navajos resisting forcible relocation from their homes around Big Mountain, Arizona, one non-Indian performer took the opportunity between each of her songs to "explain" one or another element of "Navajo religion" to the audience. Her presumption in this regard deeply offended several Navajos in attendance and, during an intermission, she was quietly told to refrain from any further such commentary. She thereupon returned to the stage and announced that her performance was over, and that she was withdrawing her support to the Big Mountain struggle because the people of that area were "oppressing" her through denial of her "right" to serve as a self-appointed spokesperson for their spirituality. "I have," she said, "just as much right to spiritual freedom as they do."

Those who hold positions of this sort go often beyond assertion of their supposed rights to contend that the arguments of their opponents are altogether lacking in substance. "What does it hurt if a bunch of people want to believe they're the personification of Hiawatha?" asks the manager of a natural foods store in Boulder, Colorado. "I will admit that things can get pretty silly in these circles, but so what? People have a right to be silly if they want to. And it's not like the old days when Indians were being killed left and right. You could even say that the attention being paid to Indian religions these days is sort of flattering. Anyway, there's no harm to anybody, and it's good for the people who do it."

The traditional Indian perspective is diametrically opposed to the idea that no harm is done by this interest. As Barbara Owl, a White Earth Anishinabe, recently put it, "We have many particular things which we hold internal to our cultures. These things are spiritual in nature, and they are for *us*, not for anyone who happens to walk in off the street. They are *ours* and they are *not* for sale. Because of this, I suppose it's accurate to say that such matters are our 'secrets,' the things which bind us together in our identities as distinct peoples. It's not that we never make outsiders aware of our secrets, but *we*—not *they*—decide what, how much, and to what purpose this knowledge is to be put. That's absolutely essential to our cultural integrity, and thus to our survival as peoples. Now, *surely* we Indians are entitled to *that*. Everything else has been stripped from us already.

"I'll tell you something else," Owl continued, "a lot of things about our spiritual ways may be secret, but the core idea never has been. And you can sum up that idea in one word spelled R-E-S-P-E-C-T. Respect for and balance between all things, that's our most fundamental spiritual concept. Now, obviously, those who would violate the trust and confidence which is placed in them when we share some of our secrets, they don't have the slightest sense of the word. Even worse are those who take this information and misuse or abuse it for their own purposes, marketing it in some way or another, turning our spirituality into a commodity in books or movies or classes or 'ceremonials.' And it doesn't really matter whether they are Indians or non-Indians when they do such things; the non-Indians who do it are thieves, and the Indians who do it are sellouts and traitors."

Former American Indian Movement (AIM) leader Russell Means not only concurs with Owl but further clarifies her argument. "What's at issue here is the same old question that Europeans have always posed with regard to American Indians, whether what's ours isn't somehow theirs. And, of course, they've always answered the question in the affirmative. When they wanted our land they just announced that they had a right to it and therefore owned it. When we resisted their taking of our land, they claimed we were being unreasonable and committed physical genocide upon us in order to convince us to see things their way. Now, being spiritually bankrupt themselves, they want our spirituality as well. So they're making up rationalizations to explain why they're entitled to it.

"We are resisting this," Means goes on, "because spirituality is the basis of our culture; if it is stolen, our culture will be dissolved. If our culture is dissolved, Indian people *as such* will cease to exist. By definition, the causing of any culture to cease to exist is an act of genocide. That's a matter of international law; look it up in the 1948 Genocide Convention. So, maybe this'll give you another way of looking at these culture vultures who are ripping off Indian tradition. It's not an amusing or trivial matter, and it's not innocent or innocuous. And those who engage in this are not cute, groovy, hip, enlightened, or any of the rest of the things they want to project themselves as being. No, what they're about is cultural genocide. And genocide is genocide, regardless of how you want to 'qualify' it. So some of us are starting to react to these folks accordingly."

For those who would scoff at Meanss' concept of genocide, Mark Davis and Robert Zannis, Canadian researchers on the topic, offer the following observation:

> If people suddenly lose their 'prime symbol,' the basis of their culture, their lives lose meaning. They become disoriented, with no hope. A social disorganization often

follows such a loss, they are often unable to insure their own survival...The loss and human suffering of those whose culture has been healthy and is suddenly attacked and disintegrated are incalculable.

Therefore, Davis and Zannis conclude, "One should not speak lightly of 'cultural genocide' as if it were a fanciful invention. The consequence in real life is far too grim to speak of cultural genocide as if it were a rhetorical device to beat the drums for 'human rights.' The cultural mode of group extermination is genocide, a crime. Nor should 'cultural genocide' be used in the game: 'Which is more horrible, to kill and torture; or remove [the prime cultural symbol which is] the will and reason to live?' *Both* are horrible."

Recreating Indians as Destroyers of the Ecology

The analysis advanced by Means, Pam Colorado and other American Indians is substantially borne out by developments during the second half of the 1980s, as the line separating appropriation of the forms of indigenous spiritual tradition from the outright expropriation of that tradition has evaporated. Over the past few years, a major intellectual enterprise among New Age adherents has been the "demystification" of pre-contact Native America. Although the variants of this effort vary widely, they take as a common objective the "reinterpretation" of one or more positive aspects and attainments of autonomous indigenous society, proving that they never existed. Inevitably, the conclusion is reached that whatever is under discussion was "actually" introduced to the hemisphere by European invaders at some point after 1500.

Hence, we find "radical ecologists" such as George Weurthner arguing in the pages of the supposedly progressive journal *Earth First!* that, far from having achieved spiritual traditions predicated in an understanding of natural harmony and balance, ancient American Indians were really the "first environmental pillagers." This flat reversal of even the most elementary meanings of native tradition is then "explained" as Weurthner wanders through a self-contradictory and wildly convoluted monologue in which he saddles North American indigenous societies with everything from the extinction of the woolly mammoth to desertification of the Sonora. That he deviates radically from logic, known fact and even plain common sense while making his "case" does nothing to deter his stream of bald assertion.

Predictably, from this contrived springboard he is able to contend with superficial plausibility that the concept of what is now termed "ecology" did not—as is popularly imagined—spring from traditional Native American practice. Rather, in Weurthner's more "informed" view, it stems from the fertility of advanced brains such as his own. It follows that he feels compelled to demand that American Indians abandon the myth and falsity of their own belief structures in favor of the outlook he and his colleagues have expropriated from them.

In a more public vein, the thinly-veiled racism of Weurthner's sort of theorizing has set the stage for the celebrated environmentalist author (and Earth First! guru) Edward Abbey to launch himself full-tilt into avowals of an imagined "superiority of northern European culture" worthy of Josef Goebbels and Alfred Rosenberg. Perhaps more pragmatically, it has simultaneously laid the basis for Earth First! political leader Dave Foreman to declare Indian peoples a "threat to the habitat" and urge both ecologists and New Agers to actively resist their land and water rights claims. All of this might be, to some extent, dismissable as the ravings of an irrelevant lunatic fringe, were it not for the fact that, as usual, such ideas are finding their way into the realm of mainstream academia where they are being sanctioned and codified as

knowledge, truth, and scholarship. The interlock and continuity between the expropriation of the physical resources of Native America on the one hand, and the
expropriation of its spiritual/conceptual traditions on the
other, could not be more clearly revealed.

Comes now Sam D. Gill, a non-Indian professor of
religious studies at the University of Colorado/Boulder,
and an alleged specialist in Native American spirituality.
In all fairness, it should be noted that Gill has heretofore
been known primarily not so much on the grounds of his
theses on Indian religion as for his advocacy of a rather
novel approach to teaching. In essence, this seems to be
that the crucial qualification for achieving university-
level faculty status is to know little or nothing of the
subject matter one is supposed to teach. As he himself put
it in an essay contained in *On Teaching,* a 1987 anthology
of "teaching excellence:"

> In my classes on Native American religions I found I
> could not adequately describe the roles of women in
> Native American cultures and religions...To begin to
> resolve my *ignorance* about Native American women and
> to pursue research...I finally offered a senior-level course
> on Native American women and religions...This course
> formally *initiated* my long-term research on Mother
> Earth [emphasis added].

One might have thought that filling a seat as a
professor at a major institution of higher learning would
necessitate not "ignorance," but rather the possession of
some body of knowledge about or from which one is prepared to profess. Similarly, it might be thought that the
offering of an advanced course on a particular subject
implies that one is offering the results of research rather
than the "initiation" of it. At the very least, one might
expect that if a course needs to be taught for canonical
reasons, and the instructor finds him/herself lacking in
the knowledge required to teach it, he or she might retain

the services of someone who does have the knowledge. Not so, according to Dr. Gill: "student questions and concerns" are most important in "shaping" what he does. In other words, "pitch your performance to the crowd."

In any event, it was in this interesting commentary on the application of Harold Garfinkle's principles of attaining "pure knowledge" that Gill announced he had "a book in the process of being published by the University of Chicago Press. It is entitled *Mother Earth: An American Story*." He had thus assigned himself the task of articulating the "truth" of what is possibly the most central of all Native American spiritual concepts. Worse, he went on to remark that in order to "encourage my expeditious writing of the book, I committed myself to a presentation of it as a portion of a summer course entitled 'Native American Goddesses' to be offered the second five-week summer session. With that incentive I completed the writing by July 15 and was able to present the manuscript to this senior and graduate-level class. The manuscript was quickly revised based in part upon student responses and sent off to press." Again, Gill's students (the vast bulk of whom are non-Indian) inform the teacher (also a non-Indian) of what they want to hear, he responds by accommodating their desires, and the result becomes the stuff which passes as "proper understanding" of Indians in academe.

News of this incipient text induced a certain rumbling among Denver-area Indians, complete with letters of outrage from community leaders. The institutional response was that Gill, regardless of the merits of anything he may have said or written, was protected within the rubric of "academic freedom." Wallace Coffey, a Lakota who directs the Denver Indian Center, summed up community feeling at the time by observing that while the university was no doubt correct in claiming Gill's activities should be covered by academic freedom guarantees, "It's funny that every time a non-Indian wants to say something about Indians, no matter how outlandish or inaccurate, they start to talk about academic freedom. But every time an Indian applies for a faculty job, all they can talk about are 'academic standards.' I guess I'll be forgiven for saying it seems to me somebody's talking out of both sides of their mouth here. And I don't mind saying that I think this situation has a lot to do with why so few Indians ever get to teach in the universities in this state."

Not surprisingly, given the circumstances and overall context of its creation, when *Mother Earth* was eventually released it extended the thesis that Mother Earth had never been a *bona fide* element of indigenous tradition at all. Instead, the author held that the whole idea had been inculcated among American Indians by early European colonists, and had been developed and perfected since the conquest. With deadly predictability, he went on to conclude that, insofar as any special rights to North America accrue to a belief in Mother Earth, they must accrue to everyone Native and Euroamerican alike, equally. (One is left a bit unclear as to Gill's views on the proprietary interests of African and Asian Americans on the continent.) Thus, *Mother Earth* has the subtitle *An American* (rather than Native American) *Story*.

A Discussion with Sam Gill

Shortly after his book's release, I called Sam Gill on the phone. After a few moments of conversation, he asked whether I was upset by what he'd written. I replied that I was indeed quite upset and responded to his query as to why this might be with a long and somewhat disjointed discourse on the nature of cultural imperialism, the fact that he'd quoted material I'd ghost-written for others quite out of context, and my impression that he'd quite deliberately avoided including *any* American Indians directly in the research process by which he'd reached conclusions about them so profoundly antithetical to their own. "I think we had better meet in person," he said.

In response to his request to go deeper into some of the issues I'd raised on the phone, I explained at our meeting that I felt there was probably validity to the idea he'd articulated in *Mother Earth* that the interpretation and reinterpretation of the Mother Earth concept by succeeding generations of Euroamericans (such as Gill himself) had blocked any broad understanding of the original indigenous meaning of it. I also acknowledged that this additive phenomenon had, over the years, no doubt carried the popular notion of Mother Earth very far from any indigenous meaning. However, with that said, I stressed that nothing in either postulation precluded there already having been a well-developed indigenous Mother Earth concept operant in North America before contact. Further, I emphasized, he'd brought out nothing in his book which precluded an *ongoing* and autonomous Native American conceptualization of Mother Earth, divorced from popular (mis)understandings, exactly as traditionalist Indians presently claim.

"Well," he said, "this is interesting. I quite agree with you, and I think that's pretty much what I said in the book. Have you read it?" Taken by surprise, I reached across my desk for a copy and read an excerpt from page six:

> As I have come to know it, the story of Mother Earth is a distinctively American story. Mother Earth, as she has existed in North America, cannot be adequately understood and appreciated apart from the complex history of the encounter between Native Americans and Americans of European ancestry, nor apart from comprehending that *the scholarly enterprise that has sought to describe her has had a hand in bringing her into existence, a hand even in introducing her to Native American peoples* [emphasis added].

Without looking up, I skipped to page seven: "...*Mother Earth has come into existence in America largely within the last one hundred years...* When her story is told, it becomes clear how all Americans, whatever their heritage, may proclaim Mother Earth to be the mother of us all...[emphasis added]." And again, almost at random, from page 157: "Mother Earth is also mother to the Indians. This study has shown that *she has become so only recently,* and then not without influence from Americans...[emphasis added]." With the third quote, I indicated I could go on but figured the point had been made. At this juncture Gill suggested that perhaps he'd not been as clear in the writing of the book as he'd intended. I countered that while I agreed the text suffered certain difficulties in exposition, these particular passages seemed quite clear, in line with his overall treatise as I understood it, and lacking only in possible alternative interpretations. "Oh well," he said with a small shrug, "I never intended this as a book on religion anyway. I wrote it as a study in American history. Are you planning to review it?"

When I replied that, yes, I was, and as widely as possible, he said, "Then I'd very much appreciate it if you'd treat it as an historical work, not in the framework of religious studies. Fair enough?" To his surprise again, I agreed.

Gill's Historiography

There are a number of points of departure from which one might begin to assess Gill's historical project, none of them as telling as the way he defines the object of his quest. On the very first page, he declares that "Mother Earth is not only a Native American *goddess* but a *goddess* of people the world over...[emphasis added]." Two things are striking here:

- First, Gill seems from the outset simply to disregard the obvious literal meanings of statements by three different American Indians—the 19th-century Wanapum leader Smohalla, contemporary Navajo politician Peterson Zah, and AIM leader Russell Means—whom he quotes on the same page. In each of these diverse utterances, the speaker refers to the earth *herself* as being "the mother." All allegorical references to human anatomy—*e.g.*, the soil as "skin," rocks as "bones"—are clearly extended *from* this premise in an effort to allow the (non-Indian) listener to comprehend the concept at issue. *No* attempt is being made to utilize the earth as an allegory by which to explain some humanesque entity.

- Second, Gill immediately insists upon precisely this reversal of polarities, quoting Edward Tylor to the effect that, "among the native races of America the Earth Mother is one of the great *personages* of mythology [emphasis added]." He then reinforces this by quoting Ake Hultkrantz, a major topical Swedish scholar on American Indian religions: "The belief in a *goddess,* usually identified with Mother Earth, is found almost everywhere in North America [emphasis added]."

This is what is commonly referred to as "setting up a straw man." By thus "establishing" on the opening page that the Native American conception of Mother Earth assumes the Eurocentric form of a "goddess"—rather than the literal "earth deity" embodied in the articulated indigenous meaning—Gill has contrived a false context for his historical examination which allows him to reach *only* the conclusions he desires, *i.e.,* Mother Earth did not exist in Native North America prior to the European invasion.

Therefore, *ipso facto,* it follows that Europeans had as much or more to do with the creation of the indigenous conceptualization of Mother Earth than did the Indians themselves.

The conclusions will be "true," of course, given how the author has framed the questions. But one could as easily decide that, insofar as the yin and yang principles of Hinduism and Zen Buddhism embody male and female principles, they too "must" signify a god and goddess. Self-evidently, no amount of "historical scrutiny" will reveal the existence in these traditions of a god named Yin or a goddess named Yang (albeit, it may be possible to locate both "personages" at the Nairopa Institute in Boulder). Notwithstanding the fact that such god and goddess entities never had a place in the Buddhist or Hindu lexicons themselves, are we not bound by Gillian "logic" to conclude that neither the yin nor the yang principle ever had a place in the structure of either Hindu or Buddhist spiritual concepts? And, if we do manage to reach this absurd conclusion, does it not follow that since the terms yin and yang are now employed within the vernaculars of these traditions, they must have originated in the interaction between East and West, the concepts themselves "introduced" to the Orient by the Occident? To the extent that we can accept the whole charade up to this point, won't it follow that we are now entitled to consider Buddhism to be as much a part of our own non-Buddhist heritage (read: "property") as it is for the Buddhist Vietnamese, or even the Zen monks? Such questions tend to answer themselves.

In many ways, then, examination of Gill's historiography need go no further than this. A project as flawed at its inception as his offers little hope of reaching a productive outcome, a matter rendered all the more acute when an author exhibits as marked a propensity to manipulate data as does Gill, forcing it to conform to his predispositions regardless of the maiming and distortion which ensues. Examples of this last appear not only as described with regard to page one of *Mother Earth,* but in abundance—by the sins of both omission and commission—throughout the remainder of the book.

As concerns omission, one need only turn to a section entitled "The Triumph of Civilization over Savagism" (p. 30-39) to catch the drift. Here, we find Gill making much of the female Indian ("Mother Earth") iconography produced in Europe and its North American colonies from roughly 1575 until 1765. It is not that he handles what he discusses with any particular inaccuracy. Rather, it's that he completely neglects to mention that there was a roughly equal proportion of male Indian iconography streaming from the same sources during the same period. Along the same line, and in the same section, he goes into the impact of Pocahontas (female Indian, "Mother Earth") mythology on the formation of Americana without even an aside on the existence of its Hiawatha (male Indian) corollary. This sort of skewed presentation precludes the drawing of reasoned conclusions from the subject matter, and prevents the book from serving as a useful contribution to the literature.

In terms of commission, there is a small matter of Gill putting words (or meanings) into people's mouths. The clearest examples of this lie in Chapter seven (pp. 129-50), where he sets out to "prove" that the adoption of a belief in Mother Earth has led contemporary American Indians away from their traditional tribal/cultural specificity and toward a homogeneous sort of "pan-Indianism." (This is a variation on the standard rationalization that Indian rights no longer exist as such because Indians in the traditional sense no longer exist.) To illustrate this idea, he selects quotations from several individuals, including Grace (Spotted Eagle) Black Elk, Sun Bear, and Russell Means.

Grace Black Elk died recently and is therefore no longer able to clarify or debunk the meanings Gill assigns her words. However, in my own (extensive) experience with her, she was always *very* clear that, while she strongly and unswervingly supported the rights of all indigenous peoples to pursue their traditional spirituality, she herself followed *only* what she described as the "Lakota way." Further, she was consistently firm in her desire not to see the Lakota way diluted or "contaminated" by the introduction of other traditions. Such a position is obviously rather far from the somewhat amorphous, intertribal spiritual amalgam Gill claims she represented.

Sun Bear, for his part, has also been quite clear, albeit in an entirely different way. Marketing aside, he has stated repeatedly and for the record that the eclectic spiritual porridge he serves up has "nothing to do with Indian religion," "pan" or otherwise. He also has openly acknowledged that his adherents are composed almost exclusively of non-Indians; he admits that he tends to steer well clear of Indians these days, because they would "beat me up or kill me" due to the deliberately misleading marketing strategies he employs. *This* is the emblem of Gill's "emerging pan-Indianism?" As concerns Russell Means, Gill quotes repeatedly from a single speech delivered at the 1980 Black Hills Survival Gathering. While assigning a pan-Indianist meaning to the passages he elects to use, he carefully destroys the context in which the words were spoken. This includes categorical statements, toward the end of the speech, that Means does *not* consider or intend himself to be a "leader" in the pan-Indian sense, and that his thinking and actions are guided by a view of himself as "an Oglala Lakota patriot." Again, it is difficult to conceive a much clearer statement of tribally-specific orientation and motivation—and rejection of pan-Indianism—than this.

Ultimately, the reviewer is left with the feeling that he should replay in paraphrase a scene from the film, *Apocalypse Now*. Sam Gill, echoing Col. Kurtz (Marlon Brando), asks: "Do you find my methods to be unsound?"

The reviewer responding as Capt. Willard did (Martin Sheen), says: "Frankly, sir, I can't find any valid method at all."

A Question of "Revisionism"

The point has been made by Roger Echohawk, a Pawnee student at the University of Colorado, that even if Gill's historiography is lacking in certain important respects, there still could be a practical value and utility to his analysis of particular themes or sub-topics. The point is accurate enough on its face, if a bit strained, and is therefore worth pursuing at least to some extent. By way of example, we will concentrate on Gill's examination of the first of the major historical occurrences dealt with in *Mother Earth*—Tecumseh's "Mother Earth statement"—the negation of which is a linchpin to the author's arguments throughout the rest of the book.

After a brief but reasonably accurate depiction of Tecumseh's diplomatic and military confrontations with the United States (p. 8-13), Gill sets out to prove that the great Shawnee leader never actually made a particular statement—"The earth is my mother, and on her bosom I will repose"—during negotiations with William Henry Harrison in 1810. On pages 13-14, he notes that he has discovered a total of 27 references to this statement in the literature of the 19th century, the first of these in an article in the *National Recorder* on May 12, 1821, by an anonymous author. The next, he says on page 15, comes in a little-read history written by Moses Dawson, a former aide to Harrison and eyewitness to the negotiations, published in 1824. Then came Henry Rowe Schoolcraft's *Travels in the Central Portions of the Mississippi Valley* in 1825. After that, there were a steady stream of references, several by other eyewitnesses.

The obvious conclusion to be drawn from all this is that so many people refer to the Tecumseh statement for the simple reason that this is what the man said. The problem for Gill in this proposition, however, is that Tecumseh's having said it would seriously unhinge a portion of the thesis presented in *Mother Earth*. Hence, he faces the need to demonstrate that the words attributed to the Indian actually came from another, non-Indian source, and that all succeeding published references merely parroted what had been said before. The logical source in this scenario would be Schoolcraft, given that he was far and away the most popular, accessible, and thus quotable of the writers in question. This is problematic insofar as both the 1821 and 1824 references were published prior to Schoolcraft's book. Gill "solves" this difficulty on page fifteen by quietly "suggesting" that for unexplained reasons Schoolcraft—who was not at all known for a tendency to write anonymous tracts, and who was a "name" any editor would have gladly afforded a byline—authored the unattributed *Recorder* article in 1821, unaccountably fabricating the Tecumseh statement.

An implication of this thoroughly unsubstantiated "historical discovery," never brought out in *Mother Earth*, is that for some equally unexplained reason Dawson then must have opted deliberately to falsify *his* historical record of the negotiations by borrowing this fictional quotation from an obscure three-year-old article that even Gill describes as "filler" in the back pages of a magazine. After Schoolcraft's book, of course, he is much freer in writing off other eyewitness accounts as fabrications (at least with regard to the Tecumseh statement). This includes the account contained in Josiah Gregg's 1844 *Commerce of the Prairies* (covered on pp. 21-22), and the accounts of Augustus Jones and Major Joseph M. McCormick, recorded by Lyman D. Draper of the State Historical Society of Wisconsin during the mid-1880s (covered on pp. 23-24). All one need do is accept Gill's utterly unsubstantiated—

and unlikely—initial speculations, and his subsequent
chronology of systematic plagiarism works out splendidly.

Having thus dismissed standard history as nothing
short of a sustained hoax involving everyone from partic-
ipants to playwrights, Gill next sets out to "correct" the
record. This he purports to accomplish by referring to a
solitary eyewitness account, this time by a man named
Felix Bouchie, published in the *Vincennes Commercial* on
January 8, 1889 (covered on pp. 25-27). The article recounts an interchange between Tecumseh and Harrison
which occurred on a bench (not on the ground), lasting
every bit of five minutes during two full days of negotiations, and in which the Mother Earth statement (an
utterance which would require less than five seconds) is
not made. Bouchie does not state that Tecumseh did *not*
make the Mother Earth statement; he is simply recounting something else, and does not bring it up.

Again, there are obvious conclusions to be drawn.
For instance, it would seem likely—since there was ample
time available—that both the bench episode *and* the
Mother Earth episode might have occurred at different
points, or even different days during the negotiations.
Bouchie does not claim to have been present during the
entirety of the sessions, and his account could well be
viewed as a valuable *addition* to the record. Gill, however,
will have none of this. Rather, he insists that Bouchie's
version of events must have occurred *instead* of the other
27 more-or-less harmonious versions. This, he says, constitutes his final "proof" that the extremely well-documented Tecumseh statement is a fiction.

One senior American Indian scholar (who wishes to
remain anonymous), upon reviewing Gill's Tecumseh material, dismissed him as "a lunatic, not worth the time and
energy to argue with." In a less emotional and more
constructive vein, an Indian historian (who also asked to
be left unnamed), offered a more thoughtful insight:

You know, what we're confronted with here is not
uniquely—and maybe at this point not even primarily—
an American Indian issue. What this calls to mind more
than anything is the sort of "historical revisionism" practiced by people like Arthur Butz and Richard Harwood,
guys who use all sorts of pseudo-scholarly sleights-of-
hand to "prove" the Holocaust never happened. Their
stuff won't hold up to even minimal scrutiny, but they
keep right on going because they're ideologically motivated.

Precisely. And with that, there seems very little left
to say concerning the possible value of Sam Gill's historical analyses.

The New Age Ideological Project,
aka The Same Old Song of Europe

And so the question naturally arises: what sort of
ideology might prompt an individual like Sam Gill to write
a book lending itself to comparison with the sordid neo-
nazi sentiments of an Arthur Butz? Certainly he would
recoil in horror at the suggestion of such a linkage. Probably, the same can be said for any of his cohorts from
Castaneda to Highwater, from Sun Bear's ersatz Indians
to the ecology movement (with the possible exception of
the Earth First! Foreman/Abbey/Weurthner group, which
seems to have found its preferred niche under the term
"eco-fascist").

By and large, it also appears just as probable that all
those mentioned would vehemently disavow the historical
processes of physical genocide and expropriation visited
upon Native Americans by the federal government. In
their own minds, they are typically steadfast opponents
of all such policies and the ideologies of violence which
undergird them. At some level, they are no doubt sincere
in their oft and loudly repeated professions of being true
"Friends of the Indian." There can be no question that

they've convinced themselves that they are divorced completely from the ugly flow of American history.

Yet, demonstrably, as much as any missionary, soldier or government bureaucrat who preceeded them, those of the New Age have proven themselves willing to disregard the right of American Indians to a modicum of cultural sanctity or psychological sanctuary. They, too, willfully and consistently disregard the protests and objections of their victims, speaking only of their own "right to know" and to victimize. They, too, have exhibited an ability to pursue courses of conduct with arguably genocidal implications, to shrug off the danger, and to argue only that genocide couldn't be genocide if they are the perpetrators. They, too, have persistently shown themselves willing to lie, distort, fabricate, cheat and steal in order to accomplish their agenda. Why? What are they after?

The answers, in a real sense, are as simple as the fact that they are here and that they fully plan to stay. While the New Age can hardly be accused rationally of performing the conquest of the Americas, and its adherents go to great lengths in expressing their dismay at the methods used therein, they have clearly inherited what their ancestors gained by conquest, both in terms of resources and in terms of relative power. The New Agers, for all their protestations to the contrary, aren't about to give up any power. Their task, then, is simultaneously to hang on to what has been stolen while separating themselves from the *way* in which it was stolen. It is a somewhat tricky psychological project to be able to "feel good about themselves" (that ultimate expression of the New Age) through "legitimizing" the maintenance of their own colonial privilege. The project is essentially ideological. As Martin Carnoy has explained it:

> The legitimation of the colonist's role requires the destruction of the colonized sense of culture and history, so

the colonized is removed [or excluded] from all social and cultural responsibility.

Albert Memmi adds:

In order for the legitimacy to be complete, it is not enough for the colonized to be a slave [or thoroughly dispossessed and disenfranchised], he must also accept his role. The bond between colonizer and colonized is thus [both] destructive and creative.

Thus, within the context of our immediate concern, Native Americans are marginalized or barred from participation in the generation of "knowledge" concerning their histories, cultures and beliefs. The realities at issue are then systematically supplanted, negated and reconstructed to suit the psychological needs of the current crop of colonizers, and the result reproduced as "truth" among both the oppressors and oppressed. As early as 1973, Jamake Highwater was telling us that, "[truth] is not simply a matter of getting the facts wrong, but of developing a credible falsehood." In 1984, he went further:

The final belief is to believe in a fiction, which you know to be a fiction. There being nothing else, the exquisite truth is to know that it is a fiction and that you believe in it willingly.

In its final manifestation, the mythology which is forged ("created") in this process *always* assumes the form of an inclusive doctrine, legitimizing the present colonial *status quo*. The invaders' "contributions," however invented they may be, inevitably "entitle" them to superior status; there may have been a problem once, but it's in the past so forget it; were all in this together now, so let's move forward (with me in the lead); I'm OK, you're OK (so long as you stay in your place and don't upset me with questions of, or challenges to my privilege), and so on. We can now name the ideology which motivates the Sam Gills of America. It is called "New Age," but as Russell Means once remarked (in another connection) it represents only "the same old song of Europe." And, in the contemporary United States, its codification has rapidly become an academic growth industry.

Hence, the living fabric of Indian society is to be destroyed as its youth are "educated" to view their heritage in exactly the same way as those who seek to subsume it. This is no rupture with, but rather a continuation and perfection of, the twin systems of colonization and genocide which have afflicted Native America for the past 400 years. From this vantage point, false as it is from start to finish, the scholarly disgrace which constitutes *Mother Earth* really *is* an "American Story."

Sources

Adams, Hank, *Cannibal Green* (on Jamake Highwater), Survival of American Indians, Olympia, WA, 1984.

Butz, Arthur D., *The Hoax of the Twentieth Century: The Case Against the Presumed Extermination of European Jewry*, Institute for Historical Review, Torrance, CA, 1977.

Carnoy, Martin, *Education as Cultural Imperialism*, David McKay Company, New York, 1974.

Churchill, Ward, "Ayn Rand and the Sioux Tonto Revisited: Another Look at *Hanta Yo*," *Lakota Eyapaha*, Vol. 4, No. 2, Oglala Sioux Community College, June 1980.

DeMille, Richard, *Castaneda's Journey*, Capra Press, Santa Barbara, CA, 1976.

DeMille, Richard (ed.), *The Don Juan Papers: Further Castaneda Controversies*, Ross-Erikson Publishers, Santa Barbara, CA, 1980.

Gill, Sam, "The Continuity of Research and Classroom Teaching, or How to Have Your Cake and Eat It Too," in Mary Ann Shea (ed.), *On Teaching*, Faculty Teaching Excellence Program, University of Colorado/Boulder, 1987.

Harwood, Richard, *Did Six Million Really Die?*, Historical Review Press, Richmond, Surrey, England, 1974.

Means, Russell, "The Same Old Song," in Ward Churchill (ed.), *Marxism and Native Americans*, South End Press, Boston, 1983.

Memmi, Albert, *Colonizer and Colonized*, Beacon Press, Boston, 1965.

Red Fox, William, *The Memoirs of Chief Red Fox*, Fawcett Books, New York, 1972.

Seals, David, *The Pow Wow Highway*, Sky Press, Denver, 1984.

Storm, Hyemeyohsts, *Seven Arrows*, Ballantine Books, New York, 1972.

"Sun Bear" and "Wabun," *The Medicine Wheel: Earth Astrology*, Prentice-Hall Publishers, Englewood Cliffs, NJ, 1980.

Wuerthner, George, "An Ecological View of the Indian," *Earth First!*, Vol. 7, No. 7, August 1987.

Spiritual Hucksterism

The Rise of the Plastic Medicine Men

Yes, I know of Sun Bear. He's a plastic medicine man.

—Matthew King
Oglala Lakota Elder
1985

The past 20 years have seen the birth of a new growth industry in the United States. Known as "American Indian Spiritualism," this profitable enterprise apparently began with a number of literary hoaxes undertaken by such non-Indians as Carlos Castaneda, J. Marks (aka "Jamake Highwater," author of *The Primal Mind*, etc.), Ruth Beebe Hill (of *Hanta Yo* notoriety), and Lynn Andrews (*Medicine Woman, Jaguar Woman, Crystal Woman, Spirit Woman*, etc.). A few Indians such as Alonzo Blacksmith (aka: "Chunksa Yuha," the "Indian authenticator" of *Hanta Yo*), "Chief Red Fox" (*Memoirs of Chief Red Fox*) and Hyemeyohsts Storm (*Seven Arrows*, etc.) also cashed in, writing bad distortions and outright lies about indigenous spirituality for consumption in the mass market. The authors grew rich peddling their trash while real Indians starved to death, out of the sight and mind of America.

This situation has been long and bitterly attacked by legitimate Indian scholars, from Vine Deloria, Jr. to Bea Medicine, and by activists such as American Indian Movement (AIM) leader Russell Means, Survival of American Indians (SAIL) director Hank Adams, and the late Gerald Wilkenson, head of the National Indian Youth Council (NIYC). Nonetheless, the list of phony books claiming

215

alternately to "debunk" or "expose the innermost meanings of" Indian spirituality continues to grow as publishers recognize a sure-fire money-maker when they see one. Most lately, ostensibly scholarly publishers like the University of Chicago Press have joined the parade, generating travesties such as University of Colorado Professor Sam Gill's *Mother Earth: An American Story.*

The insistence of mainstream America upon buying such nonsense has led Deloria to conclude that, "White people in this country are so alienated from their own lives and so hungry for some sort of real life that they'll grasp at any straw to save themselves. But high tech society has given them a taste for the 'quick fix.' They want their spirituality prepackaged in such a way as to provide *instant* insight, the more sensational and preposterous the better. They'll pay big bucks to anybody dishonest enough to offer them spiritual salvation after reading the right book or sitting still for the right fifteen minute session. And, of course, this opens them up to every kind of mercenary hustler imaginable. Its all very pathetic, really."

Oren Lyons, a traditional chief of the Onondaga Nation, concedes Deloria's point, but says the problem goes much deeper. "Non-Indians have become so used to all this hype on the part of imposters and liars that when a real Indian spiritual leader tries to offer them useful advice, he is rejected. He isn't 'Indian' enough for all these non-Indian experts on Indian religion. Now, this is not only degrading to Indian people, it's downright delusional behavior on the part of the instant experts who think they've got all the answers before they even hear the questions."

"The bottom line here," says Lyons, "is that we have more need for intercultural respect today than at any time in human history. And nothing blocks respect and communication faster and more effectively than delusions by one party about another. We've got real problems today, tremendous problems which threaten the survival of the planet. Indians and non-Indians *must* confront these problems together, and this means we *must* have honest dialogue, but this dialogue is impossible so long as non-Indians remain deluded about things as basic as Indian spirituality."

Things would be bad enough if American Indian realities were being distorted only through books and movies. But, since 1970, there has also been a rapid increase in the number of individuals purporting to sell "Indian wisdom" in a more practical way. Following the example of people such as the "Yogi Ramacharaka" and "Maharaji Ji," who have built lucrative careers marketing bastardizations of East Asian mysticism, these new entrepreneurs have begun cleaning up on selling "Native American Ceremonies" for a fee.

As Janet McCloud, a long-time fishing rights activist and elder of the Tulalip Nation, puts it, "First they came to take our land and water, then our fish and game. Then they wanted our mineral resources and, to get them, they tried to take our governments. Now they want our religions as well. All of a sudden, we have a lot of unscrupulous idiots running around saying they're medicine people. And they'll sell you a sweat lodge ceremony for fifty bucks. It's not only wrong, its obscene. Indians don't sell their spirituality to anybody, for any price. This is just another in a very long series of thefts from Indian people and, in some ways, this is the worst one yet."

McCloud is scornful of the many non-Indian individuals who have taken up such practices professionally. "These people run off to reservations acting all lost and hopeless, really pathetic. So, some elder is nice enough, considerate enough to be kind to them, and how do they repay this generosity? After fifteen minutes with a spiritual leader, they consider themselves 'certified' medicine people, and then run amok, 'spreading the word'—for a fee. Some of them even proclaim themselves to be 'official spiritual representatives' of various Indian peoples. I'm talking about people like Dyhani Ywahoo and Lynn Andrews. It's absolutely disgusting."

But her real disdain is for those Indians who have taken up the practice of marketing their heritage to the highest bidder. "We've also got Indians who are doing these things," McCloud continues. "We've got our Sun Bears and our Wallace Black Elks and others who'd sell their own mother if they thought it would turn a quick buck. What they're selling isn't theirs to sell, and they know it. They're thieves and sell-outs, and they know that too. That's why you never see them around Indian people anymore. When we have our traditional meetings and gatherings, you never see the Sun Bears and those sorts showing up."

As Thomas Banyacya, a spiritual elder of the Hopi, explains, "these people have nothing to say on the matters they claim to be so expert about. To whites, they claim they're 'messengers,' but from whom? They are not the messengers of Indian people. I am a messenger, and I do not charge for my ceremonies."

Some of the more sophisticated marketeers, such as Sun Bear, have argued that the criticisms of McCloud and Banyacya are misguided. Sun Bear has claimed that the ceremonies and "wisdom" he peddles are not truly Indian, although they are still "based on" Indian traditions. Yet, his promotional literature still refers to "Native American Spiritual Wisdom," and offers ceremonies such as the sweat lodge for $50 per session, and "vision quests" at $150.

"Since when is the sweat not an Indian ceremony?" demands Russell Means, an outspoken critic of Sun Bear and his colleagues. "It's not 'based on' an Indian ceremony, it *is* an Indian ceremony. So is his so-called 'vision quest,' the pipe, his use of the pipe, sage and all the rest of it. Sun Bear is a liar, and so are all the rest of them who are doing what he's doing. All of them know good and well that the only reason anybody is buying their product is because of this image of "Indian-ness" they project. The most non-Indian thing about Sun Bear's ceremonies is that he's personally prostituted the whole thing by turning it into a money-making venture."

Sun Bear has also contended that criticism of his activities is ill-founded because he has arrived at a spiritual stew of several traditions—his medicine wheel is Shoshoni and his herbal and other healing remedies accrue from numerous peoples, while many of his other ceremonies are Lakota in origin—and because he's started his own "tribe," of which he's pronounced himself medicine chief. Of course, membership in this odd new entity, composed almost exclusively of Euroamericans, comes with a hefty price tag attached. The idea has caught on among spiritual hucksters, as witnessed by the formation of a similar fees-paid group in Florida, headed by a non-Indian calling himself "Chief Piercing Eyes."

"This is exactly the problem," says Nilak Butler, an Inuit activist working in San Francisco. "Sun Bear says he's not revealing some sort of secret Indian ways whenever there are Indians around to hear him. The rest of the time, he's the most 'Indian' guy around, to hear him tell it. Whenever he's doing his spiel, anyway. But, you see, if there were any truth to his rap, he wouldn't have to be running around starting 'new tribes' and naming himself head honcho and dues collector. He'd be a leader among his own people."

According to Rick Williams, a Cheyenne/Lakota working at the University of Colorado, "Sun Bear isn't recognized as any sort of leader, spiritual or otherwise, among his own Chippewa people. He's not qualified. It takes a lifetime of apprenticeship to become the sort of spiritual leader Sun Bear claims to be, and he never went through any of that. He's just a guy who hasn't been home to the White Earth Reservation in 25 years, pretending to be something he's not, feeding his own ego and making his living misleading a lot of sincere, but very silly people. In a lot of ways he reminds you of a low grade Jimmy Swaggart or Pat Robertson-type individual."

Williams goes on, "Sun Bear hasn't started a new tribe. *Nobody* can just up and start a new tribe. What he's done is start a cult. And this cult he's started is playing with some very powerful things, like the pipe. That's not only stupid and malicious, it's *dangerous.*"

The danger Williams refers to has to do with the very power which makes American Indian spirituality so appealing to non-Indians in the first place. According to the late Matthew King, an elder spiritual leader among the Oglala Lakota, "Each part of our religion has its power and its purpose. Each people has their own ways. You cannot mix these ways together, because each people's ways are balanced. Destroying balance is a disrespect and very dangerous. This is why it's forbidden.

"Many things are forbidden in our religion," King continued. "The forbidden things are acts of disrespect, things which unbalance power. These things must be learned, and the learning is very difficult. This is why there are very few real 'medicine men' among us; only a few are chosen. For someone who has not learned how our balance is maintained, to pretend to be a medicine man is very, very dangerous. It is a big disrespect to the powers and can cause great harm to whoever is doing it, to those he claims to be teaching, to nature, to everything. It is very bad..."

For all the above reasons, the Circle of Elders of the Indigenous Nations of North America, the representative body of traditional indigenous leadership on this continent, requested that the American Indian Movement undertake to end the activities of those described as "plastic medicine men." The possibly sexist descriptor refers to individuals of both genders trading in the commercialization of indigenous spirituality. At its National Leadership Conference in 1984, AIM passed a resolution indicating

that the will of the elders would be implemented. Specifically mentioned in the AIM resolution were "Sun Bear
and the so-called Bear Tribe Medicine Society" and "Wallace Black Elk and [the late] Grace Spotted Eagle of
Denver, Colorado," as well as others like Cyfus McDonald,
Brook Medicine Eagle (spelled "Ego" in the resolution),
Osheana Fast Wolf and a corporation dubbed "Vision
Quest." Others, such as Dyhani Ywahoo, Rolling Thunder,
and "Beautiful Painted Arrow" have been subsequently
added to the list.

As Russell Means put it at the time, "These people
have insisted upon making themselves pariahs within
their own communities, and they will have to bear the
consequences of that. As to white people who think it's
cute, or neat or groovy or keen to hook up with plastic
medicine men, to subsidize and promote them, and claim
you and they have some fundamental 'right' to desecrate
our spiritual traditions, I've got a piece of news for you.
You have *no* such right. Our religions are *ours*. Period. We
have very strong reasons for keeping certain things private, whether you understand them or not. And we have
every human right to deny them to you, whether you like
it or not.

"You can either respect our basic rights or not respect them," Means went on. "If you do, you're an ally and
we're ready and willing to join hands with you on other
issues. If you do not, you are at best a thief. More importantly, you are a thief of the sort who is willing to risk
undermining our sense of the integrity of our cultures for
your own perceived self-interest. That means you are
complicit in a process of cultural genocide, or at least
attempted cultural genocide, aimed at American Indian
people. That makes you an enemy, to say the least. And
believe me when I say we're prepared to deal with you as
such."

Almost immediately, the Colorado AIM chapter undertook a confrontation with Sun Bear in the midst of a

$500 per head, weekend-long "spiritual retreat" being conducted near the mountain town of Granby. The action provoked the following endorsement from the normally more staid NIYC:

> The National Indian Youth Council fully supports your efforts to denounce, embarrass, disrupt, or otherwise run out of Colorado, the Medicine Wheel Gathering...For too long the Bear Tribe Medicine Society has been considered repugnant but harmless to Indian people. We believe they not only line their pockets but do great damage to all of us. Anything you can do to them will not be enough.

The Colorado AIM action, and the strength of indigenous support it received, resulted in a marked diminishment of Sun Bear's reliance upon the state as a source of revenue.

Since then, AIM has aligned itself solidly and consistently with indigenous traditionalism, criticizing Sun Bear and others of his ilk in public fashion, and occasionally physically disrupting their activities in locations as diverse as Denver and Atlanta. Those who wish to assist in this endeavor should do so by denouncing plastic medicine folk wherever they appear, organizing pro-active boycotts of their events, and demanding that local book stores stop carrying titles, not only by Sun Bear and his non-Indian sidekick "Wabun," but charlatans like Castaneda, Jamake Highwater, Lynn Andrews and Hyemeyohsts Storm as well. Use your imagination as to how to get the job done in your area, but make it stick. You should also be aware that Sun Bear and others have increasingly aligned themselves with such non-Indian support groups as local police departments, calling upon them to protect him from "Indian interference" with his unauthorized sale of Indian spirituality.

Resolution of the 5th Annual Meeting of the Tradition Elders Circle

Northern Cheyenne Nation, Two Moons' Camp
Rosebud Creek, Montana
October 5, 1980

It has been brought to the attention of the Elders and their representatives in Council that various individuals are moving about this Great Turtle Island and across the great waters to foreign soil, purporting to be spiritual leaders. They carry pipes and other objects sacred to the Red Nations, the indigenous people of the western hemisphere.

These individuals are gathering non-Indian people as followers who believe they are receiving instructions of the original people. We, the Elders and our representatives sitting in Council, give warning to these non-Indian followers that it is our understanding this is not a proper process, that the authority to carry these sacred objects is given by the people, and the purpose and procedure is specific to time and the needs of the people.

The medicine people are chosen by the medicine and long instruction and discipline is necessary before ceremonies and healing can be done. These procedures are always in the Native tongue; there are no exceptions and profit is not the motivation.

There are many Nations with many and varied procedures specifically for the welfare of their people. These processes and ceremonies are of the most Sacred Nature. The Council finds the open display of these ceremonies contrary to these Sacred instructions.

Therefore, be warned that these individuals are moving about playing upon the spiritual needs and ignorance of our non-Indian brothers and sisters. The value of these instructions and ceremonies are questionable, maybe meaningless, and hurtful to the individual carrying false messages. There are questions that should be asked of these individuals:

1) What Nation does the person represent?
2) What is their Clan and Society?
3) Who instructed them and where did they learn?
4) What is their home address?

If no information is forthcoming, you may inquire at the addresses listed below, and we will try to find out about them for you.

We concern ourselves only with those people who use spiritual ceremonies with non-Indian people for profit. There are many things to be shared with the Four Colors of humanity in our common destiny as one with our Mother the Earth. It is this sharing that must be considered with great care by the Elders and the medicine people who carry the Sacred Trusts, so that no harm may come to people through ignorance and misuse of these powerful forces.

Signed,

Tom Yellowtail
Wyola, MT 59089

Larry Anderson
Navajo Nation
P.O. Box 342
Fort Defiance, AZ 86504

Izadore Thom
Beech Star Route
Bellingham, WA 98225

Thomas Banyacya
Hopi Independent Nation
Shungopavy Pueblo
Second Mesa via AZ 86043

Phillip Deere (deceased)
Muskogee (Creek) Nation (in tribute)

Walter Denny
Chippewa-Cree Nation
Rocky Boy Route
Box Elder, MT 59521

Austin Two Moons
Northern Cheyenne Nation
Rosebud Creek, MT

Tadadaho
Haudenasaunee
Onondaga Nation via
Nedrow, NY 13120

Chief Fools Crow (deceased)
Lakota Nation (in tribute)

Frank Cardinal, Sr.
Chateh, P.O. Box 120
Assumption, Alberta
Canada T0M 0S0

Peter O'Chiese
Entrance Terry Ranch
Entrance, Alberta
Canada

AIM Resolution

Sovereign Diné Nation
Window Rock, AZ
May 11, 1984

Whereas the Spiritual wisdom which is shared by the Elders with the people has been passed to us through the Creation from time immemorial; and

Whereas the Spirituality of Indian Nations is inseparable from the people themselves; and

Whereas the attempted theft of Indian ceremonies is a direct attack and theft from Indian people themselves; and

Whereas there has been a dramatic increase in the incidence of selling of Sacred ceremonies, such as the sweat lodge and the vision quest, and of Sacred articles, such as religious pipes, feathers, and stone; and

Whereas these practices have been and continue to be conducted by Indians and non-Indians alike, constituting not only insult and disrespect for the wisdom of the ancients, but also exposing ignorant non-Indians to potential harm and even death through the misuse of these ceremonies; and

Whereas the traditional Elders and Spiritual leaders have repeaatedly warned against and condemned the commercialization of our ceremonies; and

Whereas such commercialization has increased dramatically in recent years, to wit:

- the representations of Cyfus McDonald, Osheana Fast Wolf, and Brook Medicine Ego, all non-Indian women representing themselves as "Sacred Women," and who, in the case of Cyfus McDonald, have defrauded Indian people of Sacred articles;

- A non-Indian woman going by the name of "Quanda" representing herself as a "Healing Woman" and charging $20 for sweat lodges;

- Sun Bear and the so-called "Bear Tribe Medicine Society," who engage in the sale of Indian ceremonies and Sacred objects, operating out of the state of Washington, but traveling and speaking throughout the United States;

- Wallace Black Elk and Grace Spotted Eagle, Indian people operating in Denver, Colorado, charging up to $50 for so-called "Sweat Lodge Workshops;"

- A group of non-Indians operating out of Boulder, Colorado, and throughout the Southwest, and audaciously calling itself "Vision Quest, Inc.," thereby stealing the name and attempting to steal the concept of one of our most Spiritual ceremonies;

Therefore, be it resolved that the Southwest AIM Leadership Conference reiterates the position articulated by our Elders at the First American Indian Tribunal held at D.Q. University, September 1982, as follows:

Now, to those who are doing these things, we send our third warning. Our Elders ask, "Are you prepared to take the consequences of your actions? You will be outcasts from your people if you continue these practices"...Now, this is another one. Our young people are getting restless. They are the ones who sought their Elders in the first place to teach them the Sacred ways. They have said they will take care of those who are abusing our Sacred ceremonies and Sacred objects in their own way. In this way they will take care of their Elders.

We Resolve to protect our Elders and our traditions, and we condemn those who seek to profit from Indian Spirituality. We put them on notice that our patience grows thin with them and they continue their disrespect at their own risk.

Part VI

Turning Indians into Cowboys

Fantasies of the Master Race

Categories of Stereotyping
of American Indians in Film

Now those movie Indians wearing all those feathers can't
come out as human beings. They're not expected to come
out as human beings because I think the American people
do not regard them as wholly human. We must remember
that many, many American children believe that feathers
grow out of Indian heads.

—Stephan Feraca
Motion Picture Director
1964

The handling of American Indians and American
Indian subject matter within the context of commercial
U.S. cinema is objectively racist on all levels, an observation which extends to television as well as film. In this
vein, it is linked closely to literature both fictional non-fictional, upon which many if not most movie scripts are at
least loosely based. In a very real sense, it is fair to observe
that all modes of projecting concepts and images of the
Indian before the contemporary U.S. public fit the same
mold, and do so for the same fundamental "real world"
reasons. This essay will attempt to come to grips with both
the method and the motivation for this, albeit within a
given medium and examining a somewhat restricted
range of the tactics employed. The medium selected for
this purpose is commercial film, the technique examined
that of stereotypic projection. The matter divides itself
somewhat automatically into three major categories of
emphasis. These may be elucidated as follows.

231

The American Indian
as a Creature of Another Time

We are all aware of the standard motion picture technique of portraying the Native American with galloping pony and flowing headdress. We have seen the tipi and the buffalo hunt, the attack on the wagon train and the ambush of the stagecoach until they are scenes so totally ingrained in the American consciousness as to be synonymous with the very concept of the American Indian (to non-Indian minds at any rate and, unfortunately, to many Indian minds as well). It is not the technical defects of the scenes depicted here—although often they are many—which present the basic problem. Rather, it is that the historical era involved spans a period scarcely exceeding 50 years' duration. Hence, the Indian has been restricted in the public mind, not only in terms of the people portrayed (the Plains Nations), but in terms of the time of their collective existence (roughly 1825-1880).

The essential idea of Native America instilled cinematically is that of a quite uniform aggregation of peoples (in dress, custom and actions) which flourished with the arrival of whites upon their land and then vanished somewhat mysteriously, along with the bison and the open prairie. There is no "before" to this story, and there is no "after." Such is the content of *They Died With Their Boots On, Boots and Saddles, Cheyenne Autumn, Tonka Wakan* and *Little Big Man,* to list but five examples from among hundreds. Of course, commercial film has—albeit in many fewer cases—slightly expanded the scope of the stereotype. The existence of the peoples of the Northeast receive recognition in such epics as *Drums Along the Mohawk* and *The Deerslayer.* The peoples of the Southwest have been included, to some extent, in scattered fare such as *Broken Arrow, Fort Apache* and *Tell Them Willie Boy Was Here.* The Southeastern nations even claim passing attention in efforts such as the Walt Disney *Davy Crockett* series and biographical features about the lives of such Euroamerican heroes as Andrew Jackson and Sam Houston.

The latter deviations from the Plains stereotype—which has assumed proportions of a valid archetype in the public consciousness—drives the timeline back some 75 years at most. A century-and-a-quarter selected for depiction is hardly better than a fifty-year span. Further, it should be noted that, costuming aside, literally all the geographical/cultural groups presented are portrayed in exactly the same manner, a matter we will consider in the following two sections. The point of the historical confines involved in this category, however, is that indigenous people are defined exclusively in terms of certain (conflict and demise) interactions with Euroamericans. There is no cinematic recognition whatsoever of a white-free and autonomous native past. Similarly, no attention is paid at all to the myriad indigenous nations not heavily and dramatically involved in the final period of Anglo-Indian warfare. U.S. audiences know no Aztec, Inca or Anasazi parallel to *Cleopatra, The Robe* or *Ben Hur*. Small wonder the public views the native as some briefly extant, mythic and usually hostile apparition. As a consequence, the public perception of the historical existence of Native Americans is of beings who spent their time serving as little other than figurative pop-up targets for non-Indian guns.

Nor is there an abundance of films attempting to deal with contemporary Indian realities. In effect, the native ceased to exist after the onset of the reservation period of the Plains peoples. This is evidenced by the fact that the author could find only two films listed—biographies of Jim Thorpe and Ira Hayes, both starring Burt Lancaster—released prior to 1980 which featured the indigenous experience after 1880 in any meaningful way at all. As to current events, well... There's always the *Billy Jack* series: *Born Losers, Billy Jack, The Trial of Billie Jack* and *Billie Jack Goes to Washington* (the latter, thankfully, was shelved before release), utilizing the vehicle of an ex-Special Forces mixed-blood karate expert to exploit the grisly mystique of Shaft and Superfly-type superheroes (or antiheroes, if you prefer). The result is a predictably shallow and idiotic parallel to the *Batman* t.v. series.

The single (lackluster) attempt by Hollywood to equal for American Indians what *Sounder* and *Lady Sings the Blues* have achieved for Afroican-Americans was rapidly withdrawn from circulation as an "embarrassment." So steeped in celluloid myopia are filmdom's critics—so full, that is, of their own self-perpetuating stereotyping— that they panned the characters in *Journey Through Rosebud* as "wooden Indians." This, despite the fact that most Native Americans viewing them ranked them as the most accurate and convincing ever to come from the studios. Possibly, other films of the stature of *Journey Through Rosebud* have been made but not released, in effect doing nothing to alter the time-warp involving American Indians in film. A result is that the U.S. mainstream population finds itself under no particular moral or psychic obligation to confront the fact of Native America, as either an historical or topical reality.

Native Cultures Defined by Eurocentric Values

An Anishinabe (Chippewa) friend of mine once visited the Field Museum in Chicago. While examining the exhibits of American Indian artifacts located there, she came across an object which she immediately recognized as being her grandmother's root digger, an item the museum's anthropological "experts" had identified and labeled as a "Winnebago hide scraper." She called the mistake to the attention of the departmental director and was told that she, not the museum, was wrong. "If you knew anything at all about your heritage," he informed her, "you'd know that tool is a hide scraper." My friend, helpless to correct this obvious (to her) misinformation, went away. "They never listen to the people who really know these things," she said later. "And so they never understand what they think they know."

The above sad-but-true story is not unusual. It serves to illustrate a pattern in Euroamerican dealings with indigenous people which extends vastly beyond the mere identification of objects. In terms of commercial cinema and acting, the problem may be considered on the basis of "context" and "motivation." Put most simply, the question of context is one in which specific acts of certain American Indians are portrayed in scenes devoid of all cultural grounding and explanation. From whence is comprehension of the real nature of these acts to come? The viewing audience is composed overwhelmingly of non-Indians who obviously hold no automatic insight into native cultures and values, yet somehow they must affix meaning to the actions presented on the screen. Scenes such as those presented in the John Ford "classic," *Stagecoach*, are fine examples of this stereotyping approach. Thus, the real acts of indigenous people—even when depicted more-or-less accurately—often appear irrational, cruel, unintelligent or silly when displayed in film.

Motivation is a more sophisticated, and consequently more dangerous, consideration. Here, a cultural context of sorts is provided, at least to some degree, but it is a context comprised exclusively of ideas, values, emotions and other meanings assigned by Euroamerica to the native cultures portrayed. Insofar as indigenous American and Euro-derived worldviews are radically and demonstrably different in almost every way, such a projection can only serve to misrepresent dramatically the native cultures involved and render them nonsensical at best. Such misrepresentation serves two major stereotyping functions. Since the complex of dominant and comparatively monolithic cultural values and beliefs of

Eurocentrism presently held by the bulk of the U.S. population are utilized to provide motivation for virtually all American Indians portrayed in commercial film, all native values and beliefs appear to be lumped together into a single homogeneous and consistent whole, regardless of actual variances and distinctions (the following section discusses the result of this phenomenon).

Given that the cultural values and beliefs extended as the contextual basis for motivation are misrepresentative of the actual cultural context of Native America—and are thus totally out of alignment with the actions portrayed—the behavior of American Indians is often made to appear more uniformly vicious, crude, primitive and unintelligent than in cases where context and motivation are dispensed with altogether.

A primary device used by Hollywood to attach Eurocentric values to native acts has been to script a white character to narrate the story-line. Films such as *Cheyenne Autumn, A Man Called Horse* (and its sequels), *Soldier Blue* and *Little Big Man* exemplify the point. Each purports to provide an "accurate and sympathetic treatment of the American Indian" (of yesteryear) while utterly crushing native identity under the heel of Euroamerican interpretation. To date, all claims to the contrary notwithstanding, there has not been one attempt to put out a commercial film which deals with native reality through native eyes.

"Seen One Indian, Seen 'em All"

This third category is, in some ways, a synthesis of the preceding two. It has, however, assumed an identity of its own which extends far beyond the scope of the others. Within this area lies the implied assumption that distinctions between cultural groupings of indigenous people are either nonexistent (ignorance) or irrelevant (arrogance). Given this attitude regarding the portrayal of Indians in film, it is inevitable that the native be reduced from reality to a strange amalgamation of dress, speech, custom and belief. All vestiges of truth—and thereby of intercultural understanding—give way here before the onslaught of movieland's mythic creation.

The film *A Man Called Horse* may serve as an example. This droll adventure, promoted as "the most authentic description of North American Indian life ever filmed," depicts a people whose language is Lakota, whose hairstyles range from Assiniboin through Nez Percé to Comanche, whose tipi design is Crow, and whose Sun Dance ceremony and the lodge in which it is held are both typically Mandan. They are referred to throughout the film as "Sioux," but to which group do they supposedly belong? Secungu (Brûlé)? Oglala? Santee? Sisseton? Yanktonai? Minneconjou? Hunkpapa? Those generically—and rather pejoratively—called "Sioux" were/are of three major geographic/cultural divisions: the Dakotas of the Minnesota woodlands, the Nakotas of the prairie region east of the Missouri River, and the Lakotas of the high plains proper. These groups were/are quite distinct from one another, and the distinctions *do* make a difference in terms of accuracy and "authenticity."

The source material utilized to create the cinematic imagery involved in *A Man Called Horse* was the large number of portraits of American Indians executed by George Catlin during the first half of the 19th century and now housed in the Smithsonian Institution. However, while Catlin was meticulous in attributing tribal and even band affiliations to the subjects of his paintings, the film-makers were not. The result is a massive misrepresentation of a whole variety of real peoples, aspects of whose cultures are incorporated, gratuitously, into that of the hybrid "Indians" who inhabit the movie.

Nor does the dismemberment of reality in this "most realistic of westerns" end with visual catastrophe. The door to cultural reduction is merely opened by such devices. Both the rationale and spiritual ramifications of the Sun Dance are voided by the film's Eurocentric explanation of its form and function. Thus is the Lakota's central and most profoundly sacred of all ceremonies converted into a macho exercise in "self-mutilation," a "primitive initiation rite" showing that the Indian male could "take it." It follows that the film's Anglo lead (Richard Harris) must prove that he is "as tough as the Sioux" by eagerly seeking out his fair share of pain during a Sun Dance. He does this in order to be accepted as "one of them." Just bloody up your chest and no further questions will be asked. How quaint.

This, of course, paves the way for the Harris character to become leader of the group. The Sioux, once they have been reduced to little more than a gaggle of prideful masochists, are readily shown to be possessed of little collective intellect (surprise, surprise). Hence, it becomes necessary for the Anglo captive to save his savage captors from an even more ferocious group of primitives coming over the hill. He manages this somewhat spectacular feat by instructing his aboriginal colleagues in the finer points of using the bow, a weapon in uninterrupted use by the people in question for several hundred generations, and out of use by the English for about 200 years at the time the events in the film supposedly occur. But no matter the trivial details. The presumed inherent superiority of Eurocentric minds has once again been demonstrated for all the world to witness. All that was necessary to accomplish this was to replace a *bona fide* native culture with something else.

The technique employed in *A Man Called Horse* is by no means novel or unique. Even the highly-touted (in terms of making Indians "the good guys") *Billy Jack* series could never lock in any specific people it sought to portray. The Indians depicted remain a weird confluence of Navajos and various Pueblos, occasionally practicing what appear to be bastardizations of Cheyenne and Kiowa ceremonies. All the better to trot them around as props for every non-Indian fad from the benefits of macrobiotic cookery to those of Haikido karate.

It is elementary logic to realize that when the cultural identity of a people is symbolically demolished, the achievements and very humanity of that people must also be disregarded. The people, as such, disappear, usually to the benefit—both material and psychic—of those performing the symbolic demolition. There are accurate and appropriate terms which describe this: dehumanization, obliteration or appropriation of identity, political subordination and material colonization are all elements of a common process of imperialism. This is the real meaning of Hollywood's stereotyping of American Indians.

Conclusion

It should be relatively easy at this point to identify film stereotyping of American Indians as an accurate reflection of the actual conduct of the Euroamerican population *vis-à-vis* Native America in both historical and topical senses. North American indigenous peoples have been reduced in terms of cultural identity within the popular consciousness—through a combination of movie treatments, television programming and distortive literature—to a point where the general public perceives them as extinct for all practical intents and purposes. Given that they no longer exist, that which *was* theirs—whether land and the resources on and beneath it, or their heritage—can *now* be said, without pangs of guilt, to belong to those who displaced and ultimately supplanted them. Such is one function of cinematic stereotyping within North America's advanced colonial system.

Another is to quell potential remorse among the population at large. Genocide is, after all, an extremely ugly word. Far better that the contemporary mainstream believe their antecedents destroyed mindless and intrinsi-

cally warlike savages, devoid of true culture and humanity, rather than that they systematically exterminated
whole societies of highly intelligent and accomplished
human beings who desired nothing so much as to be left
in peace. Far better for their descendants if the Euroamerican invader engaged in slaughter only in self-defense, when confronted with hordes of irrationally
bloodthirsty heathen beasts, rather than coldly and calcu-
latedly committing mass murder, planning step by step
the eradication of the newest-born infants. "Nits make
lice," to quote U.S. Colonel John M. Chivington.

Filmdom's handling of "history" in this regard is,
with only a few marginal exceptions, nothing more or less
than an elaborate denial of European/Euroamerican criminality on this continent over the past 350 years. Implicitly
then, it is an unbridled justification and glorification of
the conquest and subordination of Native America. As
such, it is a vitally necessary ingredient in the maintenance and perfection of the Euroempire which began
when the Pilgrims landed in 1620. Hollywood's performance on this score has been, overall, what one might
have legitimately expected to see from the heirs to Leni
Riefenstahl, had the Third Reich won its War in the East
during the 1940s.

As the Oneida comedian Charlie Hill has observed,
the portrayal of Indians in the cinema has been such that
it has made the playing of "Cowboys and Indians" a favorite
American childhood game. The object of the "sport" is for
the "cowboys" to "kill" all the "Indians," just like in the
movies. A bitter irony associated with this is that Indian
as well as non-Indian children heatedly demand to be
identified as cowboys, a not unnatural outcome under the
circumstances, but one which speaks volumes to the damage done to the American Indian self-concept by movie
propaganda. The meaning of this, as Hill notes, can best
be appreciated if one were to imagine that the children
were instead engaging in a game called "nazis and Jews."

That movieland's image of the Indian is completely false—and often shoddily so—is entirely to the point. Only a completely false creation could be used to explain in "positive terms" what has actually happened here in centuries past. Only a literal blocking of modern realities can be used to rationalize present circumstances. Only a concerted effort to debunk Hollywood's mythology can alter the situation for the better. While it's true that the immortal words of General Phil Sheridan—"The only good Indian is a dead Indian"—have continued to enjoy a certain appeal with the American body politic, and equally true that dead Indians are hardly in a position to call the liars to account for their deeds, there are a few of us left out here who just might be up to the task.

Lawrence of South Dakota

Dances With Wolves and the Maintenance of the American Empire

Well, here we go again. The ol' silver screen is alight once more with images of Indians swirling through the murky mists of time, replete with all the paint, ponies and feathers demanded by the box office. True, we are not confronted in this instance with the likes of Chuck Conners playing *Geronimo*, Victor Mature standing in as *Chief Crazy Horse*, or Jeff Chandler cast in the role of *Broken Arrow's* Cochise. Nor are we beset by the sort of wanton anti-Indianism which runs so rampant in John Ford's *Stagecoach, Fort Apache, She Wore a Yellow Ribbon* and *Sergeant Rutledge*. Even the sort of "rebel without a cause" trivialization of Indian anger offered by Robert Blake in *Tell Them Willie Boy Was Here*—or Lee Diamond Philips in *Young Guns* and *Young Guns II*—is not at hand. Yet, in some ways the latest "Indian movie," a cinematic extravaganza packaged under the title *Dances With Wolves* is just as bad.

This statement has nothing to do with the entirely predictable complaints raised by reviewers in the *New York Times, Washington Post* and similar bastions of the status quo. Self-evidently, the movie's flaws do not—as such reviewers claim—rest in a "negative handling" of whites or "over-sentimentalizing" of Indians. Rather, although he tries harder than most, producer-director-star Kevin Costner holds closely to certain sympathetic stereotypes of Euroamerican behavior on the "frontier," at least insofar as he never quite explains how completely, systematically and persistently the invaders violated every conceivable standard of human decency in the process of conquest. As to these media pundits who have sought to "debunk" the film's positive portrayal of native people, they may be seen quite simply as liars, deliberately and often wildly inaccurate on virtually every point they have raised. Theirs is the task of (re)asserting the reactionary core of racist mythology so important to conventional justifications for America's "winning of the West."

Contrary to the carping of such paleo-critics, Costner did attain several noteworthy breakthroughs in his production. For instance, he invariably cast Indians to fill his script's Indian roles, a Hollywood first. And, to an extent surpassing anything else ever to emerge from tinseltown—including the celebrated roles of Chief Dan George in *Little Big Man* and Will Sampson in *One Flew Over the Cuckoo's Nest*—these Indians were allowed to serve as more than mere props. Throughout the movie, they were called upon to demonstrate motive and emotion, thereby assuming the dimensions of real human beings. Further, the film is technically and geographically accurate, factors superbly captured in the cinematography of Photographic Director Dean Semler and his crew.

But let's not overstate the case. Costner's talents as a film-maker have been remarked upon *ad nauseam,* not only by the motion picture academy during the orgy of Oscars recently bestowed upon him and his colleagues, but by the revenues grossed at the nation's theaters and by the misguided and fawning sort of gratitude expressed by some Indians at their culture's having finally been cinematically accorded a semblance of the respect to which it has been entitled all along. The vaunted achievements of *Dances With Wolves* in this regard should, by rights, be commonplace. That they are not says all that needs saying in this regard.

In any event, the issue is not the manner in which the film's native characters and cultures are presented.

The problems lie elsewhere, at the level of the context in which they are embedded. Stripped of its pretty pictures and progressive flourishes in directions and affirmative action hiring, *Dances With Wolves* is by no means a movie about Indians. Instead, it is at base an elaboration of movieland's Great White Hunter theme, albeit one with a decidedly different ("better") personality than the usual example of the genre, and much more elegantly done. Above all, it follows the formula established by *Lawrence of Arabia:* Arabs and Arab culture handled in a superficially respectful manner, and framed by some of the most gorgeous landscape photography imaginable. So much the better for sophisticated propagandists to render "realistic" the undeniably heroic stature of Lt. Lawrence, the film's central—and ultimately most Eurocentric—character.

In order to understand the implications of this structural linkage between the two movies, it is important to remember that despite the hoopla attending *Lawrence's* calculated gestures to the Bedouins, the film proved to be of absolutely no benefit to the peoples of the Middle East (just ask the Palestinians and Lebanese). To the contrary, its major impact was to put a "tragic" but far more humane face upon the nature of Britain's imperial pretensions in the region, making colonization of the Arabs seem more acceptable—or at least more inevitable—than might otherwise have been the case. So too do we encounter this contrived sense of sad inevitability in the closing scenes of *Dances With Wolves,* as Lt. Dunbar and the female "captive" he has "recovered" ride off into the proverbial sunset, leaving their Lakota "friends" to be slaughtered by and subordinated to the United States. Fate closes upon Indian and Arab alike, despite the best efforts of well-intentioned white men like the two good lieutenants. ("We're not *all* bad, y'know.")

It's all in the past, so the story goes; regrettable, obviously, but comfortably out of reach. Nothing to be done about it, really, at least at this point. Best that

everyone—Euroamericans, at any rate—pay a bit of appropriately maudlin homage to "our heritage," feel better
about themselves for possessing such lofty sentiments,
and get on with business as usual. Meanwhile, native
people are forced to live, right now, today, in abject squalor
under the heel of what may be history's most seamlessly
perfected system of internal colonization, out of sight, out
of mind, their rights and resources relentlessly consumed
by the dominant society. (See the Preface.) That is, after
all, the very business as usual that films like *Dances With
Wolves* helps to perpetuate by diverting attention to their
sensitive reinterpretations of yesteryear. So much for
Costner's loudly proclaimed desire to "help."

If Kevin Costner or anyone else in Hollywood held
an honest inclination to make a movie which would alter
public perceptions of Native America in some meaningful
way, it would, first and foremost, be set in the present day,
not in the mid-19th century. It would feature, front and
center, the real struggles of living native people to liberate
themselves from the oppression which has beset them in
the contemporary era, not the adventures of some fictional
non-Indian out to save the savage. It would engage directly with concrete issues like expropriation of water
rights and minerals, involuntary sterilization, and FBI
repression of Indian activists. It would not be made as
another *Pow Wow Highway*-style entertainment venture,
or one more trite excursion into spiritual philosophy and
the martial arts *a la* the *Silly Jack* movies. Cinema
focusing on the socio-political and economic realities of
Native America in the same fashion as these themes were
developed with regard to Latin America in *Salvador, El
Norte* and *Under Fire*. Such efforts are woefully long
overdue.

On second thought, maybe it wouldn't be such a good
idea. Hollywood's record on Indian topics is such that, if
it were to attempt to produce a script on, say, the events
on Pine Ridge during the mid-70s, it would probably end

up being some twisted plot featuring an Indian FBI agent (undoubtedly a cross between Mike Hammer and Tonto) who jumps in to save his backwards reservation brethren from the evil plots of corrupt tribal officials working with sinister corporate executives, and maybe even a few of his own bureau superiors. They'd probably cast a nice blond guy like Val Kilmer as the agent-hero and call it something Indian-sounding, like *Thunderheart*. It stands to reason, after all: now that we're burdened with the legacy of *Lawrence of South Dakota,* we can all look forward to what will amount to *South Dakota Burning.*

Hi Ho, Hillerman...(Away)

Unmasking the Role of Detective Fiction in Indian Country

The literature of crime detection is of recent growth because the historical conditions on which it depends are modern.

—F.W. Chandler

My theory is that people who don't like mystery stories are anarchists.

—Rex Stout

Over the past twenty years, a string of novels—*The Blessing Way* (1970), *Dance Hall of the Dead* (1973), *Listening Woman* (1978), *People of Darkness* (1980), *The Dark Wind* (1979), *The Ghost Way* (1984), *Skinwalkers* (1986), *A Thief of Time* (1988), *Talking God* (1989) and *Coyote Waits* (1990)—have in someways changed the face of detective fiction in the United States.[1] Each of them is set against the backdrop of the Navajo Reservation in the Four Corners region where the states of Arizona, New Mexico, Utah and Colorado meet, a remote and thinly populated desert locale about as different from the usual scene of the American detective yarn as it is possible to conceive. Each of them, moreover, features one or both of a pair of Navajo police officers, Joe Leaphorn and Jim Chee, as its central characters. They too represent an abrupt departure from the sort of sleuth we have become accustomed to expect in a "whodunit." Finally, the non-Indian author of this body of work, Tony Hillerman, is himself far from fitting the typical image of the detective writer.

Despite these anomalies, Hillerman has been cast by the *Dallas Morning News* as standing among "any list of the best living mystery writers." The *New Yorker* describes his work as being "agile...reflective...absorbing," and the *San Diego Union* calls him a "gifted, skillful and...unique writer." The *Boston Globe* asserts that Hillerman "is surely one of the finest and most original craftsmen at work in the [detective] genre today." The *Washington Post Book World* has claimed he "transcends the...genre" altogether. *People Magazine* holds that he is a "keen observer in a world that is not his own." Critic Phyllis A. Whitney states categorically that he "evokes the Arizona desert and Navajo lore as no other writer can." The *Denver Post Magazine* goes even further, proclaiming that "The magic of his mysteries is in the world he creates: a sense of intimacy he builds within a structure that seems whole, unbreakable, unassailably true." Writer Ursula LeGuin sums up, announcing emphatically: "The only mysteries I read are Hillerman's."[2]

Why do Tony Hillerman's mysteries receive so much acclaim? Do they represent a progressive political breakthrough in their treatment of American Indians, as their endorsement by LeGuin and other alleged opponents of the status quo might lead one to infer?

The equally effusive praise by more right-wing papers should arouse suspicions that the novels represent something less than an advance in the portrayal of American Indians in fiction. Conservative newspapers like the Ashville, North Carolina *Citizen Times* have concurred with the East Coast liberal perspective, solemnly intoning that the essential purpose of Hillerman's thrillers is "to teach." The Oklahoma City *Oklahoman* has advised that "readers who have not discovered Hillerman should not waste one more minute."[3] To explore this paradox of mainstream endorsement for novels widely held to be progressive and that break the mold of detective fiction, it is useful to examine the more orthodox detective novels and writers who preceded Hillerman.

Tough Guys Writing Tough Guy Novels

Since the 1840s with *The Murders in the Rue Morgue* and other short stories by Poe, who has been considered a bit mad by even his most devout admirers, detective fiction has been forged and perfected, for the most part, by individuals as antithetical to Hillerman's staid temperament as is possible to imagine.[4]

Not that all writers of the genre were off balance. During the late 19th and early 20th centuries it was mainly the purview of social dilettantes, fallen British aristocrats like Wilkie Collins and Arthur Conan Doyle.[5] Theirs was the age of the "soft-boiled sleuth" and manor house murders, habitually captured, as G.K. Chesterton once noted, in the genteel, impossibly sentimental tones of snobbish rural ambience derived from landed gentry and country estates.[6]

That was when England was still the reigning world power, before the Great War and at the very beginnings of real U.S. international muscle-flexing. By the late 1920s, the detective venue had been largely taken over by commoners across the Atlantic, appropriated as *the* exemplary American literary enterprise, and redeployed in emblematic urban landscapes like San Francisco, Los Angeles, and New York. It was honed and polished by a school of writers perfecting their craft in the pages of pulp magazines like *Black Mask* and *The Phantom,* creating a style of exposition stretched so taught and descriptive as to sometimes make the sparse sentences of Hemmingway seem flabby by comparison.[7] Their idiom set the stage for Humphrey Bogart to play Sam Spade in the Hollywood adaptation of Dashiell Hammett's *The Maltese Falcon* and Philip Marlowe in Raymond Chandler's *The Big Sleep.*

These and other movies indelibly stamped upon the American consciousness notions of "heroically" bare-fisted, lead-slinging, hard-drinking, chain-smoking, wise-cracking and womanizing "hard-boiled private eyes."[8]

The authors of the stories, books and scripts making up the formative body of American detective fiction often, both as a matter of ego and as a calculated promotion of the "realism" embodied in their work, associated themselves personally and directly with the characters they created. Chandler, Cornell Woolrich, Paul Cain and Jim Thompson, were all inveterate alcoholics and carousers who typically dressed in the manner attributed to their characters.[9] Hammett, anchored by his real-life status as a former Pinkerton detective, was—despite a severe lung disorder which eventually killed him—a three-pack-a-day smoker and near-legendary consumer of straight scotch.[10] In the end he was so possessed of the carefully-nurtured image that it was generally believed he actually served as the model upon which his *Thin Man* character was based. At least one writer has taken the cue, producing a novel in which Hammett himself appears as the chief protagonist, a seedy but somewhat sexy synthesis of pulp writer and private eye.[11]

Mickey Spillane (Frank Morrison), to take another prominent example, tied his own persona so closely to that of Mike Hammer, the central figure in his novels, that he tended to speak in his character's salty vernacular during radio and t.v. interviews. Similarly, he refused to appear in public without the trenchcoat and snap-brimmed fedora which were Hammer's trademarks. Rumors, untrue but well cultivated, that Spillane packed a pistol in a shoulder holster and helped the New York City Police Department solve some of its difficult cases were far-flung during the 1950s and on into the '60s, during the period when the *Mike Hammer* t.v. series was a weekly event.[12]

It seems most unlikely, then, that a paunchy, sedate, middle-aged family man *cum* reformed journalist-gradu-

ate student and all-round "nice guy" like Tony Hillerman
should become premier detective novelist of the moment.
Little in the history of the genre would lead one to conclude the man would ever secure such a lofty place within
it. On the surface, his success seems even more far-fetched
when one considers the ideological function of his chosen
school of writing.

The Ideological Function of Detective Fiction

Despite appearances to the contrary—its main characters often appearing to flaunt both social convention
and the bounds of legality—the purpose of detective fiction has always been to reinforce the status quo. It was
thus no accident that the genre arose when, where, and
in the forms that it did. In late 19th-century England, a
mature but decaying empire, it was useful as a popular
medium through which to transmit the message that the
aristocracy, whatever its defects and idiosyncrasies, was
inherently smarter and more able than those of lower
station. The latter, it was explained, when left to their own
devices, would inevitably engage in all manner of self-de-
structive mayhem. The function of the *private* detective
whether a semi-pro like Sherlock Holmes or an amateur
like Agatha Christie's Miss Marple, was and is to provide
voluntary investigative acumen to an often less competent
body of state officials seeking to preserve institutional
authority. The underlying theme has always been that it
is everyone's responsibility—and in everyone's best interest—to see the existing order maintained.[13]

The United States of the early 20th century, on the
other hand, represented a very different setting, a bur-
geoning empire preparing to assume a "world historic
role" as first a dominant and then a hegemonic global
power. A premium was placed upon the savvy, individual

initiative and ability to project the sheer physical force needed by an as yet unconsolidated imperialist structure. The private eyes in 1930s American fiction and film were supposed not only to enhance the bumbling and often corrupt incompetents institutionally-assigned to impose order. The role required them to insure the job was done by any and all means, usually taking matters into their own hands, vigilante-style. They were to "walk point" on the fringes of official authority, serving that "higher law" from which the codified civic version derives, expanding the frontier of the state at every step along the way.

Whatever the imagined tension between those "unconventional" methods utilized by tough guy fiction's private eyes and the supposedly "tame" orthodoxy of regular police investigators, both sides ultimately realize they are the *same* side. Each is necessary if an implicitly understood "greater good" is to be accomplished. Ends inevitably justify the means. By the time Spillane came along in the aftermath of World War II, with America standing supreme on the world stage and seeking to keep it that way, the whole pathology was thoroughly established:

> Power is the law of the world to Spillane's Mike Hammer, who says, "The cops can't break a guys arm to make him talk, and they can't shove his teeth in the muzzle of a .45 to remind him that they aren't fooling." Hammer, however, can and often does do these things, and they are described with relish. When he breaks a man's fingers and then smashes an elbow into his mouth, the "shattered teeth tore my arm and his mouth became a great hole of welling blood" while "his fingers were broken stubs sticking back at odd angles."[14]

This writing serves fundamentally similar functions to the characters and thematics developed by novelists—from James Fenimore Cooper to Ned Buntline—who concerned themselves with the "frontier." The material produced by Cooper and Buntline was used to rationalize for public consumption the conquest and domination entailed in Euroamerica's "Manifest Destiny" of expanding across the face of the North American continent. The work of Spillane and his associates was employed to the same end with regard to the subsequent U.S. globalization of its ambitions. The linkage is direct:

> Actually, as critics have pointed out, the private detective [in the United States] is a direct carryover from the lone western gunfighter, that mythic folk hero who righted wrongs with a weapon at his hip and who preserved the ideals of justice in the face of raw frontier violence. In later years, as *Black Mask* put its full emphasis on big city crime, the old and new West blended into the figure of the mythic private eye who rode into the sunset at the wheel of a Ford and who packed a .45 in his armpit in place of a Colt at his hip. But, basically, he was the same man.[15]

"Savage" Indians, "dirty" Mexicans, "greasy" Latins—usually "spics" or Italian gangsters—and other such barriers to the orderly progression and functioning of American empire had been the typical targets of WASP heroes in previous western and detective fiction. But Spillane's work assumed an increasingly overt and reactionary political cant. "I killed more people tonight than I have fingers on my hands," Mike Hammer recounts in *One Lonely Night* (1951). "I shot them in cold blood and enjoyed every minute of it...They were commies...red sons-of-bitches who should have died long ago."[16] "Criminality" had by then—echoed by western and detective novels—become identified primarily with "Un-American" deviation from the "values" underlying presumptions of "natural supremacy" by North America's ruling elite. This was amply reflected in the McCarthyite witch-hunting of the same period. Whatever "Senator Joe" and the boys dished out to those guilty of thinking impure thoughts was okay; subversives were deserving of far worse in the mass fantasizing inspired by Spillane's "gritty" phrasing.[17] The books sold by the millions.

Such conditioning helped shape the mentality that went into the FBI's COINTELPROs (Counterintelligence Programs)—extralegal operations involving everything from blackmail to assassination as a means to "neutralize" politically objectionable individuals and organizations—and into Middle America's tacit acceptance of them. COINTELPRO functioned full-force from 1955 through 1971, and has been continued ever since.[18] In tandem, the CIA has run various programs to destabilize or destroy popular movements and governments abroad, often through the murder of selected organizers, leaders and heads of state.[19] The CIA's prosecuting of the "Cold War" was neatly rationalized (and sanitized) for public consumption through a whole new sub-genre of detective novels and films dubbed "spy-thrillers."[20]

The purpose of the novels extended beyond coaxing the body politic to agree with and applaud the systematic "excesses" of investigative, intelligence and police operatives. Citizens were expected, upon demand by "higher authority," to put such sentiments into practice by participating directly. During the Vietnam War, U.S. troops widely expressed the adage: "If it's dead, it's a Viet Cong."[21] Or as an American colonel stated in 1968, "We had to destroy the village in order to save it."[22] Yes, and Wyatt Earp, Philip Marlowe and Mike Hammer *must* habitually ignore the law in order that it be upheld against those who would violate it. The government *must* destroy its political opposition to guarantee "our political liberty." And everyone else *must* "do what they're told," meekly taking their assigned places within the carefully-crafted American social order so that we may all "live free."[23] Obviously, if detective fiction had never come to exist on its own, it would have been necessary for the status quo to have invented it.

The Values Upheld by Detective Novels

If the ideological function of the detective novel is to mirror and reinforce existing social and political values, it is critical to consider the question just which values? Among them are the personal codes which elites considered useful for those who comprised the core of its military capacity. The critic Julian Symons puts it this way with regard to the sexual dimension of Spillane and other tough guy detective writing:

> Women are seen as sexually desirable objects, and there are a good many descriptions of their bodies, but intercourse is often replaced by death or torture. In *I, the Jury* (1947), Charlotte, the beautiful psychiatrist, makes several unsuccessful attempts to get Hammer into bed. At the end, when she turns out to be a multiple murderess, he shoots her in the stomach with pleasure. "How could you?" she asks incredulously, and he replies: "It was easy." At the end of *Kiss Me Deadly* (1952), the apparently lovely Lily reveals herself as "a horrible caricature of a human" whose body has been burned so that it is "a disgusting mass of twisted, puckered flesh from her knees to her neck." Hammer goes on to burn her to death, so that she becomes "a mass of flame tumbling on the floor with the blue flames of alcohol turning the white of her hair into black char and her body convulsing under the agony of it."[24]

There can be no doubt that the "ideal" represented in such admiring—one is tempted to say *masturbatory*—depictions of extreme psychosexual violence has incalculably deformed gender relations in the United States. It intensified a pre-existing subjugation of women as a group and reinforced the tacit social sanction which not only okayed rape as a male "sport" (within certain parameters), but led unerringly to all manner of other misogynist atrocities.

However, it's not only misogyny that is at issue here.

In the structure of the tough guy detective genre, strength and power (hence superiority, and, by extension, "good") are invariably equated to masculinity. Weakness and powerlessness (inferiority and, by extension, "evil") are equated to femininity.[25] The metaphor of equating power to justice and good, weakness to evil extends beyond gender relations, encompassing virtually *any* set of power relations (race, international affairs, or matters concerning class and ideology) in which "we" are to project our "innate" strength and goodness.

This same formula that power equals justice was a driving force behind nazi ideology. It led nazi leader Heinrich Himmler to attempt the transformation of his SS officers into a group of "supermen." According to Himmler, it is possible for a relatively small group of superior types to assert their "proper" role of domination over multitudinous inferiors by realizing the "vision, and most of all, the *will*" to adopt a posture of "utmost hardness, even cruelty," to be "merciless" and overwhelmingly "virile."[26]

"Achieving the correct attitude of harshness" by which average people can be made to "do what must be done" to become dominant, Himmler concluded, "is by no means inevitable." It requires concerted psychological conditioning, through constant bombardment with "parables," projection of "culture figures" (role models) appropriate to the purpose, and so forth.[27] A requisite orientation and sensibility must be created in the target population as a whole. It can then be "sharpened" through more overt ideological indoctrination, at least among selected subgroups such as police and military personnel, for purposes of practical application by the state.

The nazis used tales of the Teutonic Knights and other Germanic legends to accomplish this psychological shift.[28] In the post-war United States, detective fiction and the accompanying deluge of films and t.v. programs served equivalent purposes. They were a major component of a drive by socioeconomic and political elites to inculcate the desired sense of "toughness" into the public at large.

In both Germany and the United States, the outlook sewn into the collective consciousness was as logically perfect as it was monstrous: Those who prove most masterful at inflicting torture and death are able to do so only out of a sense of duty to what is good, and because they are willing to assert the power to do so. Turning to the victims, this mindset holds that those who are tortured and/or killed are weak. Because their weakness makes them axiomatically evil, they *deserve* their fate. These psychological metaphors afford not only the essential justification necessary for systemic torture and murder, they also provide a basis for satisfaction, pride, even glee, on the part of the torturer/murderers.

Nazi-like reflections of Spillane's burning women may be glimpsed in the flaming peasant huts and napalmed children of Southeast Asia during the Vietnam War. Similarly, echoes of Mike Hammer permeated U.S. troops' habitual references to Vietnamese victims of the massive American use of incendiary weapons as "crispy critters," and the jovial, self-congratulatory descriptions of these same soldiers as "a damn fine bunch of killers" by officers like Brigadier General George S. Patton, III.[29] More recently, we see the same reflection in the charred corpses of 250,000 fleeing Iraqis in 1991, accompanied by haunting descriptions by U.S. pilots, leering at recollections of their roles in slaughtering already-defeated Iraqi opponents: "It was fun, kind of like a video arcade."[30] Needless to say, Himmler's SS troops would have felt perfectly at ease in such company.

Does Hillerman Break the Mold?

What do these tough guy novels, and their function of supporting elite interests, have to do with Tony Hillerman? Far from wandering about in a trenchcoat and slouch hat, he usually appears casually attired in slacks and a sports shirt. He does not suffer from the macho speech impediment which mysteriously caused a number of his predecessors to utter clipped phrases from the corner of their mouths. He lays no claim to a real-life background in police or intelligence work, nor even to having covered these areas during his stints as a journalist. His stories do not incorporate the quasi-surrealist misogynism marring so many of Chandler's plot lines or the alcoholic self-degradation permeating Hammett's more autobiographical works. Certainly, he avoids the twisted sadism of Spillane. In conversation, his political orientation seems blandly liberal and he appears almost squeamish about discourses on blood and guts. The one time he was asked to appear as an expert witness in a murder trial, he declined, citing lack of expertise.[31] If he doesn't fit the mold, how is it that he has attained such standing and credibility as a writer of modern American detective novels?

Let it be said, first of all, that the man can write. This is certainly an element of his success. While not the literary equal of either Hammett or Chandler, the last of whom he claims as a figurative mentor,[32] Hillerman can at least hold his own with the "second tier" standards of wordsmithing set by Spillane and, more recently, Ross Macdonald and Charles Willeford.[33] His material far surpasses that of assembly-line hack writers like S.S. Van Dine, Leslie Chartiris, Earl Stanley Gardiner, Rex Stout, and Ellery Queen.[34] The spare style of structure and exposition he acquired as a journalist have stood Hillerman in good stead while penning novels. His books are, technically speaking, always an abundantly "good read."

Yet good writing alone does not a famous writer make. One cannot escape the impression that far more is involved in Hillerman's popularity than merely his ability to turn a tidy phrase. Before leaping to the conclusion that his success rests on some profound shift in function—by no longer representing elite interests, for instance—it is useful to examine some critical factors affecting the ways in which power is exercised. Among them is the debacle of the U.S. defeat in Southeast Asia and concomitant exposure of the sheer falsity bound up in the myth of white male invincibility this entailed. Certainly, the agonizing process of losing in a major military adventure precipitated a temporary crisis of confidence (and loss of consensus about how to proceed), even among U.S. elites.[35] This loss brought on a lengthy period during which America's imperial ideology was reconstructed in an effort to overcome what was called the "Vietnam Syndrome."[36] One means to this reconstruction was a new sense of "participation and inclusiveness" centered on the imperial core of North America itself, a structure in which the oppressed themselves would be increasingly solicited and employed to impose the order which formed the basis of their oppression. Popular literature and the electronic media, of course, played primary roles in bringing about this necessary transition in public sensibilities.

Roger Simon, creator of the Moses Wine detective character portrayed by Richard Dreyfus in the movie version of *The Big Fix*, explains that the nature of U.S. power reinforced in Chandler, Hammett and Spillane novels has changed. During the 1988 International Crime Writers Conference, he noted that after the U.S. military loss in Indochina, Watergate, the rise of feminism, the black liberation movement, the new left and gay rights activism, those famous "mean streets" of Philip Marlowe and Mike Hammer are at best passé. Indeed, they are downright embarrassing, the omnipotence of Euroamerican masculinity they represent having been thoroughly discredited over the past thirty years through successful defiance by everyone from Ho Chi Minh to Rita Mae Brown.

The history of t.v. detective and police shows chronicles the shift. In 1958, the public was glued to its collective t.v. set watching *M-Squad,* an unabashed celebration of white male violence proudly proclaimed by its star, Lee Marvin, to portray "Chicago's SS."[37] By 1968, such fare had been replaced with programs like *The Mod Squad,* a much less graphically-violent series featuring three young "countercultural" figures, including a woman and a black man, "doing the right thing" by working as snitches for the police.[38] The detective genre that once composed the core symbology of Americana is doomed to an increasingly shrinking marketability. It will be ignored—or in some cases openly attacked—by those upwardly mobile multitudes who wish to continue sharing in the existing order's profitability precisely by pretending to have become too enlightened to believe in its traditional mythos.[39]

The writer who wishes to succeed in employing detective themes and imagery within the contemporary American *zeitgeist* must do so by creating characters which eschew traditional formulas in favor of "alternatives." The hero may be a heroine, as in the works of Sara Paretsky and Sue Grafton, but never (ever!) in the clichéd, frumpy manner of Miss Marple.[40] He or she may be gay or lesbian, as Joseph Hansen and others have lately demonstrated, but only when portrayed in a manner reflecting "credit" on the preference.[41]

In the event a heterosexual male is selected as a lead character, he need be "sensitive," not particularly good looking, frequently fallible, and usually "not-quite-white." It is helpful to provide such characters with a slightly stale but still noticeable "rad-lib" political cant.[42] Another helpful twist is that he have been married but that his wife left him because of obvious shortcomings. A sizeable portion of his usually meager earnings should go by court order to the support of his several children, preferably daughters requiring expensive dental work.[43] Neat bourbon by the shot should be replaced by Perrier water (or at least white wine) whenever possible. Appreciable time and emotional energy should be spent trying to kick a persistent smoking habit, and firearms should be treated as objects to be fumbled with in moments of extreme peril (proving, of course, that brain rather than brawn, although it sometimes works slowly, *always* wins the day).[44]

Part of the mystery surrounding Hillerman's success is thus solved. Rather than breaking the mold demanded of old-line, tough-guy writers like Spillane, Hammett, and Chandler, he has simply recast it in conformity to the requirements of post-Vietnam American power. His set and settings, characters and characterizations, sense and sensibility—the tone and tenor of his work as a whole—mesh perfectly with the public tastes inculcated in the process of reconstituting a U.S. imperial consensus in the wake of the defeat in Vietnam.

While first appearances may suggest these trends represent a thoroughgoing deconstruction and disposal of everything Hammeresque in detective fiction, the reality is quite the opposite. In the manner of George Bush's speech writers, the new stable of "innovative" detective novelists have simply offered up a "kinder, gentler" impression of business as usual. The central values defended by today's private sleuths—regardless of their race or ethnicity, gender, sexual proclivities, degree of addiction to health food, or inability to place a bullet in the center of the target—are exactly those held by earlier tough guys like Spade and Marlowe. While the attentions of the "new breed" may be more often devoted to the ills of official corruption than to the threats represented by subversives and street criminals which preoccupied their predecessors, their purpose remains firmly focused on making the system work, sometimes in spite of itself. Although they might never agree on the menu for lunch, yesterday's private eyes and today's "more diverse" roster share an inherent consensus about who the bad guys are and who are the good.

How Tonto Became Chief of Tribal Police

As was remarked previously in this book, genocide has several distinct stages. In the beginning, troops arrive to butcher the indigenous population. Later, the "savages" are seen worthy of being "educated" and "civilized" to white, Western standards, dealing a devastating blow to the cultures possessed by the survivors of the slaughter. Finally, indigenous cultures are assimilated into the dominant society, stripped of many of their inherent values and sold as commodities.

Corresponding to the stages of genocide, are the phases of colonial control. Direct rule is replaced by indigenous rule under in the service of the colonizers. This is a lesson the British learned long ago, when they discovered that, "properly oriented," the Gurkha Rifles and Bengal Native Infantry might serve as better, more efficient keepers of England's colonial order than could English troops themselves.[45] The French, too, arrived at such a realization, developing as a result the concepts of the Foreign Legion and the use of Algerians rather than Frenchmen as colonial police.[46] The same thrust in thinking is readily apparent in the U.S. "Public Safety Program" of the 1960s, training Latin American police operatives to "autonomously" impose the order of North American interests upon their own people.[47] Another example is the Nixon-Kissinger "Vietnamization" project of the early 1970s, the intent of which was to field an almost exclusively Asian force to fight and finish a war in Indochina initiated by U.S. elites for their own geopolitical reasons.[48]

The principle at work here is straightforward. The extent to which those who are most oppressed by a given socioeconomic and political order can be convinced that the route to their liberation lies in service to that order, the greater the extent to which the order can be rendered efficient, rational and self-perpetuating in its essence.

Such thinking tends to signify the post-conquest period of maturation in all colonial systems.[49]

The success of any such colonizing effort rests in some part on fostering the delusion among the dominant population that the emergence of such tendencies within various oppressed groups represents a dimension of "good." Simultaneously, pre-existing notions that tendencies going in other directions—those resisting or seeking dismantlement of the oppressing system—are "bad" must be reinforced in the minds of those who comprise the oppressing society. In this way, the oppressing system can avail itself of an increasing obedience—including approved sectors of selected out groups—while confusing and diminishing all natural opposition to itself.[50] The new detective fiction, and the characters who inhabit it, are an integral aspect of this process of U.S. imperial maturation, and it is here that Tony Hillerman may be said to have truly come to the fore.

Figuratively, the script needed for this purpose might be anticipated as following a course straight out of *The Legend of the Lone Ranger*, that time-honored medium for explaining the proper roles of Indians and whites to children of both groups. In the newly required, "enlightened and adult" version, Tonto—having long-since aligned himself with the Ranger's (Euroamerica's) intrinsic goodness (superiority) by habitually ("faithfully") licking his better's boots—finally reaches the point of "realizing himself as a total human being." The route to this end will not be found in some reassertion of Tonto's original identity and autonomy as a nonwestern being. No such ending of the degradation he has experienced at the hands of the Ranger will come through, say, a richly-deserved slitting of his master's throat. With the Hillerman mystery novel as a vehicle, Tonto demonstrates that his polished self-denigration and subservience has at last prepared him, the Indian, to assume his master's mantle. The Ranger can thus retire to enjoy the fruits of his labor, the long, lonely and often brutal toil of imposing the hallowed virtues of a rational order upon a world filled with the irrational evils of disorder. Meanwhile, Tonto is allowed at last to prove once and for all that he, too, can be "civilized," is "just as good" as the Ranger ever was, and has become a pretty likeable guy to boot.

The audience can thus relax, secure in the cunningly implanted knowledge that even the most obviously and viciously colonized sector of the North American population, the Indians, now agree "the system works" for one and all. What appeared to be a problem demanding redress by people of conscience really isn't an issue after all. It took a while to figure it out, but we really *do* share the same essential values and beliefs when you get right down to it. At a "gut level," we all want the same things, for the same reasons, and are prepared to do the same things to get them. Exotic little differences in pigmentation aside, we all—"black, white, yellow, red, brown, purple and polka dot"—distinguish ourselves primarily on the basis of mere cultural particularities, diversity around a common theme, the spice of life in a "pluralistic society" which is moving (or has moved) "beyond substantial questions of race and ethnicity." I'm okay, you're okay.

We can all sit back within our respective niches in the order of things, "feeling good about ourselves" and the way things have worked out in the end. Why worry? Be happy. Everything is as it should be. If this is not exactly the best of all possible worlds, it's at least the best that can be had. Meanwhile, despite the pleasurable hallucinatory sensations engendered by this narcotizing façade, the perpetual hemorrhaging of Native America (detailed in the preface) goes on and on, unconstrained by public outcry, safely out of sight and mind.

Repression on the Reservation: Whodunit?

The conventional wisdom holds that Hillerman's singular achievement, aside from bringing the western and the detective novel together in a uniquely sustained fusion, has been "humanitarian," even "liberatory" with regard to Native America. His books, beginning with their main characters, are populated by American Indians who, in ways and to an extent previously absent in the tradition of Euroamerican letters, are provided the dimensionality, motivation and nuance necessary to establish them as bona fide people rather than mere props in the popular mind. Further, for one of the very few times in popular fiction, the Indians in Hillerman's work—the lead characters at least—are projected unqualifiedly as good guys; they are honest, courageous, courteous and strong, beset by just enough doubt, confusion and frailty to make them wholly believable. By contrast, the white folk who inhabit these tales, from anthropologists to FBI agents to erstwhile girlfriends, come off rather the worse for wear, at least in terms of personal integrity and likability. Such "role reversal" takes on a tidy semblance of "pro-Indianism."

Indeed, at one level, Hillerman has managed—almost singlehandedly, to hear his enthusiasts tell it—to reverse the stream of the kind of anti-Indian sentiment which has flowed virtually without interruption across the pages of American literature since the first British colonist set foot in Virginia in 1607. Through his efforts, an appreciable portion of the American reading public, few of whom are actually Indians, have for the first time found themselves identifying directly with native characters, thereby understanding at least some aspects of the modern Indian circumstance in ways which have never before been possible for them.

All of this is true enough. And that is precisely why

the books and their author are so dangerous. Questions, not of *whether* Hillerman deals sympathetically with Indians, but of *which* Indians he chooses to treat so sympathetically—and the implications of this choice—must be posed. In other words, exactly what *sort* of "understanding" of Native America is being promoted? The issue of how the author fits into the scheme of stories mirroring the needs of ascending, consolidated, and declining empires should by now be coming into focus, at least for those familiar with the roles of Chee and Leaphorn. The query leads to the form and function of the Navajo Police, an entity in which both of Hillerman's major heroes are "responsible members." The nature of this police force begs examination if we are to truly appreciate the richness of the colonialism the Leaphorn/Chee novels support.

The police units in question, at Navajo and everywhere else, were formed during the 19th century, not by the indigenous people they were designed to "regulate," but by the U.S. Army in collaboration with an assortment of agents sent by the Departments of War and Interior. Plainly, the rationale in creating and maintaining these paramilitary elites among peoples the United States had recently conquered was never remotely concerned with seeing to it that they retained (or regained) a capacity to enforce their own laws among themselves. To the contrary, the express intent of the exercise was from the outset to usurp and destroy native concepts of legality and order, imposing in their stead a system of rules devised in Washington, DC, all of them meant to subordinate indigenous nations to the will of the United States, to undermine their sociocultural integrity and destroy their ability to resist Euroamerican domination.[51]

The role of these Indian surrogates for U.S. power has never been abstract. In a number of instances, those who were to become the nucleus of the original police units had served as scouts for the army, fighting against their own people's struggles to remain free and independent.

Subsequently, they were used, notably in the cases of the great Lakota patriots Crazy Horse and Sitting Bull, to assassinate key leaders of the ongoing indigenous resistance to U.S. rule.[52] During the late 19th and first half of the 20th centuries, they also lent themselves consistently to putting teeth into programs meant to eradicate even deeper layers of internal cohesion within native cultures, targeting the traditional spiritual leadership by arresting and sometimes imprisoning those "guilty" of conducting such central religious ceremonies as the Sun Dance and Potlatch.[53] Once the governments were created by the Indian Reorganization Act (IRA), the Indian police were incorporated as subparts. As recently as the mid-1970s, they played a key role in repressing efforts by traditional Oglala Lakota people on the Pine Ridge Reservation to depose an exceptionally corrupt IRA regime; approximately 70 Indians were murdered during this counterinsurgency campaign, mostly at the hands of Leaphorn and Chee's real-life counterparts.[54]

In a manner typical of imperial literature everywhere, the sympathetic portrait Hillerman draws of the tribal police carries in it undeniable implications regarding how he *must* depict the remainder of the native societies with which he deals. Put simply, if his heroes are to be those most sold out to the colonizing order, then it stands to reason that the less sold out, more traditionally-oriented a character is, the greater the degree of silliness and/or negativity must be assigned to him or her. Hence, a theme running like a river through the Leaphorn/Chee novels is that traditional Navajo and Hopi societies are predicated in an inexplicably irrational complex of beliefs infested by all manner of goblins and demons. These child-like outlooks give rise to a steady series of innately evil individuals, "witches" who adopt the personae of "skinwalkers," "bad kachinas" and the like. Because of the inordinate power supposedly held by these witches within their own cultures—traditional folk are as a whole usually terrorized by them to the point of trauma in Hillerman's stories—they are often selected for manipulation by sinister non-Indians pursuing an assortment of nefarious ends.

Since the traditional Indian characters are automatically incapacitated by the evil ones among them, and thus subject to endless victimization by a seemingly infinite array of villains, it falls to a nice college-educated, Euro-oriented boy like Jim Chee—or his older and crustier, but equally Euro-oriented police mentor, Joe Leaphorn—to save them, protecting them from their own naïve fallibilities over and over again. (*Listening Woman* is a prime example of this emphasis developed to its full potential, a novel to which we will return.) Small wonder that Leaphorn professes a near-total disinterest in Navajo tradition. Chee, for his part, is cast as being curious but perpetually baffled by the sheer and often perverse stupidity imbedded in the culture of which he is allegedly a part. It is easy to understand why he might be given to endless deep contemplation of the meaning of it all, perched as he is upon the peak of superior knowledge provided him by the anthropology department at Arizona State University. He is bound up irretrievably in the world of Kipling's discourses of "wogs" and "white man's burdens."

The Politics of the Hillerman Formula

Hillerman, as even his staunchest admirers have been sometimes willing to admit, has had to engage in considerable distortion of Navajo ethnography in order to make the good and evil dimensions of his heavily value-laden moral plays work out.[55] And there is much more to it than that. The author deploys two absolutely unbreachable rules while developing every one of his "Indian" novels (most emphatically in *Skinwalkers, Talking God* and *Dancehall of the Dead*).

- First, Euroamericans are *always* the smart guys, manipulating Indians in criminal endeavors, *never* the other way around. Although usually understated in Hillerman's work, this is no more than a conventional ploy to reinforce the smug sense of Euroamerican supremacism permeating the U.S. reading mainstream. The only reasonably intelligent Indians on the scene are invariably Leaphorn and Chee, adherents to the rules of the Euroamerican status quo. The implication is that if Indians wish to stop suffering, they should abandon all this odd "other cultural" claptrap, and buy into the system as rapidly as possible. As a whole, Hillerman's construction speaks sly volumes about the "inevitability" of native subordination to Eurocentric values and ideologies. Such themes play well these days, not only among Wall Street conservatives, hard-hat types and federal officials, but especially among liberal yuppie readers who have "grown tired" of hearing that their position and mobility are based in the oppression and exploitation of non-white people.

- Second, Euroamerican bad guys are *always* individuals, "criminals," who have deviated from the rules of procedure laid down by the status quo while striking out on their own for unapproved purposes. (In other words, their actions stand to interfere with more orderly and institutionalized forms of criminal conduct.) They are *never* representatives of the governmental/corporate entities—the Bureau of Indian Affairs, Bureau of Reclamation, Bureau of Land Management, Army Corps of Engineers, U.S. Marshals Service, FBI, Peabody Coal, Anaconda, Kerr-McGee, Westinghouse, *et al.*—which have been demonstrably victimizing In-

272 FANTASIES OF THE MASTER RACE

dians far more extensively and systematically than any individual(s). This too is a standard device, consistently used by detective novelists and other propagandists to divert attention away from the real nature of the problems suffered by "common people," replacing it with the illusion that "real" issues are caused by the "deviant" actions—often on the part of the victims themselves—which are always solvable without rocking the boat of the larger system in which the crimes take place. Resolution of these fictional problems can thus be located in the very structures which generate the real world problems of the oppressed. Needless to say, both conservative and liberal Euroamericans are delighted to learn that the source of daily agony for oppressed people of color lies not in the structure of white supremacism, but in deviation from its order and values.

So conscientious has Hillerman been in the latter regard that he has managed to write *nine consecutive novels* providing ostensibly detailed descriptions of the habitat of Navajoland, and the people who reside in it, without ever once mentioning the vast proliferation of uranium tailings piles abandoned by U.S. corporations— with full government complicity—on the reservation since 1952. He makes no remark at all upon the cancers, congenital birth defects, and other health problems among the Navajo resulting from governmental-corporate practices, matters which presently constitute a major crisis for the Navajo Nation.[56] Nor does he refer in any way to the massive and ongoing stripmining for coal which is destroying the Navajo and Hopi land bases, or the forced relocation of more than 10,000 traditional Navajo sheepherders which is accompanying this mining in the Big Mountain area.[57] Missing too is mention of the cata-

strophic depletion of ground water, chemical and radioactive contamination of surface water, rapidly deteriorating
air quality due to the location of massive coal-fired elec-
trical generating facilities on Navajo land, destruction of
sacred sites, and all the rest of the damage done by the
Euroamerican system of "liberty, freedom, and justice for
all" to the land and peoples depicted so "sympathetically"
in the Chee/Leaphorn novels.[58] The list of omissions might
be continued at length, but suffice it to say that such
"politically sensitive" issues are strictly off-limits within
the framework of the author's literary project.

Premeditated Propagandist or
Innocent by Reason of Stupidity?

Hillerman pulls off his novels with such sincerely
posed dexterity that one might almost be willing to accept,
despite the highly politicized nature of his cross-cultural
characterizations, his own oft-repeated assertion that his
intent is apolitical. Depiction of the colonial police as
honorable and value-neutral figures might, after all, be
merely a regrettable, perhaps reprehensible, but a nonetheless unwitting regurgitation of Indian-white stereotypes, subconsciously absorbed during a life-time's
furtherance of "objective journalism." It might also be
plausible that his decision to avoid completely the questions of governmental-corporate impact upon the land and
lives he purports to reveal has been borne more by some
sort of weird ignorance or an unwillingness to face facts;
something other than a politically-motivated desire to
obfuscate certain fundamental truths.

Hillerman's innocence might be believable, were it
not for the fact that—denials notwithstanding— he *does*
frequently venture into the domain of overt political
content. Here, he tips his hand in ways to refute any
possible disclaimer, depicting—sometimes at great

length—the politics of indigenous resistance to colonial rule. This is *always* done in a manner both devoid of contextualization and framed in the most viciously demeaning and inaccurate ways. Take, for example, *Talking God*. Hillerman opens with perhaps the finest chapter he's ever written, having a young, mixed-blood Navajo who works for the Smithsonian Institution, weary of fruitless arguments against the museum's practice of desecrating Indian graves and "collecting" native skeletal remains. The character makes his point by digging up the curator's grandparents and shipping them to her in a box. The administrator is properly aghast at being treated in a fashion she is plainly accustomed to reserving for others. The message seems clear and appropriate. But, having thus flashed his credentials of understanding in the matter, Hillerman devotes much of the rest of the book to administering a raft of punishment to the Indian, whom he plainly considers guilty of a deep transgression against institutional order and authority.

The character is developed as being tragically confused about his identity, a weak and pathetic creature desperately grasping for a cause, and ultimately one of the villains. In the end, we are left to conclude there was nothing actually wrong with the Smithsonian's systematic grave robbery, all protests by similarly misguided "wannabe" Indians notwithstanding. "Real" natives like Jim Chee, who helps track the boy down, are unconcerned with such things. In fact, Hillerman has Chee explain at one point that the Navajos—afflicted as they are with a host of rather sublime superstitions about the dead—might actually *prefer* that the bones of their ancestors be gathered up and warehoused in remote Euroamerican facilities like the Smithsonian. Consequently, what becomes inappropriate and offensive in this thinly-veiled polemic is the "arrogance" and "wrongheadedness" of real-life Indian "militants" attempting to challenge the colonial order's self-proclaimed "right" to take from native people not only the remains of their dead, but whatever else it desires as well.

Listening Woman provides an even more striking example of his treatment of Indian resistance to colonization. Here, we find Hillerman busily deploying an imaginary "splinter group" of the American Indian Movement. He derived this from an actual 1976 FBI counterintelligence operation designed to discredit "Indian radicals." Known as the "Dog Soldier Teletypes," disinformational documents were secretly leaked to the press by the Bureau's "media liaisons" to fix in the public mind that AIM was a supremely bloodthirsty outfit, a portion of which was preparing to commit all manner of random, gratuitously violent acts against innocent non-Indians. FBI Director Clarence M. Kelley was subsequently forced to admit in open court that there was "not one shred" of evidence supporting this characterization of any known element of the movement. The whole thing was nothing more than an elaborate and highly illegal hoax perpetrated by the Bureau as a means to garner popular support for the lethal campaign of political repression its agents were waging against the movement at the time.[59]

Having been so thoroughly and publicly debunked, one would think this particularly malignant lie might have been left to wither away into the nothingness it obviously warrants. Perhaps it would have been finally laid to rest, had Hillerman not elected to utilize his rising popularity as a platform upon which to give it new life in somewhat amplified form. In the resuscitated, retooled and revitalized—but hardly disguised—version developed for *Listening Woman,* the AIM Dog Soldier fable once again cloaks native activism in the garb of psychotic terrorism. The author uses a character, referred to throughout as "gold-rims," to recruit an odd assortment of misfits to an absurdly postulated "program" entailing the kidnapping and murder of more-or-less randomly selected whites.

The numbers of intended victims correspond to the casualties recorded as having been sustained by various Indian peoples in massacres occurring a century and more ago. As it turns out, gold-rims himself has never believed for a moment in the bizarre concept of justice to which he attracts others. To the contrary, Hillerman has him using his depraved adherents as mere cannon fodder in a cynical scheme to make himself rich. Plainly, folk of this ilk are unworthy of support by anyone, Indian or non-Indian. Equally clearly, the author wishes to lead his readers to the conclusion that a public service was performed through the extermination visited upon these mad dogs by Joe Leaphorn at the end of the book. From there, it is an easy step to applying the same rule to real AIM members who have suffered the same fate at the hands of real Indian police.

Nor does it end there. By discrediting radicals, the topical issues of AIM and related groups—such as the uranium contamination, water depletion and compulsory relocation that Hillerman so deftly ignores—are completely delegitimized. Indian radicals are depicted as wanton killers trapped in a pointless obsession with visiting retribution upon innocent people for "tragedies" occurring in the distant past. Hence, they have nothing constructive to offer anyone, including themselves. Best to "put them out of their misery," the sooner the better, and get on with the business of making the system work.

Fascist Mysteries Legitimate the Final Solution

The man is nothing if not consistent. Without exception, American Indian resistance to conquest and colonization, whether active or passive, signifies that which is evil and therefore to be overcome in Hillerman's books. Indian resistance has become the evil that replaces the

"Communism" used by Spillane and "labor agitation" used by Hammett in some of his earliest work. Indigenous compliance with the existing system is always good, and direct participation in or service to it is even better. The "best" among his Indian characters no longer even require direction from their Euroamerican overlords; they simply enforce colonialism's dictates upon themselves.

Now, having come full circle, we can return to our exploration of the fascist ideology that might makes right in detective fiction. In the context of other nations—Norway, say, or France—the word normally used to describe such outlooks and behaviors of indigenous people carrying out the will of an invading population is "treason." It follows that, if Hillerman were to write a novel set in occupied Norway during World War II, and remain consistent with the character formulations he has used throughout the Chee/Leaphorn novels, he would have no alternative but to script a character filling the role of the notorious nazi collaborator and puppet leader, Vidkun Quisling, as the book's most heroic figure. Perhaps a better analogy would be a hypothetical novel set in nazi-occupied France. Then the heroes would have to be the police of the Vichy puppet regime, enforcing Hitler's New Order upon the people, working closely with the Gestapo to wipe out the French resistance. In context, these *are* the only counterparts to Chee and Leaphorn. One might find interesting precedents to such "unique" and "innovative" story lines in the material produced by Josef Goebbels' nazi propaganda ministry during the period in which Germany occupied both countries.[60] Certainly, there are more than ample antecedents to Hillerman's characterizations of American Indians in *Gunga Din* and others of Rudyard Kipling's literary apologetics for British colonialism in East India.

Ultimately, despite all the superficial and misleading distinctions with which he has been so careful to clothe his image, there is nothing incongruous in Tony

Hillerman's presence among the peculiar roster of personalities making up detective fiction's list of noted authors. Fundamentally, there is no difference whatsoever between the logic and meaning of a Hillerman novel and that of a Mickey Spillane. The end is the same, and for precisely the same reasons, no matter whether the main protagonist is an enthusiastically efficient practitioner of torture and homicide like Mike Hammer or a better-natured cop like Jim Chee who must always fumble for the gun locked in his glove compartment. And, if the way in which Spillane has Hammer impose order upon the disorderly oppressed can be properly termed "reactionary and sadistic," how much *more* sadistic is it for Hillerman to dispense with Hammer altogether? The maneuver changes nothing other than to remove the colonizers from direct participation in the colonial process by eliminating their figurative representative as a key player. Much crueler in its subtle way is Hillerman's tactic of imparting willing complicity—often even full responsibility—to the colonized for the fact, continuation and perfection of their own colonization.

Spillane at least was more-or-less open about who he was and why, as were Hammett and Chandler before him. Hillerman's charade of not only providing fictional characters completely opposite to the heroes created by Spillane, Chandler, and Hammett, but also *being* the opposite number to those authors—capturing as it does the loyalties of a much broader contemporary audience—is far less honest. It is also much more sophisticated, efficient and dangerous. The literary celebration of brute force has been replaced by the logical next step reflecting the culminating phase of America's imperial pretensions.

When all is said and done, one need not be a master detective to solve the "mystery" of why the Jim Chee/Joe Leaphorn novels have received such accolades from establishment reviewers. Because he has been canny enough to rationalize the context of U.S.-Indian relations which is of such vital importance to the maintenance of the status quo, and because he holds the requisite proficiency to make the project work, Tony Hillerman has been anointed to a position at the very crest of his chosen genre. It follows that his books lack even the slightest connection to the literature of liberation. They are instead the very quintessence of modern colonialist fiction in the United States.

Notes

1. All of Hillerman's Leaphorn/Chee novels have been published by Harper and Row.

2. The quotes are taken from the dust jacket of *A Thief of Time.*

3. *Ibid.*

4. Poe, who suffered from chronic depression and hallucinations, never managed a book length effort. Further, many of his stories, written between 1837 and 1849, would be more properly classified as horror than detective fiction. For the literary output, see Poe, Edgar Allan, *Complete Stories and Poems of Edgar Allen Poe,* Doubleday Publishers, Garden City, New York, 1966. Biographically see Hoffman, Daniel, *Poe Poe Poe Poe Poe Poe,* Houghton-Mifflin, New York, 1972.

5. Collins's *The Moonstone,* first published in 1868, is generally credited as being the first "real" detective novel, although others, such as William Goodwin's *Things as They Are; or, The Adventures of Caleb Williams* (London, 1794) were written earlier. Conan Doyle's four novels and 56 short stories featuring Sherlock Holmes and Watson, written in a stream which encompassed the last quarter of the 19th century and first quarter of the 20th, established detective fiction as a viable form in its own right. For the complete works, see Barring-Gould, William S. (ed.), *The Annotated Sherlock Holmes,* 2 volumes, Clark N. Pottinger, Publisher, New York, 1967. For context see Peterson, Audrey, *Victorian Masters of Mystery: From Wilkie Collins to Conan Doyle,* Frederick Ungar Publishing, New York, 1984.

6. Chesterton, G.K., "A Defense of Detective Stories," in his collection of essays entitled *Twelve Types* (London, 1902). See generally, Barker, Dudley, *G.K. Chesterton: A Biography,* Stein

and Day, New York, 1973.

7. The best first-hand account of the *Black Mask* days is Guber, Frank, *The Pulp Jungle*, Sherborne Press, Los Angeles, 1967. A fine sampling of the material published therein is included in Ruhm, Herbert (ed.), *The Hard-Boiled Detective*, Vintage books, New York, 1977. Ample bibliographical information may be found in Hageman, E.R., *Comprehensive Index to Black Mask, 1920-1951*, Bowling Green University Popular Press, Bowling Green, OH, 1982.

8. The films were based on Hammett, Dashiell, *The Maltese Falcon* (Alfred A. Knopf, New York, 1930) and Chandler, Raymond, *The Big Sleep* (Alfred A. Knopf, New York, 1939). For an overview of the mergence of the detective cinema genre, see Tuska, Jon, *The Detective in Hollywood*, Doubleday, Garden City, NY, 1978. Also see Naremore, James, "John Houston and The Maltese Falcon," *Literature/Film Quarterly*, No. 50, 1973.

9. See Madden, David (ed.), *Tough Guy Writers of the Thirties*, Southern Illinois University Press, Carbondale, 1968. Also see Wolfe, Peter, *Beams Falling: The Art of Dashiell Hammett*, Bowling Green University Press, Bowling Green, OH, 1979, and Gardiner, Dorothy, and Katherine S. Walker (eds.), *Raymond Chandler Speaking*, Houghton Mifflin, Boston, 1962.

10. On Hammett's history as a Pinkerton, his alcoholism, his smoking and tuberculosis, see Layman, Richard, *Shadow Man: The Life of Dashiell Hammett*, Harcourt, Brace, Jovanovich, New York, 1981. See also Nolan, William F., *Hammett: A Life at the Edge*, Congden and Weed, New York, 1983.

11. For the character with which he most heavily imbued his own persona, see Hammett, Dashiell, *The Thin Man*, Vintage Books, 1975; originally published by Alfred A. Knopf in 1934, and *A Man Named Thin*, Ferman, New York, 1962. MGM produced six movies based on Hammett's Thin Man Character— beginning with *The Thin Man* and ending with *The Song of the Thin Man*—between 1936 and 1947. The novel is Gores, Joe, *Hammett*, G.P. Putnam, New York, 1975.

12. The NBC *Mike Hammer* series, starring Darren McGavin as Hammer, ran from 1958-60, following in the footsteps of such gumshoe groundbreakers as *Martin Kane, Private Eye*, (NBC, 1949-53, 57), *Man Against Crime* (CBS, 1949-53, 1956), *The*

Adventures of Ellery Queen (1950-54), *The Thin Man* (1957-60), *Richard Diamond, Private Detective* (CBS, 1957-59; NBC, 1960), and *Perry Mason* (CBS, 1957-67). It appeared in the midst of an outright glut of t.v. detective series—including such staples as *Peter Gunn* (NBC, 1958-1960, 62), *Hawaiian Eye* (ABC, 1959-62), *Surfside Six* (ABC, 1960-63), and *The Defenders* (CBS, 1961-65). When viewed in the context of a mass of private eye also-rans, reruns of Hollywood movies and a similar wave of tough guy cop shows—*Dragnet (NBC, 1951-59, 1967-71)*, *Highway Patrol* (NBC, 1956-60), *State Trooper* (ABC, 1957-60), *M-Squad* (NBC, 1957-61), *The Line-Up* (CBS, 1954-60), *The Naked City* (ABC, 1957-63), *The Untouchables* (ABC, 1959-63)—running along with a number of failed efforts in the police genre at the same time, the full dimension of public conditioning to accept an essentially and brutally lawless sort of "order" can be appreciated. For further detail, see Meyers, Richard, *TV Detectives*, The Tantivy Press, London, 1981.

13. For an incisive view of the English social milieu in which the detective fiction arose, see Watson, Colin, *Snobbery with Violence: English Crime Stories and Their Audience*, Eyre & Spottiswoode, London, 1971.

14. Symons, *op. cit.*, p. 214.

15. Nolan, *op. cit.*, p. 60. For further elaboration and analysis, see "The End of the Trail: The American West of Dashiell Hammett and Raymond Chandler," *Western Historical Quaarterly*, October, 1975.

16. Quoted in Zinn, Howard, *A People's History of the United States*, Harper and Row Publishers, New York, 1980, p. 248. For context, see Reilly, John, M., "The Politics of Tough Guy Mysteries," *University of Dayton Review*, No. 10, 1973.

17. For personal recountings of how the process worked, see Schultz, Bud, and Ruth Schultz, *It Did Happen Here: Recollections of Political Repression in America*, University of California Press, Berkeley, 1989. A supreme irony of McCarthyism was that no less than Dashiell Hammett himself was caught up in the witch-hunt and sentenced to six months in federal prison for "contempt" for refusing to testify before the House Un-American Activities Committee. The best handling of this may be found in Johnson, Diane, *Dashiell Hammett: A Life*, Random House, New

York, 1983. Also see Nolan, William F., *Dashiell Hammett: A Casebook*, McNally and Loftin, Santa Barbara, CA 1969.

18. For a detailed overview of what went on under the rubric of COINTELPRO—and what continues to occur as part of its legacy—see Churchill, Ward, and Jim Vander Wall, *The COINTELPRO Papers: Documents from the FBI's Secret Wars Against Dissent in the United States*, South End Press, Boston, 1990.

19. A concise account of CIA operations during the entire period may be found in Blum, William, *The CIA: A Forgotten History*, Zed Press, London, 1986.

20. Actually, the first known example of the form is probably James Fenimore Cooper's failed novel, *The Spy*, published in 1821. The genus of literary merit attending spy fiction did not occur until publication of Erskine Chambers' *The Riddle of the Sands* in 1903. Joseph Conrad tried his hand at spies in *Secret Agent* (1907) and *Under Western Eyes* (1911). This was followed by John Buchanan's *The Thirty-Nine Steps* (1915), *Mr. Standfast* (1919) and *Bulldog Drummond* (1920). Occasional forays were made over the next two decades by noted writers like Eric Ambler in *The Dark Frontier* (1936) and *Epitaph for a Spy* (1938), Graham Greene in *The Confidential Agent* (1939), Geoffrey Household in *Rogue Male* (1939), and Michael Innes in *The Secret Vanguard* (1940), but basically the embryonic genre languished (especially in comparison to detective and western fiction). Things really began to move only with the advent of the Cold War and publication of Ian Fleming's first James Bond novel, *Casino Royale*, in 1953. Graham Greene then weighed in with *The Quiet American* (1955) and was followed by a spate of books by John Le Carré (David John Moore Cornwell), notably *The Spy Who Came in from the Cold* (1963) and *The Looking Glass War* (1965), and Len Deighton with *The Ipcress File* (1963) and *billion-Dollar Brain* (1966). By the mid-1960s, the spy thriller was nearly as well established as detective and western yarns in both pot-boiler and serious literary modes. And, of course, Hollywood capitalized quickly on the newly popular format.

21. See note 29.

22. See Lewy, Guenter, *America in Vietnam*, Oxford University

Press, London/New York, 1978, p. 278.

23. This theme is developed rather well in Ruehlmann, William, *The Saint with a Gun: The Unlawful American Private Eye,* New York University Press, New York, 1974.

24. Symons, Julian, *Mortal Consequences: A History From the Detective Story to the Crime Novel,* Harper and Row, New York, 1972, pp. 214-5.

25. For related analysis, see Brownmiller, Susan, *Against Our Will: women, Men, and Rape,* Simon and Schuster, New York, 1975. Also see Janeway, Elizabeth, *Man's World, Woman's Place,* Delta, New York, 1971.

26. Quoted in Manville, Roger, and Heinrich Frankel, *Heinrich Himmler,* Mentor Books, New York, 1965, p. 163. Exhaustive analysis of how these principles were applied in Germany may be found in Mosse, George L., *Nazi Culture: Intellectual, Cultural and Social Life in the Third Reich,* Schocken, New York, 1981.

27. Quoted in Manville and Frankel, *op. cit., pp. 162-63.*

28. See Mosse, *op. cit.*

29. These and dozens of comparable quotations from U.S. military personnel in Indochina will be found in Boyle, Richard, *Flower of the Dragon: The Breakdown of the U.S. Army in Vietnam,* Ramparts Press, San Francisco, 1972. A classic illustration was reported in the *New York Times* on June 5, 1965: "As the Communists withdrew from Quangngai last Monday, United States jet bombers pounded the hills into which they were headed. Many Vietnamese—one estimate is as high as 500—were killed by the strikes. The American contention is that they were Vietcong soldiers. But three out of four patients seeking treatment in a Vietnamese hospital afterwards for burns from napalm, or jellied gasoline, were village women." Brigadier Patton is the namesake of his much more famous father, the legendary tank commander called "Old Blood and Guts" during World War II.

30. Quotes of this sort were relentlessly telecast by CNN and other news networks throughout the Gulf War.

31. Information about the trial and other aspects of Hillerman's personal make-up are contained in Bulow, Ernie, *Talking Mys-*

teries: A Conversation with Tony Hillerman, University of New Mexico Press, Albuquerque, 1991.

32. Hillerman's reference to Chandler's influence upon his writing occurs in *ibid.,* p. 27; he also acknowledges strong influences from Eric Ambler and Graham Greene.

33. Ross Macdonald began his Lew Archer series in the late 1950s, and continued it until rather recently. Some of his earlier efforts, such as *The Zebra-Striped Hearse* (1964), hold up favorably in comparison to Chandler. He was, however, unable to sustain such quality and degenerated into something of a formula writer. Willeford, creator of the Hoke Mosely series, is probably best known for his 1984 *Miami Blues.* He had several better efforts, including *New Hope for the Dead* (1985).

34. S.S. Van Dine (Willard Huntington Wright) is known for having written the Philo Vance detective series during the 1920s. Leslie Chartiris (Leslie Charles Boyer Yin) created the "Saint" series during the 1930s. Earl Stanley Gardiner wrote the Perry Mason series of nearly 120 books, selling upwards of 150 million copies in total. Rex (Todhunter) Stout launched his Nero Wolf series, beginning with *Fer-de-Lance* in 1934. "Ellery Queen," supposed author of an unending series of stories and short novels about his own cases, and editor-publisher of a crime magazine bearing his name, is actually the invention of a pair of writers, Nelson Lee and Frederick Dannay.

35. See Joseph, Paul, *Cracks in the Empire: State Politics in the Vietnam War,* South End Press, Boston, 1980.

36. See Chomsky, Noam, and Edward S. Herman, *The Political Economy of Human Rights, Vol. II: After the Cataclysm—Postwar Indochina and the Reconstruction of Imperial Ideology,* South End Press, Boston, 1979.

37. Marvin is quoted in Meyers, *op. cit.,* p. 43.

38. *The Mod Squad* (ABC, 1968-1973) starred Clarence Williams II, Peggy Lipton and Michael Cole. A "reunion" movie, entitled *Return of the Mod Squad,* was aired in 1979.

39. Quoted in the introduction to McCullough, David Willis (ed.), *City Sleuths and Tough Guys: Crime Stories from Poe to the Present,* Houghton-Mifflin, New York, 1989, pp. xv-xvi.

40. Paretsky's V.I. Warshawski, recently portrayed by Kathleen

Turner in a rather dismal movie of the same name, does follow standard female stereotypes in that she solves cases by intuition rather than logic. (For a sample, see the story in "Skin Deep" in McCullough, *op. cit.*, at p. 461.) Sue Grafton's Kinsey Milhone, on the other hand, is more of a "tried-and-true granddaughter of Marlowe and Spade," demonstrating that in the new American sensibility, it's sometimes okay for women (but never men) to comport themselves like macho thugs (see "The Parker Shotgun," in McCullough, *op. cit.*, at p. 425). Both female detective characters indulge themselves amply in such approved yuppie pastimes as jogging.

41. Although Dave Brandstetter, the central character of Joseph Hansen's novels, was not the first example of a gay detective character—being predicated by four years with George Baxt's Pharaoh of Love in *A Queer Kind of Love* (1966)—he was the earliest to find general public acceptance. For a sample of Hanson/Brandstetter, see "Election Day," in McCullough, *op. cit.*, at p. 398.

42. Simon's own depiction of Moses Wine, the imaginary Jewish student radical become private sleuth, has worked quite well in this regard. A more extreme example, Ernest Tidyman's John Shaft (*Shaft*, Macmillan, New York, 1970), a black detective based in Harlem, ultimately failed, not on racial grounds per se, but because he was projected as a sort of African-American Mike Hammer.

43. Simon's Moses Wine fits this mold to a certain extent. Willeford's character, Hoke Mosely, however, is the very epitome of the genre's new white male detective figure. He is of middle-age, pudgy, and wears false teeth, white socks, and polyester leisure suits. His wife has left him to move in with a wealthy pro baseball player, but continues to "assert herself" by compelling him to spend an appreciable part of his meager police salary underwriting the costs of dental work for the eldest of his two daughters. He lives in a sleazy hotel room in the wrong part of town, drives a battered old clunker of a car, and experiences almost continuous self-doubt concerning his own worth as a human being. This is obviously a far cry from Same Spade and Philip Marlowe.

44. For example, in *The Big Fix*, while driving his children

around in his Volkswagen during a visit permitted by his estranged wife (who has moved in with a brainy psychiatrist), Moses Wine is stopped for a routine traffic violation. After disclosing to the traffic cop that there is a licensed but never used .38 revolver in the glove compartment, Wine is asked to produce it for inspection. It turns out to be rusty, minus its cylinder, its barrel filled with the children's crayons. The cop threatens to arrest Wine for "abuse of a weapon." One can be sure that Mike Hammer would never be found in anything resembling these circumstances.

45. See Boldt, David, *Gurkhas* (Weidenfield and Nicholson, London, 1967) and Barat, Amiya, *The Bengal Native Infantry* (Firma K.L. Mukmopashyay, Calcutta, 1962). It should be noted that earlier, and quite successfully, British experiments along this line had been conducted using Highland Scots as guinea pigs; see. for example, Howard, Philip, *The Black Watch* (Hamish Hamilton, London, 1968); Sinclair-Stevenson, Christopher, *The Gordon Highlanders* (Hamish Hamilton, London, 1968); Sutherland, Douglas, *The Argyll and Sutherland Highlanders* (Leo Cooper, London, 1969); and Oats, L.B., *The Highland Light Infantry* (Leo Cooper, London, 1969). Overall, see MacRoy, Patrick, *The Fierce Pawns,* J.B. Lippincott, Philadelphia, 1966.

46. See Young, John Robert, *The French Foreign Legion,* Thames and Hudson, New York, 1984. A broad view of the history of the use of troops from colonized or otherwise oppressed social sectors may be found in Enloe, Cynthia, *Ethnic Soldiers: State Security in a Divided Society,* Penguin Press, Baltimore, 1980.

47. On "The Public Safety Program," see Langguth, A.J., *hidden Terrors: The Truth About U.S. Police Operations in Latin America,* Pantheon, New York, 1978.

48. For one of the better handlings of the Vietnamization process and rationale, see Chapter 4, "'An Army with a Country': Thieu's Vietnam," in Isaacs, Arnold R., *Without Honor: Defeat in Vietnam and Cambodia,* Vintage, New York, 1984, pp. 101-22.

49. Perhaps the best explanation of the psychological process at work may be found in Fanon, Frantz, *Black Skin/White Masks,* Grove Press, New York, 1966. Also see Memmi, Albert, *Colonizer and Colonized,* Orion, New York, 1965.

50. Fanon again provides excellent insight into the process

involved. See his *Wretched of the Earth*, Grove, New York, 1965.

51. See Hagan, William, *Indian Police and Judges*, University of Nebraska Press, Lincoln, 1966.

52. See Clark, Robert (ed.), *the Killing of Chief Crazy Horse*, University of Nebraska Press, Lincoln, 1976. Also see Vestal, Stanley, *Sitting Bull: Champion of the Sioux*, University of Oklahoma Press, Norman, 1957.

53. See Cole, Douglas, and Ira Chaikan, *An Iron Hand Upon the People: The Law Against Potlatch on the Northwest Coast*, University of Washington Press, Seattle, 1990.

54. The Indian police on Pine Ridge were doubling, in the classic pattern of the CIA-sponsored Latin American death squads, as GOONs (Goons Of the Oglala Nation), liquidating political targets among their own people selected by the FBI. See Churchill, Ward, and Jim Vander Wall, *Agents of Repression: The FBI's Secret Wars Against the Black Panther Party and the American Indian Movement*, South End Press, Boston, 1988. Also see Matthiessen, Peter, *In the Spirit of Crazy Horse*, Viking Press, New York, (2nd Edition) 1991.

55. See Bulow, Ernie, "Introduction," in *talking Mysteries, op. cit.*

56. See Churchill, Ward, and Winona LaDuke, "Native America: The Political Economy of Radioactive Colonization," in M. Annette Jaimes (ed.), *The State of Native America: Genocide, Colonization and Resistance*, South End Press, Boston, 1992.

57. See Kammer, Jerry, *The Second Long Walk: The Navajo-Hopi Land Dispute*, University of New Mexico Press, Albuquerque, 1980. Also see Parlow, Anita, *Cry, Sacred Ground: Big Mountain, USA*, Christic Institute, Washington, DC, 1988.

58. For a fine exposition on the nature of the water crisis in Navajoland, see Reisner, Mark, *cadillac Desert: The American West and Its Disappearing Water*, Viking, New York, 1986. On Sacred sites, see Parlow, *op. cit.*

59. For a reproduction of the main Dog Soldier Teletype and excerpts from Director Webster's testimony, see *The COINTELPRO Papers, op. cit.*, pp. 275-80.

60. For a sample of such writing—in an ostensibly nonfiction

vein—see Jacobsen, Hans-Adolf, and Hans Dollinger (eds.), *Der Zweite Weltkrieg, 1941-43,* Verlag Kurt Desch München Wien Basel, 1943.

Index

About the Author

Ward Churchill (Creek/Cherokee Métis) has, since 1980, served as Codirector of the Colorado Chapter of the American Indian Movement. He is an associate professor of American Indian Studies and Communications with the Center for Studies of Ethnicity and Race in America (CSERA) at the University of Colorado/Boulder. A prolific writer and lecturer on American Indian affairs, he is a regular columnist for *Z Magazine* and editor of the journal *New Studies on the Left*. His previous books are listed at the front of this volume.

About the Editor

M. Annette Jaimes (Juaneño/Yaqui) is a lecturer in American Indian Studies with CSERA, presently on leave to pursue a post-doctoral study on the structure of scientific racism with the Society for the Humanities at Cornell University. Widely published in various journals and periodicals, her books include *The State of Native America: Genocide, Colonization and Resistance* (1992).

About Common Courage Press

Books for an Informed Democracy

Noam Chomsky once stated in *Necessary Illusions: Thought Control in Democratic Societies* that "Citizens of the democratic societies should undertake a course of intellectual self-defense to protect themselves from manipulation and control, and to lay the basis for more meaningful democracy." The mission of Common Courage Press is to publish books on the syllabus of this course.

To that end, Common Courage Press was founded in 1991 and publishes books for social justice on race, gender, feminism, economics, ecology, labor, and U.S. domestic and foreign policy. The Press seeks to provide analysis of problems from a range of perspectives and to aid activists and others in developing strategies for action.

You can reach us at:

Common Courage Press
P.O. Box 702
Monroe, ME 04951
207-525-0900

Send for a free catalog!